For Love of

Soysambu

The Saga of Lord Delamere
& his Descendants in Kenya

Juliet Barnes

ISBN# 978-9966-757-66-1

Cover design: Andrew Denman
Interior layout & design: Blake Arensen

Old Africa Books
Naivasha, Kenya

Dedication

*For Soysambu and all Kenya's unique ecosystems
that face an increasing struggle for survival*

'An extraordinary and ultimately deeply moving saga of one family's contribution to the foundation of the Kenyan nation, and the conservation of one of its most paradisal landscapes'
Graham Coster, author of *The Flying Boat That Fell to Earth*

'A must read for Kenyans and non-Kenyans, assisting us to objectively understand Kenya's forgotten history and its makers, beginning with an exceptional generation that left the comfort of their country and came to start a new life in Kenya, while their descendants became Kenyans, becoming even more Kenyan than the Kenyans'
- Prof. X N Iraki, Lecturer at Nairobi University and columnist with *The Standard*

'Accurate and well-written'
Lord Delamere

About the Author

Juliet Barnes is a Kenyan writer, born in Nyeri and educated in Nairobi before going to St Andrew's University in Scotland to do an MA (hons) in English Language and Literature. Back in Kenya, she completed a correspondence course with the London School of Journalism, and has written for newspapers and magazines in Kenya and the UK, as well as publishing fiction and non-fiction in both countries.

Her short story *Broken Glass* was runner-up for the Commonwealth Short Story Award and *Lake of Smoke*, for Kenyan teenagers, was runner-up for the Jomo Kenyatta Prize for Fiction. *The Ghosts of Happy Valley* (Aurum Press, London, 2013) was shortlisted for the Spear Book Award in 2014, and she was named one of Hatchard's "Authors of the Year" in 2016. *Hillcrest: A History*, the story of a Kenyan school was commissioned in 2014. Juliet Barnes has also edited *The East African Private Schools Guide* and *Ndege News* magazine, and was Kenya editor for *Good Schools Guide International*.

She has two adult children, has taught English, music and drama in many parts of Kenya, and now writes full time from her rented home on Soysambu, where she has lived for 20 years. She has known the Delamere family for over forty years and attended numerous court hearings during the murder trial of Lord Delamere's son, Hon. Tom Cholmondeley.

In epochs of expansion, epochs such as that in which we now live, epochs when always the warning voice is again heard: Now is the judgement of this world - in such epochs aristocracies with their natural clinging to the established fact, their want of sense for the flux of things, for the inevitable transitoriness of all human institutions, are bewildered and helpless.

Matthew Arnold, *Culture and Anarchy*

The safest shield is honesty.

Delamere family motto

Generations of the Delamere Family in Kenya

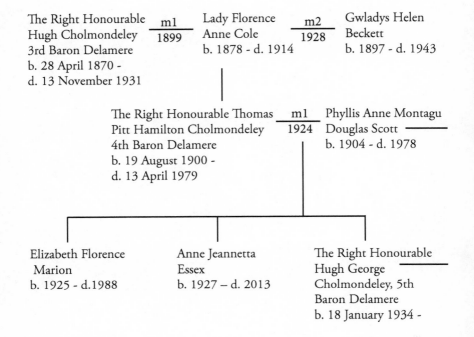

The Right Honourable
Hugh Cholmondeley
3rd Baron Delamere
b. 28 April 1870 -
d. 13 November 1931

m1
1899

Lady Florence
Anne Cole
b. 1878 - d. 1914

m2
1928

Gwladys Helen
Beckett
b. 1897 - d. 1943

The Right Honourable Thomas
Pitt Hamilton Cholmondeley
4th Baron Delamere
b. 19 August 1900 -
d. 13 April 1979

m1
1924

Phyllis Anne Montagu
Douglas Scott
b. 1904 - d. 1978

Elizabeth Florence
Marion
b. 1925 - d.1988

Anne Jeannetta
Essex
b. 1927 – d. 2013

The Right Honourable
Hugh George
Cholmondeley, 5th
Baron Delamere
b. 18 January 1934 -

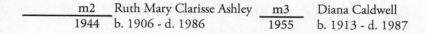

m2	Ruth Mary Clarisse Ashley	m3	Diana Caldwell
1944	b. 1906 - d. 1986	1955	b. 1913 - d. 1987

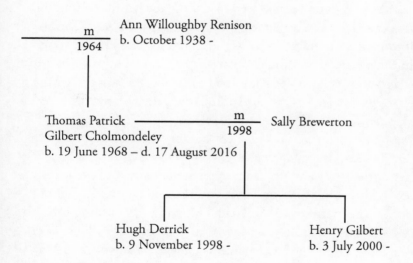

m	Ann Willoughby Renison
1964	b. October 1938 -

Thomas Patrick — m — Sally Brewerton
Gilbert Cholmondeley   1998
b. 19 June 1968 – d. 17 August 2016

Hugh Derrick   Henry Gilbert
b. 9 November 1998 -   b. 3 July 2000 -

Acknowledgements

First and foremost my heartfelt thanks go to Lord and Lady Delamere for their unstinting kindness and hospitality – including many meals, cups of coffee, and drinks - and their patience when answering questions, telling me stories about their own lives and those of their ancestors; for lending me books from their library; and to Lady Delamere for digging out various letters, booklets and photographs, even during some very stressful times. My special thanks to Deborah Colvile for her hospitality and memories, and Kathryn Combes for telling me stories over many dinners and glasses of wine, as well as lending me her file containing newspaper articles and notes pertaining to the trial of Hon. Thomas Cholmondeley. I remain eternally grateful to the late Hon. Thomas Cholmondeley for his enthusiasm and encouragement to write this book, and above all for enabling me to move to live on Soysambu back in 1999, where he and Lord and Lady Delamere made me feel so welcome.

I am indebted to many writers before me, but especially to the late Elspeth Huxley for her meticulous research on the history of East Africa, so carefully documented in so many beautifully written books, and for her legible notebooks; and the Weston Library for their preservation of Huxley's papers, including the 3rd Baron Delamere's handwritten letters to Gwladys, as well as other assorted letters and typed leaflets/press releases dating back to Mau Mau. I was most grateful for their efficiency, assistance and the ease with which researchers can access historical documents in such a tranquil setting in the atmospheric city of Oxford. In particular I thank Lucy McCann, then Senior Archivist at Oxford's Bodleian Library, for her assistance and advice. Errol Trzebinski is another writer whose detailed research has been invaluable, and I'm further grateful for her advice, encouragement, friendship and for sharing the memoir of Michael Cunningham-Reid.

My gratitude extends to London Agent, Robert Smith, for believing in this book from the start; to Graham Coster for his invaluable advice and editing expertise; to Shel Arensen and his team for creating the final version of the book; to my husband Patrick van Oudgaarden for his support which enabled me to abandon more lucrative writing jobs in order to write this book; to Andrew Denman for his creative work on the cover design; to Simon Thomsett for his beautiful photograph of three flamingo in flight, for his dedication to raptors and Kenya's wild places, and all he has taught me; to Lotte Hughes for allowing me to use those interview notes relating to 3rd Baron Delamere, and for her extensive research on the Maasai moves of the early 20th century; to my mother, Margery Barnes and Philip Coulson, for both reading first drafts and offering suggestions; to Rupert Watson for casting a wise eye over the manuscript; to my Godfather John Fowler for his interest and for bequeathing me his historical book collection; to Tom Lawrence for his research assistance and for demystifying certain names in the Huxley notes, as well as on certain key characters in the book; to the late Liza Long for sharing her memories and allowing use of her photographs; to David Markham for sharing his stories and giving me access to his grandmother's visitors book, letters and portrait; to the helpful staff at the Vale Royal Golf Club and especially Debbie Howard for introducing me to General Manager Ian Embury, who kindly showed me around and sent me old photographs taken by the late Edward Chambre Hardman and shared by Keith Roberts who was researching the history of Vale Royal; to Andrew Nightingale for showing me around historic Njoro and sharing some interesting documents and stories; and to my dear friend, the late Frank Draper, for his generous hospitality during my many trips to London.

My thanks are also extended - in random order - to so many who have assisted, granted me interviews or written me letters, sharing their stories and/or photos: Sally Cholmondeley, Hon. Hugh Cholmondeley, Mandy Newton, Robert Newton, Anne Fitzmaurice, Nelson Rotich, Benson Ngugi, Stephen Koigi, Joseph Mwangi Wakaba, Peter Ndung'u, Muiruri, Jonny Havelock, Anthony Rowan, Lendani, John Weller, Annie Dunn, X N Iraki,

Keith Roberts, Sally Dudmesh, Suzanne Woodward, Henry Ole Sanoi, Joseph Kodonyo, the late Tobina Cole, Linda Muir, the late Monty Brown, Jenny Pont, Guy Combes, Brian Macoun, Don Rooken-Smith, Margaret Dalton, Lucy Shilstone, Susan Mackain-Bremner, Tony and Sarah Seth-Smith, Jennifer Falkiner, the late Patrick Waweru, the late "mganga" David, Ken Doig, Barbara Terry, Peter Ouko, Lady Jay Hewett, Amyra Mah, and Hugh Cran. If there's anybody I've unintentionally forgotten, please accept my apologies.

Finally, my thanks to Soysambu, that special sanctuary that always offers a healing space in between many happy times, for offering me periods of tranquillity in which to write, and for exposing me to the miraculous wonders of our natural world.

CONTENTS

ABOUT THE AUTHOR

Juliet Barnes is a Kenyan writer, born in Nyeri and educated in Nairobi before going to St Andrew's University in Scotland to do an MA (hons) in English Language and Literature. Back in Kenya, she completed a correspondence course with the London School of Journalism, and has written for newspapers and magazines in Kenya and the UK, as well as publishing fiction and non-fiction in both countries.

Her short story Broken Glass was runner-up for the Commonwealth Short Story Award and Lake of Smoke, for Kenyan teenagers, was runner-up for the Jomo Kenyatta Prize for Fiction. The Ghosts of Happy Valley (Aurum Press, London, 2013) was shortlisted for the Spear Book Award in 2014, and she was named one of Hatchard's "Authors of the Year" in 2016. Hillcrest: A History, the story of a Kenyan school was commissioned in 2014. Juliet Barnes has also edited The East African Private School's Guide and Ndege News magazine, and was Kenya editor for Good Schools Guide International.

She has two adult children and has taught English, music and drama. She now writes full time from her rented home on Soysambu, where she has lived for 20 years. She has known the Delamere family for over forty years and attended numerous court hearings during the murder trial of Lord Delamere's son, Hon. Tom Cholmondeley.

PRELUDE
An Urgent Cleansing

I first fell in love with Soysambu in the 1970s - albeit from a distance. I was ten, and my father was driving us to the small farming town of Nakuru. An hour earlier we'd descended into the Great Rift Valley on an escarpment road built by Italian Prisoners of War, winding steeply down its forested walls as the landscape fell away to our left, revealing enormous views into hazy distance - what Martha Gellhorn called 'the paradise section of Africa.' Once on the valley's floor, we'd driven on past giant pimples and scars scattered by its volcanic past, leaving the placid expanse of Lake Naivasha behind. We were about 140 kilometres from Nairobi when suddenly Lake Elmenteita revealed itself.

A small irregularly-shaped lake reflected the innocent blue of the sky, with pink froth around its rim and pink dots spattered over its surface, seeming as if an artist on drugs had experimented with Impressionism, adding in a dose of pointillism. I find it impossible to see a flamingo without smiling, and here were hundreds of thousands, occasionally rising in colourful wafts in between feeding on the rich soup of microorganisms in the lake's alkaline waters.

Across the lake, straddling its northern, western and south western reaches, lay the arid yellow expanses of Lord Delamere's farm, Soysambu, a landscape often swept by whipped-up funnels of dust. Shimmering in the heat haze, this was shadowed by dark green swathes of Jurassic-looking vegetation and extraordinary-shaped hills the imagination could sculpt into pyramids, puddings or amphitheatres. The biggest, my father told me, was called 'Delamere's Nose.' It did look a little like a mummified head on its back. I tried to work out whether he had a receding or prominent chin. It depended on whether his mouth was open or not.

I never imagined that one day I'd come to know this area so

intimately it would begin to feel that its fate could define my own well-being.

In 1989 I got married in a small stone church, close to the old Nairobi-Nakuru road no longer in use. It was some way south of Nakuru where my parents lived, but I'd fallen in love with the little colonial relic that had been built by a friend of my grandfather's. And the first thing I saw when I emerged on the arm of my new husband was Lake Elmenteita, reflecting the midday sun, like a blinding and beckoning jewel. I ignored a strange feeling of premonition, averting my gaze to the indigo escarpment above which late morning clouds were massing.

By then we'd got to know the Delamere family, sometimes staying with them on Soysambu. Theirs was an important name in Kenya, partly for historical reasons, but they were also extensive landowners, with another farm in Naivasha, through which we'd driven earlier. Delamere Estates was renowned for its high-quality beef and dairy cattle, while its titled owners, titles being something of a rarity in Kenya, were seen by land-hungry Kenyans as enormously wealthy, although this hadn't been in evidence when we'd visited Lord and Lady Delamere, whom I knew as Hugh and Ann. Always hospitable, regardless of class, colour or creed, they lived in a rambling home, its mix of cheap plastic chairs and priceless family heirlooms reflecting an unpretentious lifestyle and a lack of spare cash. A smaller version of it had been built almost a century earlier by Boy Long, a handsome young manager who'd worked for Hugh's grandfather. Women had adored Long, whose lovers had included Lady Idina, doyenne of the infamous Happy Valley set. The house was later expanded and upgraded, most notably by Hugh's stepmother, Diana, third wife of the 4th Baron Delamere. Diana had rocketed to fame when her high-profile lover, Lord Erroll, had mysteriously been murdered, thus tenuously linking the Delamere name to the Happy Valley scandals. A portrait of the 4th Baron hung in the drawing room, a room decorated by Diana. Hugh had disliked his stepmother to the extent that her own portrait had been banished to the furthest guest house, where her icy-blue eyes glared at you wherever you stood.

In the dining room the walnut table was overlooked by some

sizeable paintings; a busy winter scene by Breughel, and some ancestral portraits - Charles I and the 1st Baron Delamere. A portrait of the 3rd Baron hung in the drawing room: pioneer settler, farmer and politician, Hugh's grandfather had in the early years of the twentieth century contributed enormous amounts of money and knowledge to British East Africa. A large bronze statue of him by Kathleen Scott, wife of the Antarctic explorer, had stood on Nairobi's Delamere Avenue until 1963, when Kenya became independent and the treed precincts were renamed Kenyatta Avenue. Now it stood at Soysambu, where it looked pensively across plains towards the white soda-encrusted lakeshore.

These days, as the 5th Baron Delamere, Hugh preferred a modest life: mid-morning coffee on the west-facing back veranda, running on into pre-lunch vodkas; post-siesta afternoon tea and cake taken on the front veranda overlooking Lake Elmenteita; ('Kenya or China?' Ann would say); a drive around the farm in the cool of evening, before whisky time in the living room where the plump golden Labrador, Teddy, snored before the fire. In between, Hugh's favourite place to unwind was his train room, where he displayed childlike enthusiasm for the tangle of electric wires that sometimes managed to work a complicated model railway.

By 1989 I had struggled through a difficult divorce and was looking for a house as far away as possible from Nairobi. Soysambu seemed a good place to start. With its 48,000 acres of fragile ecosystems and a harsh beauty that drills its way into your heart, Soysambu had already penetrated mine.

'You must have an isolated house somewhere,' I begged Tom, Hugh and Ann's son and heir to the title.

'Well,' he pondered, 'there's that old place on Ol Jolai...'

'You couldn't possibly live there!' said his more practical wife.

But soon afterwards I delightedly took up the lease of the half-derelict mud-walled house. It was perfect: five kilometres from its nearest neighbours, down a barely discernible track, and it didn't bother me that there was no power. Water was unpredictable, draining into a leaking tank if it rained, or erratically pumped in from a borehole. Bathwater was heated in a metal drum with firewood, delivered weekly by ox-cart.

When giraffe stood completely still to watch me doing yoga beneath the tree where the Red-headed Weavers raised their babies in precariously dangling nests and the Striped Kingfisher perched to eat its grasshopper, I felt I'd found the life I'd always sought. Here was my place to live simply, write, and heal.

A decade later, still at Soysambu, I'd seen some extremes; enormous bush fires raging through dry seasons, with choking dust storms forerunners to torrential rain that melted roads into impassable swamps. During droughts, my nights were punctuated with eerie whoops and giggles of feasting hyena or bellows of bull buffaloes, fighting at my small waterhole. When the moon was full, the birds sang all night, and I could see formations of flamingos, grunting softly as they flew south to breed. But after rain, a chorus of frogs drowned all other sounds as the sun-scorched plains transformed. Acacias blossomed and grass turned green, spangled with wild flowers, some so minute you needed to kneel down to identify them, while the larger white *cycnium tubulosum*, the 'waste paper flower,' scattered itself carelessly over the plains. During these verdant times, there was grazing for cattle, as well as thousands of wild zebra, antelopes and buffalo.

But there was a darker side to this Eden: poachers from impoverished surrounding communities hung hundreds of wire snares in the scrub to catch the smaller antelopes or warthogs. They set other snares along fences and would then drive herds of eland through and wait until these giant antelopes died slowly of strangulation. Often, taking my children back to school on a Sunday evening, we'd be late for chapel because we stopped to fill the back of the Land Rover with deadly nooses. When I drove home again the following morning, scores more would be hanging along the fence like another Monday's dirty washing.

In 2008 multiple disasters had affected the Delameres, Soysambu and indeed the entire country. Disputed elections had erupted in violence, people's anger exacerbated by droughted conditions in a backdrop of a country embroiled in corruption scandals and land-grabbing. Amidst all this the Delameres had fared badly in the press after Tom had been accused of murder - twice. I had a call from David. He was what they call a *mganga* (Kiswahili for witchdoctor) from western Kenya, albeit a Christian version, but most of the time he did his own alternative work; cleansing places and people, lifting curses using a curious mixture of religious utterances, traditional herbs and ground-up bones or stones. I'd met him through a friend. He would sniff out thieves and liars, if they hadn't run a mile before he arrived, but he was also unnervingly psychic. In the latest incident at Soysambu some skulls had been dug up and stolen from the family graveyard.

'Of course!' said David. 'They are valuable in witchcraft; it is believed that if you take the skull of a rich and powerful man, you will get his power! I need to clean Soysambu,' he declared.

It had been over a hundred years since Tom's great grandfather had come here with his grandiose schemes and single-minded determination to create a white man's country out of untamed wilderness, disposing of wildlife to make way for crops and livestock. And now, in the early 21st century, when history had tipped the scales and Soysambu was struggling to protect its threatened species while surrounded by a burgeoning human population who questioned its very existence as a white man's farm, there were those who felt that Delamere's descendants were meeting their nemesis. A series of overwhelming circumstances, including Tom's recent incidents, both related to his stance as a conservationist, had cast a dark cloud of gloom and foreboding over those who lived on Soysambu. Did it indeed need to be cleansed as it faced this time of reckoning?

If Hugh and Ann were sceptical of David's mission they were too polite to say, and invited me to bring him to stay, pledging payment in cows as he wished. After our introductory lunch at Soysambu, David and I walked around the garden, dry grass crunching beneath our feet, and he went into one of his reveries.

'Delamere's grandfather, he comes here at night,' he then announced, as if he was speaking about somebody who was still alive. 'He was a very good man. He loved his bulls.' (I later discovered that Hugh's grandfather used to house his prize bulls in the guest house we were passing, though nobody had told David that). We walked on beneath a spreading jacaranda, where two Spotted Eagle Owls snoozed on a branch. We stopped by Delamere's statue, as a dry wind carried up the rotten-egg smell from the alkaline lake. David put his large dark hand on the cold bronze one. 'This was a man of great strength.'

The statue looked impassively across the vast view; the multi-coloured herd of cows, their hooves raising dust, the pink ribbons of flamingos and the indigo hills beyond. Behind Delamere's Nose, an increasing number of tin roofs flashed in the sunlight; almost two years after Kenya's post-election fracas had been quashed, there was still a camp on the far escarpment where displaced people somehow survived in ragged tents. It had evolved dramatically since the third Baron Delamere first saw - and fell in love with - this land.

'He must have many stories to tell,' I said, touching the statue too.

'Yes,' replied David, 'and you will write them.'

BOOK I

1897-1931

Finding Soysambu

"Delamere had two great loves - East Africa and the Masai People."
- Beryl Markham, *West with the Night*

CHAPTER 1

From an English Stately Home...

Kirinyaga, Kirinyaa, Kiinya, it was called by the Kikuyu, Embu and Kamba peoples. God's resting place. It was the richly forested source of rivers, and in just over two decades the country would be named after it. The notion of snow so close to the equator on this sacred mountain had been dismissed by scientists after it had first been reported by German missionary Ludwig Krapf in 1849. The fertile highlands that lay around, including the Great Rift Valley, were discovered by the young Scottish explorer Joseph Thomson, risking everything to get through country occupied by warlike Maasai, who'd prohibited plenty of newcomers before him. In 1883, when Thomson returned to London to confirm Krapf's stories, a young Hugh Cholmondeley had been a schoolboy at Eton. He would grow up to become the Right Honourable Hugh Cholmondeley, 3rd Baron Delamere, grandfather of the present Hugh and, in the verdict of Sara Wheeler in her biography of his contemporary Denys Finch Hatton, 'the most influential white man ever to settle in Kenya.'

It's confusing trying to work out a who's who of Delameres, as they were mostly called Hugh or Thomas. The 3rd Baron, for example, born in 1870 and christened Hugh Cholmondeley, took the same name as his father, son of Thomas Cholmondeley, 1st Baron Delamere. But there was only one family seat of the Delameres, and that was Vale Royal in Cheshire.

In 1263, when Prince Edward's ship happened to be hit by terrible storms, he vowed that if they survived he would found an abbey in gratitude. Thus in 1277, now King, he consecrated a site at Over, near Winsford, naming it Vallis Regalis. Plans for an elaborate Gothic cathedral with multiple chapels and cloisters were sabotaged by dwindling finances, lack of interest and a hurricane, but Richard II finally agreed to finish a more 'modest' version that was nevertheless larger than Westminster Abbey.

Vale Royal Abbey became a byword for mismanagement, ill-discipline and scandal before it was pulled down in 1539 during the Reformation. Sir Thomas Holcroft, one of King Henry VIII's commissioners, purchased the site and land for a mere £450 and built himself a sizeable mansion around the remaining parts of the south and west cloisters and the monks' refectory, using timber and stone from the ruin. In 1615 it was bought by Lady Mary Cholmondeley, widow of Sir Hugh Cholmondeley, for an expensive £9,000. Amongst other highbrow guests, she entertained James I, who granted knighthoods to two members of her family, offering to advance their political careers, and named her "the Bolde Lady of Cheshire" when she refused. When she died in 1625, her younger son Thomas inherited Vale Royal. Her eldest had been created Earl of Leicester, while another son would become forebear of the Marquesses of Cholmondeley.

**

How, I asked the present-day Hugh, did the Vale Royal line of Cholmondeleys acquire their barony? Hugh cut an imposing figure, very tall, long-limbed and thin, with a prominent nose and a severe, sometimes sardonic expression, giving way to a slight curl of the lip when amused. His hair was white and thinning, and due to the onset of Parkinson's Disease, he walked with two sticks, but he was quick witted and observant, his deep blue eyes bright. I'd seldom seen him wear anything more formal than his worn khaki trousers, with an aging cardigan or fleece over a cotton shirt.

'My great, great grandfather bought it for £5,000 in 1821, or rather he was invited to contribute money to the Conservative Party and the Duke of Wellington conferred the title upon him. Being a provincial boy from Cheshire he didn't know the going rate was only £1,500! He thought being a lord was fashionable. All it did was put up the grocery bills.' Hugh indicated the portrait of the 1st Baron through the open doors of their dining room. 'Pompous-looking chap. He was so proud of being able to read he had books and candles put in. A lot of Cholmondeleys couldn't read!' He pointed out the portrait of Charles I beside it, the oblong mark showing where his head had been tactically removed before the Roundheads' attack. 'You can't choose your ancestors. During the Civil War, when all the Cholmondeley men were off fighting for him, one of the Cholmondeley ladies defended the house with a bunch of housemaids, firing a musket out of the window every ten minutes until eventually Cromwell - or his men - brought up a ten-pound cannon and fired it up into the chimney. So then she thought, Well, this can't go on, and she hung up a white sheet. The cows were taken, but one ran back and it was in milk, so that kept them alive all winter. Vale Royal was famous for its red cows...'

Ann, her expression glazed from having heard these stories in various versions many times, said, 'Wasn't a pony driven into a cupboard in the house to hide it from the troops?'

'A pony or a cow,' Hugh shrugged. 'It's all a long time ago.'

Hugh had been the last Cholmondeley to live at Vale Royal, 'if only until the age of five. Ah, the stink of bad drains and dry rot!' But, he added, his grandfather had seen it in its prime: 'The estate was quite large for England back then: five acres short of 6,000.'

There was no sign of dry rot or smell of drains at the elegant Vale Royal Golf Club, a magnificent Georgian red sandstone building, when I visited in 2016. Newer houses and roads covered much of the former estate; the stables had been converted into residences, as had the south wing, rebuilt in the 17th century after the Roundheads' assault, its garden today retaining the formal rose beds and large rectangular pond. The apartments' names harked back to family history (Delamere) and grand visitors of yore (King's Rooms). The ground floor of the north wing was now a members' bar; the first floor, with its tall bay windows and carved fireplaces, was the dining area, and through a towering doorway a vast room with a vaulted roof was a private dining room. The outdoor staircase had gone, the entrance now a magnificent wooden studded door on the ground floor, opening onto a stone-flagged corridor with a stained glass window. In the golf club's offices at the south end a weathered red sandstone arch revealed part of the original cloisters.

A celebrity footballer was teeing off at the 12th hole, beside the

Great Ditch that once ran down to the river Weaver, the northern boundary to the abbey precincts. All that was left now of the abbey was a pile of mossy grey stones, alleged to be the 14th-century grave of a nun said to haunt Vale Royal. An oak-lined lane led to the river with its railway viaduct and double locks. A mile or so along an avenue of beech trees to the south, beside the old entrance to the abbey, the Church of St Mary had been reinvented in 1875 when the 2nd Baron Delamere hired the famous Cheshire architect, John Douglas, who also upgraded Vale Royal. The graveyard holds the Delamere vault, with space for more, although no more Delameres would die in England. Close by, two 19th-century gravestones commemorated Essex Cholmondeley and Caroline Elizabeth Cholmondeley. Beyond the churchyard wall, built with stones from the demolished abbey, Whitegate village had grown up, the adjacent mews once housing the Delamere horses and carriages.

As we looked at my photographs of the golf club, Hugh told me he'd only returned once to Vale Royal - with Ann and their young son Tom, after it had been sold. 'It doesn't look anything like it did in my day, apart from the Adam-like engravings along the edge of the ceiling. Ah, yes - The library! It was a terribly cold room - we didn't go into it in the winter. The room next to it was the billiard room, full of stuffed animals. There was a pair of lions fighting. All the hair started to fall out so they went to the Chester Museum.' The dining room he remembered was now absorbed into the residential wing: 'We used to have breakfast at a bay window in the dining room at a table which is now our dining room table here!'

'I had it chocked by Ikanyi,' Ann put in, 'so it didn't wobble.' Soysambu's odd job man, Ikanyi still climbed ladders to repair roofs at the age of eighty-something, although Hugh was always trying to persuade him to let his son, his apprentice, do the dangerous stuff.

'Before my grandfather dissipated the family fortunes, we owned good, rich, fertile farms; about 12 of them, first-class new-potato land, rented out at the best rates,' Hugh continued, still looking at photographs of Vale Royal. Then, pausing at the grand salon, originally the monks' refectory, he said: 'The ceiling was renewed in the nineteenth century into these 25 neo-Gothic sections with coats of arms. In the middle was the coat of arms of Edward I and around it those of the abbots, then the Cholmondeleys. One coat of arms was never put up - my father's.' He recalled huddling around one of the two fireplaces. 'The chimney smoked so mother had it cleaned, and out came the six-pound cannon ball fired by Cromwell.'

I showed Hugh the photo of the flat named Delamere.

'That was the door into the servants' quarters! We called the South wing the Elizabethan wing. James I stayed there and hunted until the park ran out of game. He arrived with 200 servants and 50 horses. The royal visit was like paying income tax.'

'Of course it wasn't a nun's grave at all,' Hugh pointed out as we progressed through photos, 'It was the base of an abbey pillar they pulled down.' He raised an eyebrow at a plaque's translation of the Cholmondeley motto: Integrity is my sure protection. 'That's one way of putting it.'

***

Back in 1887, when Hugh Cholmondeley was just 17, his father died, and he returned to the family seat at Vale Royal, where he'd grown up with his younger sister Sybil and a series of exasperated governesses, until he started at Eton, where he became notorious for his hot temper, truancy and extreme pranks. His parents had sent him on to a crammer's. But now, the new 3rd Baron Delamere embarked on a series of spending sprees, once losing £3,000 (equivalent to almost £390,000 nowadays) in a single bet at the races. He had altercations with his mother, spurning their social obligations - hunting in Cheshire in winter, shooting in autumn and going to London in spring for the season - and refused to join the Life Guards. At the age of 19 Delamere began travelling, the Australian bush sparking his interest in sheep and the enticing freedom of a simpler life. When he turned 21, his mother could no longer legally restrain him, not that she'd had any success thus far, and in 1891 he selected some companions and made his first trip to Africa, to Somaliland via the Cape and Zanzibar. At Aden the horses had to swim to this relatively new, mostly unexplored and unmapped British Protectorate.

"Ten times my salary would not again induce me to go

with such a crowd of undisciplined, foolish, wasteful, reckless youngsters," wrote the British hunter, whom Delamere had employed. "With Delamere, when I can get him alone, I can do things: he will then - with persuasion - listen to reason or, at worst, acquiesce in suitable arrangements after a wild explosion of dissent: but as soon as others come on the scene he is worse in waste and expenditure than all of them."

Delamere himself, he added, was partly redeemed by being "a thorough, keen, hard-working sportsman...happy as the day is long..."

His ginger hair and pale complexion were unsuited to tropical sun, inducing infected blisters and dehydration, but Delamere was nonetheless thrilled by Africa, staying on four months after his companions left, even thinking of settling near Hargeisa in the interior of Somaliland, although his annual income was less than £1,500 – not enough even to maintain Vale Royal.

Debts didn't stop him heading back to the interior of Somaliland repeatedly, returning with typhoid, malaria and peritonitis. When he was mauled by a lion, his Somali gun bearer, Abdullah Ashure, built a shade over him, caring for him as he lay motionless for five days. As they finally boarded a cattle boat to Aden, the English skipper, outraged to see a Somali using the same ladder as Lord Delamere, kicked Abdullah in the face. Delamere punched the skipper into the sea before being forced back home to rest, his leg strapped in irons, disregarding his trustees' letters of impending financial disaster.

Determined to venture south into East Africa, Delamere planned his fifth trip, using the vague maps and books of earlier explorers, notably Dr Donaldson-Smith and Count Teleki. After the usual arguments with his mother, he agreed to take Arthur Edward Atkinson, a clever, well-read doctor who'd almost qualified at the Royal College of Surgeons. Their trip was delayed after Delamere caught dysentery while tiger-shooting in India. Then his horse fell during a fox-hunt in Cheshire. With an injured spine, he was obliged to spend six months flat on his back - to his fury. After months of playing piquet with Atkinson and reading copiously, as a diversion from the complete works of Charles Darwin, Delamere ordered the precursor of an X-ray machine, regardless of expense.

While Delamere was thus confined, a young woman visited Vale Royal, a meeting no doubt engineered by Lady Delamere as an attempt to keep her son in England. Lady Florence Anne Cole, daughter of Lowry Egerton Cole, 4th Earl of Enniskillen, was 18. Delamere was eight years older and, with his oversized nose and undersized mouth and hands, not remotely good-looking, and he had a maddening habit of fiddling with his pen or whatever he was holding. As he was confined to bed, Lady Florence Cole might have failed to see how small a man he was, but she noticed a sparkle in his blue eyes when he talked about Africa. These were times when the most subtle of flirtatious gestures became loaded with meaning, with "suitable" marriages all but arranged amongst the aristocracy. The result of a beautiful girl being obliged to talk extensively to a bored young man was an engagement.

Finally Atkinson headed to Aden, Delamere following three months later with a photographer, taxidermist, 100 rifles, twenty dogs, a consignment of cloth and beads, and a Hotchkiss gun, to venture south into un-administered territory. An Italian count and 35 men had been massacred at Warebode some years before, but Delamere was an optimist. They left Berbera in December 1896, arriving at Lugh, Italy's only upcountry station, in March, already short of cloth and beads with which to trade. Atkinson, who felt Delamere was ridiculously generous in his random disposal of largesse, resignedly headed for Zanzibar for more supplies, carrying half a sheet of notepaper on which Delamere had scribbled in pencil: Kindly oblige bearer with whatever he wants up to £1,000. Delamere indicated a blob on a French sketch-map and told Atkinson it was Lake Rudolph, and to find him somewhere between here and there, sometime in May.

A few months later Delamere entered a corner of the future East African Protectorate, still unclaimed no-man's land. 1890 had seen the partitioning of East Africa under the Anglo-German agreement, although Great Britain had been less than enthusiastic about administering territories. However, by now a combination of the Church Missionary Society and influential figures like Cecil Rhodes had persuaded it to occupy Uganda. The "most courageous railway in the world" as Elspeth Huxley, one of the best chroniclers of this period of East African history, calls it, was heading out from Mombasa, aiming to reach Lake Victoria, with shiploads of Indian coolies arriving to build a project that would cost the British taxpayer five and a half million pounds. As well as hoping to finally eradicate the slave-trade, Britain realised it needed Uganda, as it would mean controlling the Nile, the Suez - and trade with India.

Armed with coffee, beads and cloth, Atkinson miraculously reunited with Delamere in May, and found him busy slaughtering goats to make skin bags to carry enough water for the long walk to the next wells. He'd evaded an Abyssinian attack, only to find the first well polluted by a rotting elephant carcass, and had been saved by some Boran tribesmen who'd exchanged milk for cloth. Noting their exceptionally well-built cattle, he'd headed on to less barren country with more frequent waterholes. Now the two explorers roughly followed what would later become the Abyssinian border, to the mysterious rock wells of Le, subject of a local legend about an extinct race of giants. Delamere painstakingly measured these reservoirs - it satisfied his restless mind to plot, plan and work things out - and later noted in his photo album: "The Boran say that these wells, which are numerous all over this bit of country, were dug by some people called Madanle... Every time one looks at these wells one is more astonished at the extraordinary perseverance of a people who made such enormous excavations with the tools they would be likely to have."

***

'Your grandfather was quite an explorer,' I observed to Hugh one evening in April 2016.

Hugh looked up from his book. 'He was useless as an explorer. He never kept a diary or a map of his travels. He just went to Africa to shoot elephant. There was nobody to tell him NO, so he simply spent money.'

'He was almost finished off by a lion,' said Ann, 'but his gun bearer hit the lion on the head with a champagne bottle which was full of methylated spirits. The lion got it in his eyes and walked off.'

'You see, my grandfather didn't trust the water, so he drank champagne.'

Muiruri, their elderly Kenyan butler, came in to light the living room fire, stepping over the dog that jealously guarded its bone.

But there had apparently been photo albums documenting Delamere's pioneering expeditions, hadn't there?

'One used to be in the office,' said Hugh. 'I think the rats ate it.'

Later, in England in Oxford's Weston Library, I found an album of the 3rd Baron's photographs, dating from January 1897. Its yellowing pages had plenty of hyena heads, lion corpses and dead antelope, including Soemmerring's gazelle (now a highly threatened species in the horn of Africa), an "antbear that took two days to dig out of its hole," a huge crocodile and a "boa constrictor" (actually a python), as well as pictures of camps they'd pitched, people they met, villages and surrounding landscapes, and Abdullah posed atop a camel beside a vast anthill - all with long captions in black ink. "The man on the right," writes Delamere beside a photo of ten mounted Somalis, recently returned from a massive loot, "gave me the white pony Maidal Gore that he is riding."

I felt grateful the album was safe from Soysambu's rats.

***

Eventually Delamere was sick of shooting, uniquely breaking away from the obsession with hunting game that gripped so many white men in Africa. Casting aside his 4-bore muzzle loading rifle for good, he talked at length to the Somalis every evening, intrigued by their history, culture and cattle husbandry. By the firelight he was compiling a dictionary and learning their language. Their adventurous trek continued to the placid crater lake atop the 5,000-foot Marsabit mountain, later named Lake Paradise. Two years earlier Donaldson-Smith had camped here, but no white man had trodden its forest-fringed shores since, the nearest British administrative post being 300 miles away.

After Atkinson had shot 21 elephant in as many days, they continued into desolate country, frequently charged by black rhino, to the eastern shores of Lake Rudolph, with its undrinkable green waters and hot wind, diverting around the southern end to its western shore. On reaching the Turkwell's dry river mouth Delamere headed south, meeting their first Turkana people, before crossing the Kerio river, ascending the escarpment and descending to the orange-brown waters of Lake Baringo. Using a mix of sign language and porters' attempts at translation, Delamere asked local Njemps if there was a white man anywhere in the vicinity.

'Yes,' they said. 'Martini, at Eldama Ravine.'

A messenger delivered an unaddressed letter to Delamere the following day: "Sir. Please take notice that you are now on British soil. Any act of aggression on your part will be sternly resisted. J. Martin."

Puzzled, they climbed up to Eldama Ravine, which so appealed to Atkinson that he instantly decided he wouldn't return to England to complete his medical career. Here, James Martin, more correctly Martini as he was Maltese, apologetically explained that he'd received notice that a large mounted Abyssinian army with 1,000 camels was advancing.

Back at Baringo, Delamere sent Atkinson back to Somaliland with half their oversized entourage, and soon afterwards climbed the escarpment rising to the eastern side of Baringo to what would later be called the Laikipia plateau. He had come by an entirely different route from any previous white missionary or explorer, and the entire trek south through the desert sands had taken eleven months. Now from the plateau, where the air, thin at 7,000 feet, would have felt sparkling fresh, he beheld an undulating green country that extended into blue distance, apparently empty of human life. The foreground was freckled silver with stunted whistling thorn and vast herds of wild animals, the far horizon a heap of clouds erupting into the two jagged peaks of Mt Kenya.

CHAPTER 2

...To the Dark Continent

When Delamere finally arrived back at Hartford station near Northwich, after two years' absence, his mother didn't recognise the man with the thick red beard. He married Lady Florence Cole at St Paul's in Knightsbridge in July 1899. No-one was more surprised than Atkinson. Delamere had his charms, Atkinson later told Elspeth Huxley: a 'very pleasing voice and manners', although he abandoned this 'disarming' veneer with his 'always disapproving' mother and sister. But for all Delamere's extravagance Atkinson had observed a very abstemious side, which seemed to extend to women: during all those travels he'd never even mentioned a woman, let alone taken any interest. Atkinson had concluded that his friend was 'entirely sexless.'

Delamere wasted little time taking Florence to East Africa, accompanied by a taxidermist, to collect birds for the British Museum. At Aden some of his Somali friends joined them, along with a few hardy ponies. They drew into Mombasa's harbour on 25th October 1899, with strong black arms carrying Florence ashore from a rowing boat. Mombasa island was largely forested, brightly coloured birds flitting between giant baobabs; small buck, even leopard, hiding in its shaded depths. An old stone town clustered around the harbour where Arab dhows had come and gone for centuries, blown by trade winds. At its entrance loomed the vast walls of Fort Jesus, built by the Portuguese during their rule. Now Mombasa and the coastal strip of the protectorate fell under the Sultan of Zanzibar.

The Uganda Railway had reached a swamp called Nairobi, Maasai for place of cold water, so they took a first class berth on the train, the sixty porters Delamere had hired travelling in the cramped confines of third class. Green palms faded into desiccated bush before the sun set vividly over the waterless Taru desert, its colours magnified in trillions of dust particles. Darkness fell faster than it did back home, and when they stopped there was a multitude of strange sounds. The train only travelled in daylight, so it took three dusty days to cover the 275 miles to Athi River, just short of Nairobi. Delamere was impatient to get going, but due to a smallpox epidemic their porters were quarantined for a month. Dust devils whirled through camp and Florence constantly had to pick ticks from her stockings and long skirt, unnerved by being in close proximity to the coolie camps.

Finally they moved to the tin shacks of Nairobi, a temporary railhead while engineers paused to plan the railway's ascent into the highlands followed by a challenging descent into the Rift Valley. Here they camped for a week, then walked to Fort Smith, following the railway's planned route. By now Delamere had sent back approximately 386 birds, 178 varieties, to the Museum. Descending, passing Lake Naivasha, they followed the old Uganda road up onto the 8,000 foot high Kinangop plateau, where their drinking water grew a skin of ice at night. They climbed Kinangop mountain, following elephant trails through grassy glades carpeted with flowers and bamboo thickets, returning to Naivasha on Christmas day. Then they proceeded to Nakuru, where they paused for their first sight of Elmenteita, rimmed with pink flamingos, its soda-encrusted shores shaded by yellow-barked fever trees, a curious clefted hill on its southern shore. Maasai folklore told how a lion had stampeded the cows of the chief, the cattle creating this deep cleft as they fled. Back in 1884 Joseph Thomson had noted that at "Ol-muteita" Maasai had annihilated a caravan a few years before, leaving "a fearful spectacle of skeletons and dried skins." He only saw some small gazelles - later they'd be named after him.

Delamere's party followed the Molo River to Baringo, back up the escarpment to Laikipia. As young Delamere looked at this wilderness for the second time, he saw it as a new world for white men to tame, an attitude typical of those empire-building times. In the preface to her two-volume biography of Delamere, *White Man's Country*, published three and a half decades after Delamere's first sighting of the highlands, Elspeth Huxley quotes Sir Charles Eliot, Commissioner for the East Africa Protectorate from 1900-5:

"The main object of our policy and legislation should be to found a white colony."

While camping by a stream, Florence had spotted a game bird with a cocked tail, and the next day Delamere managed to catch one for the Museum: *Ptilopachys florentiae* it was later named.

***

A century on, more modern bird books listed this Stone Partridge as merely *Ptilopachys petrosus*.

'Boffins love getting one up on each other by changing the names of species,' Hugh complained, when I pointed this out, adding. 'I don't think it matters. My grandfather wouldn't mind. I don't think he really *discovered* the birds.' D was still honoured in one of the bird books, however: The *Eucleptes progne delamerei*, more commonly the Long-tailed Widowbird. We were drinking strong black coffee on their back veranda. Creepers and shrubs shielded us from the bored gateman dozing in an old chair beside the dusty drive. 'You know the empire was simply built with red, white and blue and brass bands,' continued Hugh. 'They could just dish out bits of Africa as they felt like it, and Laikipia was just another bit - nobody quite knew who owned it.' A century earlier the Maasai had been controversially moved from Laikipia to what was called the southern reserve. 'It was the most terrible swindle. Colonialism didn't come out at all fairly – I know the British thought they brought civilization to Africa, but they didn't half bugger the natives about.' He glanced with irritation at his Kenyan newspaper, then looked up again. 'My grandfather is the worst thing that hit our family since 1715.'

'What happened in 1715?'

'The battle of Culloden, when two Cholmondeley brothers fought on one side and two on the other!'

***

When they left Mombasa on 24th of April 1900, Delamere, who was in the throes of another bout of malaria, had to be carried

20

there on a stretcher. Five months' pregnant, Florence nursed him throughout the long voyage.

Thomas Pitt Hamilton Cholmondeley was born on the 19th August at Vale Royal. While his wife was confined to home, Delamere's mind wandered back to East Africa, where the Commissioner for Uganda had refused land applications of over two acres because of the Foreign Office's decision to wait until the railway was completed. Undeterred, a few pioneers had begun cultivating. When Sir Charles Eliot was appointed first Commissioner of the Protectorate, his headquarters were moved to Mombasa from Zanzibar, where he faced a challenging job. Fiercely under the control of the Foreign Office, not even a tin shed could be built without permission from Whitehall. It seemed that the only white men who could do as they wished were the big-game hunters - and Eliot shared Delamere's opinion that it was criminal to kill wild animals for pleasure.

Finally, in December 1901, the railway reached Kisumu. It had taken four years to complete 580 miles. Eliot moved to Nairobi, built a basic house, and dedicated himself to persuading the British Government to adopt a policy of encouraging settlers. The following year the area east of Lake Victoria was taken from the kingdom of Buganda and joined up with the Protectorate. Eliot started a land department.

After almost two years of failing to enjoy England, Delamere announced that they were returning to East Africa. The life of an English country gentleman bored him and he'd continued to dream of returning to a more challenging life in a place that had captivated him with its beauty and inspired him with its endless possibilities. Determined to pioneer new farming methods, he'd already sent a prize Shorthorn bull from Vale Royal as a gift to Atkinson. It had sired eight calves, the protectorate's first half-breeds, then died of pneumonia. As this new country wasn't yet known to be safe or healthy for European children, 18-month old Thomas had to be left with his maternal grandmother at Florence Court in Northern Ireland. Galbraith and Berkeley Cole, two of Florence's brothers, arrived in Mombasa in January 1903, a month later than Florence and Delamere, who'd left for Nairobi with four horses and two tonnes of luggage.

The northern part of the East African Protectorate remained uncharted; a 1902 map labels much of it "Boran (not yet divided into Provinces or Districts)." Nairobi had grown; the one road - still a cart track but flanked by Indian shops - was now Government Road. The town had been burned down by a medical officer during a bout of bubonic plague, but had mushroomed up again. There were now 100 settlers - many of them from South Africa, with 30 more in the highlands.

The Delameres set up home at their old camp across the Nairobi River, not far from today's National Museum. After visiting Eliot, who'd voiced his disappointment at the minimal interest from potential settlers, Delamere wrote a pamphlet criticising the government's refusal to make things easier for them; they currently faced stock theft, rigid game laws preventing the killing of vermin, prohibitions on keeping goats, and obligations to use imported timber for fencing because all standing timber was crown property. The Foreign Office, Delamere concluded, treated the country like a private estate, and settlers as small tenant farmers.

Florence settled into a life of washing in buckets of muddy river water, making do with limited provisions from Indian stores and chasing off scavenging hyenas in between serving tea to numerous officials and new settlers, all vying for her husband's advice. Strongly against being referred to by his title, Delamere was now known as simply D. He became President of the new Farmers' and Planters' Association, determined to take an active part in opening up the country. But while he was riding on the Athi plains his galloping pony stumbled into a pig hole and he was thrown off, returning to Nairobi by stretcher. This time D was incapacitated in plaster, doomed to lie on his back for the rest of the year.

Eliot offered him a job and a government bungalow, but D declined - he was having a mud hut built above Ainsworth bridge, the only one across the Nairobi River. As the April long rains turned everything to muddy chaos, he wrote pamphlets and held court in his hut, applying for land in Laikipia - duly refused as it was too far from the railway or any administrative centre. He then tried for

100,000 acres running down from the Aberdare mountains to Lake Naivasha, refused on grounds it might cause problems for itinerant Maasai ("the most important and dangerous of the tribes," Eliot had noted back in 1901), and finally an unoccupied block of 100,000 acres further north in Njoro, just over 50 kilometres northwest of Elmenteita, viewed as virgin land with little worth, where the Maasai seldom grazed their stock. In between D wrote lengthy and detailed letters to Jackson, his Vale Royal agent, requesting he send out a specified selection of rams, ewes, bulls, cows, boars, sows, turkeys, ducks, geese and pheasants - and a good manager.

Finally D was granted his land in Njoro; a 99-year lease at an annual rent of just over £200, with a guarantee that £5,000 be invested in the farm in five years. "In fact," Lord Cranworth would write in his memoir *Kenya Chronicles*, "Delamere must have spent on his concession at least ten times the amount guaranteed." Concerned about D's health, Eliot added a special proviso that if he died within five years the land would revert to the government.

It was here at Njoro that the Delamere family began to establish their name, creating a legacy in the agricultural sector that would last over a century. D had already decided that the country needed someone to conduct large-scale farming experiments; the settlers were broke and the government wouldn't risk any money. "At present there is no one in the country with any capital except myself and some of the coast merchants," he wrote to Jackson in September 1903, outlining his plans to set up a refrigerating plant, making butter and cheese for export, "so none of these things are being developed." And thus, he concluded, it would have to be himself.

This "capital," of course, was money borrowed from the bank, leaving his mother the impossible task of running a huge house with no money. (Hugh took a dimmer view of his ancestor's motives. 'Grandfather wanted to prove things which are quite impossible,' he said. 'Like that you can farm in Kenya just like in England.')

As a result of Jackson's and Eliot's respective efforts, around 200 British settlers and hundreds of South Africans arrived by ship or ox-wagon. The government was far from ready with land surveys.

There'd been various proposals and pie-in-the-sky ideas: to hand over a large part of the protectorate to Jewish refugees from Russian slums; even to create a colony of Finns or Indians. D had made his disapproval known, further criticising the government for stating that no settler should come with less than £300 in cash, and then proposing penniless immigrants who spoke a foreign language and weren't even coming voluntarily! He was single-mindedly determined that his chosen country should become an economic success, repaying its debts to Britain, his reason for opposing the idea of resettling Jews; he wasn't against them as a people. When he'd met a struggling young Jew, Abraham Block, who would later become a notable business name in Kenya, he'd given him financial and material assistance, all on account at a local shop. Not expecting to be paid back, D would be astonished in 1906 when Block would repay his loan, with interest.

In spite of still being unable to walk properly, D moved to Njoro in early January 1904. It was perfectly possible to stop the train anywhere to shoot a lion or any other good reason, so D stopped it at a level crossing between Njoro and Elburgon stations. He was then carried by stretcher to two rough grass-thatched mud-walled huts built by Atkinson's brother, who'd arrived four years earlier. The steep olive- and cedar-forested slopes of the Mau escarpment behind D's farm were ideal for logging, while the rich soil on the mostly treeless and waterless expanse below stretching into the distance seemed perfect for agriculture or stock-raising. "This area is uninhabited and of great extent," the explorer Lugard had written in *The Rise of our East African Empire* in 1893: "Here, if anywhere in Central Africa, in my opinion, would be the site upon which to attempt the experiment of European settlements."

D decided to call his farm at Njoro "Equator Ranch," marvelling that such high land with its pleasantly cool climate had the equator running through one corner.

CHAPTER 3

Pioneering Amongst the Maasai

The Maasai, with their handsome warriors and nomadic lifestyle, tended to be romanticised and admired by white settlers, who viewed them as the nobility of African tribes - while keeping them at arm's length. D, on the other hand, astounded other Europeans by inviting Maasai warriors and elders into his home, spending long evenings talking with them. According to Huxley, the Maasai arrived promptly at Njoro to see what he was up to, asking through a translator how long he planned to stay. When D replied forever, this didn't seem to upset them, and Huxley claims they agreed to assist him. Thomas O'Shea, an early settler from Eldoret, told her that D was the first European to actually employ Maasai, who generally refused to work for white men.

D learned to speak Maa, and further shocked his fellow settlers when he bought greatcoats for his scantily clad employees to ward off the Njoro cold, even turning a blind eye to their stock thefts, mindful of their traditional belief that all livestock belonged to them. In spite of being extremely well read and never short of schemes, D didn't have much experience with livestock, but now he began to learn a great deal more from the Maasai.

Sammy McCall, an experienced shepherd, was shipped in with some sheep, a pony, pigs and a turkey cock. When the Scotsman arrived at Njoro Station, bowler-hatted, cigarette dangling from his lips, he was taken aback; D looked so small and eccentric, with his worn khaki trousers and moth-eaten woollen cardigan, long ginger hair flowing from a huge pith helmet. D was more interested in the animals McCall had bought, muttering under his breath when he found a dead ram. He'd learned how difficult native breeds were to acquire - the Maasai would only exchange them with cattle.

Immediately he decided to send McCall to New Zealand to get

1,000 merinos. Dying stock and marauding wild animals didn't deter D from continually importing more domestic animals, as well as seeds, and wire to make paddocks to deter zebra, hartebeeste and other pests. Settlers were only permitted to kill four antelopes a month - and to D's irritation he had to pay 375 rupees for a sportsman's license for this privilege. "I am too much in an experimental stage here to say anything definite yet," he wrote to Jackson, "but if the country is worth anything (and I believe it is) I think I have got the best stock farm in it."

Apart from the Maasai, whom settlers didn't really count as they had no fixed abode, initially the only neighbours were Atkinson and his brother, Eustace, with whom D had partnered in a sawmill. Gradually a few more arrived, including Trevor Sheen; he'd come from India in 1898 with some opium, exchanged it for a camel, transported missionaries until he'd built up a camel herd and could afford a farm. His land was best accessed on an old track passing through one corner of Equator Ranch. He got a shock when D galloped up on a mule, accusing him of trespassing. They argued under the midday sun until D suddenly invited him for tea. When they arrived at D's huts Sheen looked at Florence with surprise. How did she survive here - and with such a difficult man? The river - the only source of water - was three miles away. Ablutions were in buckets, while the prowling leopard had to be avoided on nocturnal visits to the long-drop.

D was now crossing imported cattle with tougher native breeds, struggling as his sheep became riddled with worms, not to mention lung trouble, foot rot, running noses, and mysterious black and yellow grubs behind their eyes. Much of this land was also deficient in minerals, especially iron. The Maasai had good reason to avoid lingering too long in the pastures of Nakuru and Njoro; the name Nakuru derived from the Maasai for 'the place of swayback disease;' they'd even named part of what was now Equator Ranch *ongata natai emuny* - "the plain of the female rhinoceros without milk" - because even black rhinos couldn't survive as browsers. Hardier wild animals brought ticks, notably the brown one transmitting East Coast Fever. Then there was redwater disease, and pleuro-pneumonia brought by the native oxen D bought to plough parts of his land, while his crop experiments unearthed yet more diseases. Labour was cheap (four rupees a month, plus clothes and food) although willing labourers were difficult to find and the Maasai were not willing to stoop to what they considered menial tasks.

In spite of substantial losses D remained optimistic and determined, and by the end of 1904 he had about 1,500 cattle, kept at night in a boma built around his huts, poking their heads in through the windows as their hooves churned the grass into a quagmire, their dung attracting flies. Equator Ranch was able to advertise for sale its broken bullocks (50 rupees each), unbroken ones (40 rupees) and Yorkshire pigs. D built a dairy - the first working dairy in East Africa, supplying Mombasa with fresh butter - and eventually accommodation for his cattle that was far superior to his own. Every day before dawn he drove his four mules and cart, at breakneck speed, the seven miles to supervise milking. After an incident when he was thrown out of the cart, but miraculously spared further injury, he employed Charles Clutterbuck, who'd arrived in mid-1904. It wasn't easy to work with D, Clutterbuck later told Huxley, with his 'violent temper!' On one occasion when D was away, sixty cattle disappeared. Clutterbuck sacked one of the Maasai herdsmen, at which news D flew into a blind rage, siding with the Maasai.

In mid-1905, after being summoned to Nairobi to pay a fine for shooting marauding zebra, D claimed damages for crop loss and lost, but the publicity assisted in the subsequent amendment of game laws. In 1906 he was on the wrong side of the law again over 500 acres outside Nairobi he'd tried to buy from a double-dealing character, losing his temper and tearing up the title deeds. The case was dismissed. By now he was planting maize in the Rongai valley, at the northern end of Equator Ranch, still experimenting with wheat varieties. Frustrated by his oxen, he bought the powerful steam engine that had been used for the building of the railway. Nobody could work it, so a man from England had to be imported at vast expense, although the protectorate's first large-scale ploughing was short-lived; the engine proved too heavy.

During a wet 1906 another British peer who had capital to invest, Lord Cranworth, arrived. Lake Naivasha was so high the water almost reached the railway; you could throw a cigar end into the lake from the train. D was away, but Florence hosted Lord and Lady Cranworth. "I do not think that I have ever met a more delightful companion or a more devoted wife," Cranworth wrote of their visit to the "little mud hovel" at Njoro. "Uncomplaining and extremely witty, Florence loved hunting, dancing, every form of society and every joy of life. Yet she shared an existence of the utmost discomfort without any one of these amenities with the utmost cheeriness... Two poor mud huts, which would have been condemned instanter by any Housing Authority in England, served them for years, and there was no garden nor indeed any other amenity whatever."

D, adds Cranworth, was "never a man of many personal friends, as opposed to acquaintances and admirers," but "an entrancing companion when he was in the mood." He didn't talk much, "but when he did it was talk worth listening to."

They returned the following year, by which time Clutterbuck was running the sawmill. Although Equator Sawmills brought in some much-needed cash, however, Cranworth could see D's heart wasn't in it: "he aspired to be, and was, a creator, and a penny made by some new development was more to him than a hundred pounds made by the destruction of an asset." Clutterbuck was also training and breeding D's imported racehorses, he and Jim Elkington running the only training stables in the protectorate. "I don't think that Delamere was ever really keen on racing," Cranworth added, "but, needless to say, he was President of the Turf Club." According to Shel Arensen's *And They're Off*, D was a generous supporter, donating half of his one hundred sovereign prize in 1904, while the following year Clutterbuck had won on D's horse, Dawn, and in 1906 Florence's brother rode her horse, Kathleen, imported from Australia - and won.

Florence loved racing, escaping to the stables to discuss equestrian matters with Clutterbuck. His wife Clara, who couldn't take to life in a thatched hut behind the dairy, had left in 1905 with her ailing son, but leaving behind her three-year-old daughter, Beryl. Beryl, who would later as Beryl Markham become a renowned pilot and racehorse trainer in Kenya, most famous for her solo flight from east to west across the Atlantic, became devoted to D: "To the country he gave his genius, most of his substances, and all of his energy," she writes in her classic memoir *West With the Night*. "To the Masai he gave the help and understanding of a mind unhampered by the smug belief that the white man's civilization has nothing to learn from the black man's preferred lack of it." Growing up to prefer the company of men, Beryl hardly mentions any women in her book; not her mother, nor the governess who became her stepmother, but of Florence she writes: "She was, in a sense, my adopted mother... and over a period of several years there were few days when I did not visit... Equator Ranch. I cannot remember a time when her understanding of my youthful problems was lacking or her advice withheld." Dropping English formalities, Beryl called her adopted parents Florence and D, happy to be in their home, in spite of no proper doors or windows and having earth floors, the whole place thoroughly infused with a strong smell of cow.

Watching Beryl grow up might have dropped a little balm into Florence's heart as she lived in much discomfort so far away from her only son, trying her best to make a pleasant home. Clutterbuck later told Huxley that the main living room hut had 'some very good pieces of furniture brought out from home, leaning at drunken angles against the walls,' Two other huts served as sleeping quarters for them and their guests, and Florence 'was very keen on the garden,' but the cows sabotaged her efforts. Another early Njoro resident, Bo Fawcus, added that you were obliged to cross the Delamere boma to get to their dwellings, the buggy always getting stuck during the rain. The boma was enclosed in corrugated iron 'to protect the cattle from the Nandi,' a tribe who had frequently caused trouble for the British further north and west, and sometimes ventured as far as Njoro to raid D's cattle. 'His boys drove them away,' explained Fawcus, and they 'only got away with Lady Delamere's underclothes,' (Calling male employees "boys," even elderly ones, was one way of assuming European superiority). Fawcus records that in 1906 Florence persuaded D to add 'shuttered windows' (to stop the cows looking in) and 'Persian rugs on the muddy floors.'

Florence persisted with her garden, even though D had planted water-sucking blue gums (for financial rather than aesthetic reasons). As she coaxed a vine up the side of one hut, D announced, nose in an agricultural book, that bone meal was good for vines. Since this was generally unavailable, he shot an ox beside the hole, where it fell in. 'There,' he concluded; Florence had her bone meal.

***

Some of Florence's furniture remained scattered throughout Hugh and Ann's Soysambu home. 'I'm talkative but not walkative!' Hugh complained as he hobbled up two steps to show me. His Parkinson's disease was making him increasingly paralysed. He indicated the tallboy in the sitting room: 'My grandmother, who I never met, put its feet in tin plates to stop them rotting on the mud floors.'

'The Dower chest in the drawing room is Italian,' said Ann, 'inlaid and extremely old.'

'She didn't have it easy,' I said, marvelling at Florence's ability to abandon luxury for a rough pioneering life.

'No - my grandfather killed her pretty quickly!'

***

Indeed, it wouldn't seem surprising if Florence found solace in any kindness or affection offered by other men. She certainly spent much time at the stables talking horses with Clutterbuck. Atkinson also claimed that her relationship with him was more than friendship. Huxley left all such intimate details out of *White Man's Country* but, with the characters long gone, I was grateful they had all been so well-preserved in her interview notes. According to neighbours at the time, Atkinson was a better-looking man than D, with a kind face beneath dark receding hair. Several decades later Atkinson would tell Huxley the story of when he'd accompanied D to Nairobi to meet Florence, who'd been away almost a year. D was more concerned about his sheep: 'I know that bloody fool McCall will be dosing them with arsenic or something,' he kept grumbling. 'Will you meet Lady Delamere?'

When Atkinson explained D's absence to Florence she laughed.

'How history does repeat herself,' she had replied. 'Do you remember Arthur sent Lancelot to meet Queen Guinevere?'

When they had disembarked from the train after dark, obliged to walk down the slopes with a safari lamp and a revolver, Florence had started as a large animal bounded across the path. She'd loosed off a few rounds, then said breathlessly; 'What was that, doctor?'

'I think it was a large antelope of some sort,' Atkinson had lied.

'You know perfectly well it wasn't. It was a lion!'

'Well, if you know what it was why do you ask me?'

'You've nothing to be alarmed about, anyway. You know perfectly well that you're safe enough?'

'Why am I safe?' asked the puzzled doctor.

'Because no self-respecting lion would even look at you if it had any chance!'

Perhaps Atkinson told Huxley this story because it amused him - and maybe their easy banter proved her reciprocal feelings for him. She might also have been venting her frustration that no self-respecting man could actually look at her because she was Lady Delamere.

D was a prominent political figure, Chairman of the Colonists' Association, formerly the Farmers' and Planters' Association (of which he'd been President), although he frequently resigned when annoyed. There was a government proposal to move the Maasai away from their land flanking the railway, endorsed by Lord Lansdowne, Secretary of State for Foreign Affairs, with a grant to the East African Syndicate of 500 square miles of farming land just north of the railway. D pointed out that the Maasai occupied a large tract of the protectorate, parts of which had been settled with permission of the Foreign Office without any apparent arrangement with them, but he didn't back down on his ideal of a white man's country. 'It would seem much fairer to tell the Maasai once and for all that we have come to stay and to give them a tract of country in which they would not be disturbed,' he declared. 'The reservation would have to be carefully chosen, not by someone fresh out from home looking at the country just after the rains.' The new Commissioner, Sir Donald Stewart, held a meeting with Maasai spokesmen, and it was alleged that the Maasai agreed to move away from the railway, north to Laikipia and south to the Mara plains. In August 1904 Chief Lenana signed the Maasai Treaty, the move was completed and settlers who'd been granted land in Maasai-allocated territory were ousted, including Galbraith Cole.

Land continued to be an emotive issue; by 1906 Indian immigrants, who'd continued arrived by the dhow-load to join relatives brought out to build the railway, were demanding equal rights, notably for land in the highlands. The committee of the Colonists' Association argued strongly against it. Lord Elgin, the new Secretary of State for the Colonies, felt that lease-transfer restrictions must remain, further suggesting that leases of grazing land should be granted for 21 years, not 99, as they had been. Settlers were horrified. A small Legislative Council was formed and a new Land Board, uniting with the Commissioner for Lands and the Colonists' Association. D was one of two non-official members on the Council, nominated by the Governor, which first met in August 1907. The Colonists' Association lost its momentum, and some members broke away to form the Pastoralists' Association in Nakuru, partly Sammy McCall's idea, with Atkinson as president. "Each district should have its own association, which would deal with any business it thought fit," D wrote to the East African Standard; "each association should send, say, one delegate to every twenty members to a half Convention in Nairobi." The following year the Convention of Associations was formed along the lines he suggested, becoming the unofficial opposition to the government, with D as leader, further building his reputation as the man who could force the hands of bureaucracy.

In between politics, he had other worries. His 6,000 native ewes were doing no better than the imports, so he began buying up other settlers' leases of drier land around Lake Elmenteita; initially 10,000 waterless acres, gradually increasing it with smaller farms lying along the banks of a river, albeit one that frequently dried up before it reached the shallow, saline lake. These purchases had to go through the long slow process of gaining government approval, and in 1906 Lord Elgin reluctantly sanctioned the transfer of 41,900 acres to D, before ruling that no more transfers be allowed. D gradually began to consolidate his land into one block by exchanging farms with settlers, swapping those with water for others without. As soon as he had enough land at Elmenteita, McCall was sent there with the dying sheep. New Australian rams arrived annually, with which McCall began to breed high-grade flocks, crossing them first with native sheep, then half-breeds, teaching Africans to shear, battling against predatory lions, leopard, hyenas and hunting dogs.

Back at Njoro, D's days began at 4 a.m., eating Thomson's Gazelle chops by lamplight while playing his favourite tune - repeatedly - on an old gramophone. Florence may not have been able to sleep through 'All Aboard for Margate,' but at least she was spared from frying the chops when D employed a Goan cook. He would plough before sunrise, then, after a long and busy day, he'd spend evenings with his Maasai herdsmen, the headman on the cushion from an American buggy, the others squatting by the fire, spears stacked beside the door. Florence would head off to bed and leave D, who barely touched alcohol and survived on minimal sleep, to many hours of conversations in Maa. He was a stickler for routine, regardless of any disapproving European guests. Cranworth referred to the Maasai as "D's favourite weakness" whom he "consistently spoilt." To the Cranworths these Maasai "detracted considerably from the pleasure of a visit. At all hours of the day, and especially before and after dinner, they would be in his sitting-room, squatting on the floor, and smelling most offensively...which never seemed to bother Delamere." Just don't insult his beloved Maasai, seasoned guests would warn new ones.

***

In 2000 the British journalist and academic historian Lotte Hughes visited Hugh and Ann to research D's interaction with the Maasai, accompanied by a Maasai translator. Charles Ole Nchoe was touched, if surprised, to be welcomed into one of the Delameres' spare rooms; some Europeans would have sent him to their considerably less comfortable staff quarters. There was a severe drought that year, and Maasai, who'd come from far away, were constantly trespassing into Soysambu with their cattle. Ole

Nchoe observed with apparent amusement Hugh's solution to the problem; splashes of coloured paint on the offending bovines - green the first time, then yellow, finally white, at which time the tri-coloured cows would be impounded, their owners fined. In gratitude for their hospitality Ole Nchoe asked his mother to make Hugh and Ann thank-you gifts, and thus they both wore these Maasai bracelets, beaded in green, yellow and white and emblazoned with Lord D and Lady D, until they fell apart.

Lotte interviewed 76-year old Lendani Ole Sialal, Soysambu's recently retired livestock headman. He'd worked on Soysambu for forty years, his father before that, and now several of Lendani's many daughters were still employed. From Lotte's transcriptions of her interviews I gathered that the Maasai (who traditionally and literally counted wealth according to a man's numbers of cattle, sheep and goats) had called D "Olkarsis" (rich man). Lendani confirmed that D 'liked the Maasai very much,' notably the Purko (referring to a clan), who cared for his livestock as they did their own. 'Delamere, also, was really very much taking care of the shepherds - they didn't eat *unga* (maize meal) they ate rice and milk,' D also gave each new employee a heifer, which would live in D's herd, insurance that the herdsman would be vigilant in his care of all the livestock. 'Nowadays,' Lendani pointed out, ranchers 'are not taking care of the Maasai like they did in the old days, like the first Lord Delamere was taking care of the Maasai' - changes the Maasai *laibons* (seers) had predicted, he added.

Lendani also told of D being made a Maasai blood brother, when his father was working on Soysambu. This oath only got a cursory mention from Huxley, but Lotte Hughes would expand further in her extensively researched *Moving the Maasai: A Colonial Misadventure*. According to Hughes this oath of blood-brotherhood was an important part of a complicated relationship between settlers (notably D, another early pioneer, Gilbert Colvile and possibly a few others) and Maasai; "a two-way street whereon a mutual admiration society formed, embedded in the idea of blood-brotherhood between two peoples, and shared notions of racial superiority." The ceremony, which happened some time before 1911, involved the cutting of fingers or forearms and the sucking of one another's blood, after which a big meat feast took place, probably on Soysambu.

'I'm not sure when,' Hugh told me, 'but I can show you where. It was under a fig tree just beside the bridge over the furrow on the left of the road. He had a vegetable garden down there. The fig tree is still there - it's got pinkish bougainvillea growing over it.'

The oath, delineating land boundaries, was lasting and, despite Hughes' belief that the participating settlers' motivation was greed (for land), still seen as binding by Maasai elders by the time her book was published in 2006. One Maasai interviewee told Hughes that D was close enough to the Maasai to share *enkiyieu* (brisket), which involved removing the heart and brisket from a slaughtered ox, both of which D was obliged to bite four times before handing it over to Maasai elders to do the same. Oaths were used widely amongst different tribes, and sharing *enkiyieu* created deep friendship as well as peace. The Maasai's main concern was the European's superior weaponry but, tragically, believes Hughes, they imagined settlers like D to be like government officials, and chose the wrong men with whom to strike deals.

CHAPTER 4

Dwindling Finance and Cowboy Politics

In 1907, no longer able to afford its upkeep, D's mother, Lady Delamere, was obliged to move out of Vale Royal, leasing it to Robert Dempster, a wealthy industrialist from Manchester. His granddaughter, Mary Hopkirk, later wrote a booklet about her childhood in a place by then suffering from surrounding industrialisation. "The red sandstone of the monastic wing and the red brick of the late Tudor wing were almost purple with smoke and grime," she recalled, "the trees and grass looked grey and sooty." Even the sheep were "grimy."

Hopkirk and her siblings thoroughly explored the grounds, house and cellars - where a bricked-up secret passage went under the river to Darnhall - intrigued by everything, from D's stuffed animals to the curtains in the large bay windows of the saloon, "the work of the first Lady Delamere...of velvet lavishly embroidered with gold thread and padded applique coats of arms and roses big as plates...embossed in padded satin about two inches thick." The children slept in "enormous Victorian beds with draped testers," the portrait of two Tudor Cholmondeley ladies, twins, holding their twin babies above one of the washstands. The dining room had portraits of royals and Cholmondeleys, including a 1657 Van Dyck and a "vast chandelier," cleaned daily by two footmen. There were two rabbit-fed eagles, harping back to when an eagle had sat in the turret of the library window at the time of the birth of a long-awaited heir. D's mother was superstitious about such things and, on hearing that one of the eagles had died, arranged for another to be sent from Scotland.

In 1907 Winston Churchill, the Under-Secretary of State

for the Colonies, visited East Africa. D arranged pig-sticking at Elmenteita where there was an abundance of warthogs, with lunch afterwards. "Every white man in Nairobi is a politician," Churchill later wrote in *My African Journey*. "There are already in miniature all the elements of keen political and racial discord...all these different points of view, naturally arising, honestly adopted, tenaciously held, and not yet reconciled into any harmonious general conception, confront the visitor in perplexing disarray."

The following year the provincial headquarters was moved from Naivasha to Nakuru. Another accidental town that had grown up by the railway, Nakuru offered little in the way of entertainment. After a good 1908 harvest, D rectified this, building the Nakuru Hotel (later renamed the Midlands, it was still there in 2018) and employing a French couple to run it. His unpredictability soon unnerved them, however; having refused to let in some elephant hunters arriving late from Uganda, he remorsefully paid their bill after they'd broken in and taken their fill of drink. D was also prone to sudden eruptions of dare-devil behaviour, once buying every orange in Nakuru and encouraging hotel guests to throw them at the windows until there was no glass left. Another time he organised a rugby match in the hotel's bar, standing on the bar himself before leaping into the scrum. Once, having sold 1,000 head of sheep at a Nakuru auction, he treated every hotel guest to dinner. Even back home, D's long working days and abstemious lifestyle would result in a need to let off steam, when he would race the train in his buggy along the rough track from Njoro.

The Cranworths were renting Chiromo house in Nairobi, named by its owner Ewart Grogan, an early settler famous for walking from Cape to Cairo to win the hand of his wife. Florence now joined Lord Cranworth in the production of *The Advance Flag*, a magazine sold at race meetings in aid of local charities. Held twice yearly and lasting a week, race meetings were an opportunity for revelry for hard-working settlers. D would attend in his old farm clothes, long hair flowing beneath his enormous sunhat, usually staying at the Norfolk Hotel, once locking its manager in the meat-safe after he'd announced closing time in the bar. Sometimes settlers dined at Nairobi Club, and after dinner, just after street lighting was introduced, D took a group on a rickshaw outing to watch him shooting the gas lights. ('He was imprisoned in The Norfolk as there was no prison for whites,' Hugh told me, 'and fined £12, which was a lot. He probably borrowed it from the manager who he'd let out of the meat safe. But he did not ride into the bar as some stories said.')

D certainly gave Florence inspiration for the caricatures she drew, something at which she excelled, although according to Bo Fawcus she never showed D the ones of him. Meanwhile Cranworth, who also wrote for *The Standard*, remained staunchly loyal to his fellow peer, starting up a rival paper, the *Daily Leader*, after a leading article in *The Standard* had criticised D.

D registered a small non-profit company called Unga Ltd, providing half the capital - £5,000 - to build a flour-mill in Nairobi. According to a 1903 Swahili dictionary the Kiswahili word *unga*, when used as a noun, means anything powdered or ground up, especially grain. Having arranged a plot near the railway, brought out machinery from England and begun to dig foundations, D flew into a rage when the Land Office changed its mind and ordered him to build elsewhere. He paid some loitering spectators to collect wood, heap it beneath the wooden Land Office on stilts, and prepared to set it alight. Unga Ltd didn't lose its plot after all.

D continued to sink money into East Africa, exhausting his finances and borrowing more from English banks, refusing advice from his friend Wilfred Hunter, an expert on financial affairs who also sat on the Legislative Council. "As far as his own money went he had no financial sense whatever," Cranworth writes of D, "though he was careful enough about other peoples', and especially so with public funds." When D was obliged to go to England to try to raise more money, Florence ran Equator Farm, a gun beneath her pillow after Sotik warriors had raided and massacred everyone in two nearby Maasai villages. "The rain has been awful and the cold intense," she wrote to her husband. "I hope you won't be annoyed but I couldn't stand it any longer and have bought a little house and hired a carpenter to build it. I could not stand the cold any longer."

***

As Hugh pointed out to me, his grandfather 'didn't believe in nice houses because you'd waste time sitting in them.' Elspeth Huxley had interviewed Sir George Ritchie Sandford, who knew and admired D. Sandford was in the Colonial Service, his roles including Clerk to the Legislative Council, Private Secretary to Governor Northey and Deputy Head of the Treasury. He confirmed that Florence's new house was envied by all, seen as 'a terrific luxury,' and that it would survive into the 1930s, by which time D's mud hut lower down had fallen to bits.

In early 2017 Andrew Nightingale's family were the only remaining white landowners on a drastically downsized corner of the former Equator Ranch. A collector of historical memorabilia, Andrew had two original millstones from Unga Ltd that had been displayed for decades in front of Unga House in Nairobi, the modern successor to D's flourmill. He drove me up to the railway siding at Njoro where D had been dropped off on his stretcher. Weeds straggled amongst the sleepers - only one train a month nowadays. Nearby was where the sawmill once stood.

The old Delamere homestead was now a school. It was term time but there was an eerie silence from Olive Secondary School. Hammering on the gates produced no joy, so finally Andrew stood on the bonnet of his car and shouted.

'I am Nicholas,' said the man who finally opened the gate. 'Welcome!'

Beneath a hot blue sky, a yellow-painted stone house with a red tin roof looked over D's former farm. This would have been built long after D had left, in the late 1930s or 1940s. We walked around the side, where a sprawl of hardy salvia, two large hibiscus, a coniferous tree and a poinsettia still survived, peering through a window at rows of empty bunk beds.

'The school, it cannot open,' Nicholas explained, 'because of money.'

All that was left of the original homestead was behind the house: a rectangle of old, wide-girthed cedar posts that once supported the panels of Florence's wooden hut. A large stone water tank held a few inches of murky water. Beside it, a couple of plum and lemon trees wilted in the fierce sun. As we prepared to leave, Nicholas disappeared, returning bearing two vast pumpkins: 'My grandmother told me that visitors should never leave empty handed,' he stated with touching generosity. 'I hope you will return.'

***

By 1908, public affairs increasingly engulfed D's time. Bureaucracy and its plethora of regulations and restrictions still hampered pioneers' lives. Quick-thinking, argumentative, autocratic and outspoken, and above all doggedly determined, D was very much their leader. The year had seen new settlers arrive from South Africa and the founding of Eldoret town on the Uasin Gishu plateau. Of all their problems, including excessive railway charges, a shortage of labour was the most frustrating, although D was little affected; the Maasai were still happy to work for him. While settlers believed it was the Africans' duty to help build the economy, they didn't particularly need (or want) to work, nor did the government encourage them. The Colonists' Association wrote to the Governor, James Hayes-Sadler, and when he still failed to come up with a labour policy, D led a contingent of embattled settlers towards Government House to get a definitive answer. The Governor afterwards complained to the Secretary of State that Delamere had been offensive and aggressive, and D and a colleague were suspended from the Legislative Council. D then wrote a long letter to the Governor accusing the government of worsening racial relations by taking the side of the labourers. "And is the native so very contented under the present regime?" he asked, adding that he had "hundreds of friends among the natives" averse to the government's petty regulations preventing their free movement, and often resulting in pointless arrests. "The country is on the brink of bankruptcy," D wrote, "owing to the interference of Government with the land laws and the labour supply, and it cannot be wondered at if people take strong measures to try and avert their own ruin." The Colonial Office blamed the incident between Governor and settlers on the altitude.

But D gained popularity, and after six months 'Flannelfoot,' as Florence had nicknamed the Governor, was forced to reinstate both men. A central board to review the labour situation was appointed, labourers' living conditions improved and Hayes-Sadler was dispatched to the Windward Islands after some of his junior officials had been incriminated in forcing African girls to become concubines. The new Governor, Sir Percy Girouard, was a French Canadian interested in the country's prosperity, and although he would fail to persuade the British Government to build a railway to Mt Kenya, he'd manage to get a tramway to Thika.

With less than half the country under administration, D had been trying to persuade the government to take over the neglected north. He'd spoken at length during Churchill's visit in 1907 on the Galla tribe, who were being killed, raped and enslaved by the Abyssinians, their villages looted. A railway should be built all the way up to Lake Rudolph, he said, to open up an area where few ventured - apart from the Boma Trading Company, which brought cattle to trade with Maasai sheep, but due to quarantine became a smuggling agency. The government even seemed uncertain as to the exact line of the Abyssinian border. Girouard managed to establish posts at Marsabit and Moyale, and in November 1909 the area was officially named the Northern Frontier District.

And now the protectorate's revenue finally met expenditure: Girouard reorganised finances, raising loans and finally doing away with the grant-in-aid, freeing the British taxpayer from the costs. A new pier was built at Mombasa's Kilindini harbour, railway traffic increased, coffee and sisal were doing well, a cooperative creamery and bacon factory started, and more settlers arrived. In spite of hating any obligation to dress smartly, D became a frequent dinner guest at Government House. He didn't always agree with Girouard but, as Cranworth points out, D was tolerant - "a virtue none too common in Kenya" - and "would always... listen to an opposing point of view and weigh it carefully."

A new land ordinance was passed through the Legislative Council and sent to England early in 1909. Although not passed into law until 1915, it granted the colonists 999-year leases, as opposed to 99, sold to the highest bidder. There was an obligation to develop and use land, but the Governor's consent was no longer required - although he could veto transfers between members of different races.

D began to fence his Elmenteita land in 1908. The sheep were doing better here, while he was also increasingly attracted to the stark beauty of his ranch, which he named Soysambu, a misspelling of a Maa word: it should be *soit-sambu*, Henry Ole Sanoi, a Maasai conservationist on Soysambu in 2018 told me. '*Soit* means rock,' he said 'and *sambu* is its colours, striated volcanic rocks having black, brown, white and sometimes red-orange in almost parallel lines.' According to the present-day Hugh, *soit-sambu* also describes the colouring of a brindled cow.

D imported an Australian supervisor, who gloomily watched herds of galloping zebra flattening fences overnight. His Scottish shepherd, McCall, was more concerned about being responsible for too many sheep, and threatened to resign, not for the last time. They had frequent rows, The Hon. Robert Carnegie, an early settler at Ndaragwa on the edge of Laikipia, would later tell Huxley - after which D would raise McCall's salary. But soon the first samples of East-African cross-bred merino wool were sent to England, and the following year D began sending it over in commercial quantities. Photographs of sheep and cattle grazing the bare expanse of Soysambu, captioned: "Lord Delamere's East African Estates. First cross ewes from native sheep with second cross lambs. Shorthorn and Devon cattle. Second cross cattle, shorthorn and native," were published in East Africa (British): Its History, People, Commerce, Industries and Resources, by the Foreign and Colonial Compiling and Publishing Company in 1908-1909. There were also photos of wheat and maize being harvested on Equator Ranch.

D continued his experiments: importing wattle seedlings from Natal and starting a factory; experimenting with Virginian and Turkish tobacco; and ostrich farming - all of which failed. Spotting the herd of donkey mares being led by a zebra stallion, he visualised a disease-resistant cross. But several years of effort only saw four bad-tempered 'zedonks,' although one did agree to pull a buggy in Nairobi. Remaining philosophical in the face of failures, D would also try breeding eland as pack-animals as well as for their excellent meat. He imported more pigs, sending a whole cured pig to England to be displayed at the 1909 Royal Agricultural Show. That January he'd exhibited his wheat, maize, cattle, sheep and vegetables at the Nakuru Agricultural show. "The outstanding characteristic of his operations was courage," writes Cranworth. "Having made up his mind, sometimes on somewhat scanty evidence, that a certain line was likely to prove successful, he went full speed ahead...Indeed I really believe that if he had ever found an easy way to fortune, the success would have bored him stiff."

A good wheat harvest prompted D to buy large numbers of unbroken oxen, hiring Dutchmen to drive them. Over 1,200 acres were sown to pay off the overdraft, but yellow rust destroyed over half. Using a final loan of £17,000, D imported 12 varieties of wheat from New South Wales, planning to cross them with the Italian Rietti, later engaging Gerald Windham Wright Evans. A Railways employee in East Africa since 1898, Evans was a self-taught scientist who'd been Director of Agriculture at the Government Kabete Experimental Farm. He'd gone to Cambridge during his leave, where he persuaded a renowned professor of plant breeding to teach him plant genetics. Returning to East Africa, he began experiments at Kabete to breed rust resistant strains, resigning when he was promoted to Inspector of Coffee Plantations. D stepped in to take responsibility for Evans's employment, building him a makeshift laboratory at Njoro. More wheat varieties were obtained from India, Egypt, South Africa and Canada, and Evans would finally breed a successful wheat strain, aptly named "Equator" although after the war he never returned to plant breeding.

Meanwhile, back in England, a receiver was appointed to collect Vale Royal Estate's income.

As settlers suffered stock theft, D continued to battle the government. After an incident at his Elmenteita ranch where two Indian policemen failed to deal with a reported incident, D took matters into his own hands, tracking down his stock on horseback, then sitting down under a thorn tree for lengthy discussion with Maasai elders, as was their custom. Feeling that the prevailing police ineptitude would see a problem turn into a crisis, D tried to persuade the government that less should be spent on the military, and more on the police. Eventually, in 1909, the collective punishments ordinance was passed, laying down that the community could be punished for an individual's misdemeanours. Stock theft decreased.

Ex-American president Theodore Roosevelt visited, determined to be the first white man to shoot a shy and rare antelope called the forest bongo, found in the montane forests. D was in many ways an early conservationist, although there wasn't a need for such a word in those times when Africa teemed with wildlife and hadn't yet seen the decimation of her natural resources. Although he had no desire to shoot animals for sport, D evidently had respect for the man who'd won the Nobel Peace Prize and gone through the grief of losing his wife during childbirth. Generous to a fault, as always, D ordered two Swedish elkhounds and some English collies, wasting more time and money until Roosevelt got his bongo. As Roosevelt famously said, 'In any moment of decision, the best thing you can do is the right thing, the next best thing is the wrong thing, and the worst you can do is nothing.'

A grateful Roosevelt continued to correspond with Florence after his safari, in a lengthy letter dated March 7th, 1911, telling her he'd spent the happiest four months of his life in East Africa, expressing sincere gratitude and further praising her and Delamere's "large outlook...I only wish that in England itself there was a fuller appreciation of the service." He concluded, "Whatever comes, you and Delamere have played your parts well and bravely, you have done well what was well worth doing." Roosevelt also wrote a booklet, *African Game Trails*, in which he described the Delamere home as "most attractive," particularly the library where Florence kept her books. He described D as "a practical and successful farmer, and the most useful settler, from the stand-point of the all-round interests of the country, in British East Africa."

By now D had put £40,000 (amounting to £4.6 million in today's value) into his endeavours, while struggling to live on £200 a year (£23,000 today), but he had at least proved the economic viability of ploughing large acreages in virgin country. And now he was feeling restless. Leaving Equator Ranch in the hands of his manager, in 1910 he moved to the place that would come to mean more to him than any of his other parcels of land in the protectorate: Soysambu.

CHAPTER 5

A Dusty Place

There are multiple spellings of Elmenteita. According to Hugh, the correct spelling is Elmenteita: 'The name is derived from the Maasai *Ol-muteita*, meaning "dust place." It refers to the crust of soda when the lake dries up.' Joseph Kodonyo, a Maasai naturalist and expert ornithologist at a nearby lodge, agreed with this, but Henry Ole Sanoi added another meaning: *Ol mut*, he told me, means 'terminator or finisher' while *Eitaa* means 'taking one by one.' In other words, he explained, it means 'slow killer,' referring to its mineral deficient soil and grass that slowly killed livestock.

According to a 1910 map depicting the Northern and Southern Game Reserves, Elmenteita lay in the vast Eland and Roan Reserve, which bordered with the Southern Game Reserve. Its history goes back millions of years, when the earth's tectonic movements formed the Rift Valley and one vast lake covered today's Lakes Nakuru, Elmenteita, and Naivasha, supporting our ancestors as well as large populations of diatoms, their fossils now mined as diatomite above the south eastern edge of Lake Elmenteita. A prehistoric site at nearby Kariandusi displays vanished peoples' stone hand-axes and cleavers, unearthed by paleoanthropologist Louis Leakey in 1928. As you drop into the Rift Valley, the impression is of having lost altitude, but in fact Elmenteita, lying at an altitude of around 6,000 feet, is higher than Nairobi.

After drier conditions had forced the great lake to shrivel to three smaller ones, various people, including the Maasai, passed through, but seldom lingered in *Ol-muteita* with its alkaline lake, lack of fresh water and mineral-deficient soil. In the early 1880s Joseph Thomson paused to admire its pink fringe of flamingos. Half a century later Elspeth Huxley would describe Elmenteita as "almost blinding in the intensity of its beauty. Nature seems to have spilled her colours with a wild luxuriance." And a century after D moved there, his great grandson, Tom Cholmondeley, would write, "The beauty of the landscape is sufficient to make you go mad - or to stir very strong passions."

To the east of Soysambu was the Mereroni river, then the flat-topped Sugonoi escarpment (*Losogonoy* being Maasai for the *warburgia ugandensis* trees that thickly forested the slopes). To the west lay the Mau escarpment, and to the south rose the two mountains of Eburru, more properly Oldoinyo Opurru, Maasai for "mountain of smoke" because of the hot volcanic fumaroles that riddled the craters and flanks. The Maasai and the wildlife continued to migrate through area, while Lake Elmenteita was visited by vast numbers of waterfowl. Surprisingly, hippos basked in its saline waters.

Initially D shared a hut with Sammy McCall, although he "gave that up," Fawcus told Huxley, "as McCall never washed or took off his socks." D's new hut had no door, a bed in one corner, and a "writing desk piled high with unopened letters." When Florence moved to Soysambu, she found her husband still spending evenings conversing exhaustively with the Maasai. She listened to the constant muttering of the flamingos, amplified into gentle grunts as they flew over the huts, missing Beryl's daily visits as much as the child missed her, although her brother, Galbraith Cole, was now a neighbour. He'd named his 30,000 acres Kekopey after the small river running into the lake from a hot spring at the top of the farm. Galbraith was an expert on sheep, (unlike his brother Berkeley who preferred cattle) and he and D had become friends based on a strong mutual admiration.

By now D had purchased 20,000 acres in Ndaragwa, on the northern foothills of the Aberdare mountains overlooking Laikipia, half of it from Galbraith. Galbraith's future wife would later claim in her memoir that he had exchanged some of his Ndaragwa farm for Kekopey, but according to Huxley, D gave his brother-in-law this land.

By now Soysambu had 15,000 sheep, partly descended from a few Corriedale, and over 300 merino ewes. The first year at Njoro had seen only six lambs survive out of 4,000. Now there was only a ten percent loss. D's Shorthorn and Devon bulls were also doing well in the absence of red water disease and East Coast fever. The latter, D claimed, had been originally introduced to Maasailand from the coast, but the Maasai had eradicated it by frequently changing grazing grounds, a practice now threatened by restrictions on their movements. He formed Nyama Ltd ("meat" in Kiswahili), opening butcheries in Nakuru, Nairobi and Mombasa, buying a plot in Mombasa and building the country's first cold store.

In 1911 the first Nakuru race meeting was held. D was still president of the Turf Club, winning and losing horses over poker games with Clutterbuck. So many lambs died that the farm's profits from the previous year were sucked dry. Nobody knew what caused it or how it was transmitted. Settlers called it Nairobi Sheep Disease, Huxley claims, the Africans called it *ngurutu*. Little was known about such diseases, and meanwhile worms were spread by wild animals, and these problems were compounded by malnutrition caused by soils lacking in cobalt and zinc. It wouldn't be until 1925 that researchers from Aberdeen would call this mineral deficiency in cattle Nakuruitis. ('Most of the diseases should be called Delamere-itis,' mused Hugh, 'as Grandfather found most of the cures…')

***

Dividing Maasai territory hadn't been a success; many Maasai hadn't moved, there was overstocking in Laikipia, and the road between the two sections was quarantined. A new formal treaty was signed, renouncing the 1904 one, approved by Secretary of State for the Colonies, the Viscount Harcourt, in May 1911, exchanging 4,500 square miles of Laikipia for 6,500 square miles along the Mara River. Olonana, son of a Maasai seer, felt the division had undermined discipline, that his people should be reunited, a sentiment with which his peer, Parsaloi Ole Gilisho, strongly disagreed. Land politics had also been at play: the Land Office had informed settlers that Laikipia land would be available, and after many meetings, false moves and muddles, and the death of Olonana, Governor Girouard resigned in early 1912 and by April 1913 the Maasai move was complete.

Writing almost eight decades apart, Elspeth Huxley and Lotte

Hughes tell different versions of the story, the latter correcting Maasai names and including Parsaloi Ole Gilisho's failed court case against the colonial government in 1913. Hughes' conscriptions of Lendani's interviews include the story of his father, then a young warrior, moving from Entorror (Laikipia) to N'gatet (the southern Maasai reserve, part of which is now the Maasai Mara). Lendani's boundaries of these areas are considerably larger than Huxley's, with Entorror beginning at the Rift Valley escarpment running east of Soysambu. In the end, Lendani's family returned north; Entorror was free from rinderpest and pneumonia, the pasture was better, well-watered with mineral deposits - *larjak* - that could sustain cattle for six months. N'gatet was drier, rife with disease, and thus, with their cattle dead, many Maasai sought employment with white settlers, especially D. 'He was telling the other white settlers to handle the Maasai nicely,' Lendani explained. But at the end of the day, he added, 'I really feel hurt very much, because of the land that was taken.'

***

By 1912 D had 1,750 acres under wheat. He imported seven expensive Australian harvesters, confident the crop would yield three times the Canadian average, planning for Unga Ltd to buy a plot at Kilindini and build an elevator on the wharf. But the labour shortage resurfaced with the rise in demand for farm workers. The government appointed a commission, requesting D be on it, leaving Florence to deal with endless daily problems, from doling out medicines to sick babies, to convincing men they would survive witchdoctors' spells. "It was a constant grind of hard, exhausting work without even the restfulness of a comfortable home to look forward to in the evening," Huxley writes, "a lonely, a nerve-wearing and often a monotonous life for a woman." Unsurprisingly, when Florence returned to England in early 1911 to engage an engineer for the meat freezing plant, she collapsed. At the news, D went to England for six months, the longest he'd been away from East Africa since he'd settled. "I am going to have a rest," he wrote on leaving East Africa. "I want one after ten years."

He arrived to find his wife had suffered a nervous breakdown.

Then on 25 February 1911 his mother died, aged 75, and three months later his 40-year-old sister, Hon. Sybil Cholmondeley, died too. Unable to face up to family stresses, D toured tobacco factories, read up on wheat, visited a bacon factory, then the Secretary of State to discuss Kilindini pier and the Uganda Railway, and drew up plans for a larger cold store.

The news from the protectorate wasn't much better. Having suffered continual stock theft over a long period, Galbraith Cole had shot and killed a man. He didn't deny this, but claimed he was defending his property after the police had failed. The jury who acquitted him attracted much publicity, and Cole was deported. Florence, her convalescence spiked with anxieties, entreated D not to go to the Colonial Office. Instead he wrote an unusually restrained letter to the Secretary of State, admitting that such cases were difficult, adding that he didn't care about his relative - who'd made an error of judgement. However, he argued, "You cannot hang a white colonist who defends his property when the government has failed to do so."

Ernest Caswell Long, who simplified his name to Boy Long, had now been hired to assist on Soysambu. According to Cranworth, he'd been selected by Florence to be Thomas's tutor when her son had been briefly exposed to the hazards of East Africa, before returning to England after about a year, but Long had stayed. Long's notes, now in Oxford's Weston Library, give a detailed impression of life on Soysambu, although curiously there's no mention of Florence. D returned first, still rising before dawn, bolting breakfast by the light of a hurricane lamp, bumping off at first light through rain-gouged ruts and aardvark holes in his latest acquisition, a second hand Ford. All morning he'd dose, dip or perform post-mortems on sheep, coming home for a rushed late lunch nine hours later. He'd do farm paperwork until sunset, when his Maasai herdsmen would arrive for the habitual conversations. He didn't eat until 10 pm, and the menu seldom varied: tea, those Thomson's gazelle chops, blancmange and tinned peaches. Long would "creep off to bed thoroughly tired," but D would summon the herdsmen again to discuss the next day's plans. Then he would read, do accounts or go through political matters until the small hours. When he finally lay down on a camp bed he'd keep a lamp burning to deter himself from sleep-walking.

"It was a hard life, but an enjoyable one," Long writes. "We had plenty of food, but pretty bad, and no drink. D was exacting to a degree, hardly ever satisfied...On the other hand if one was in the right he would always climb down and apologise. He had the kindest of hearts and provided one was prepared to devote the whole of one's energy to his interests there was nothing he would not do to help one. Despite his roaring temper I was devoted to him, and so were all his natives."

Long was astonished at D's trust in the Maasai, conceding that these thieving herdsmen were "devoted to Delamere and his interests," quickly learning not to criticise them. In his view the herdsmen already received excessive provisions, but D then ordered they be supplied with umbrellas biannually - to the astonishment of other settlers. He relates the story of D boarding the Nairobi-bound train at Elmenteita when an out-of-breath headman found him: he needed to move his cows and sheep to the Maasai reserve, but the District Officer wouldn't grant him permission. D, who allowed his herdsmen to herd their livestock on his land, was enraged, and vowed to sort the matter out in Nairobi. After many complicated meetings and lengthy correspondence, he finally obtained a special permit and sent it to Soysambu. A year later, Long pointed out that the cattle moved had actually been D's own, that theft was against the law, and the Maasai involved should be imprisoned. D had just laughed, and said this simply proved their intelligence.

Long's diaries are particularly critical of one "boy," whom he refers to as "Lakamyunay," although his spelling varies. D's "favourite," Lakamyunay turned up one day wearing one of D's khaki shirts. Long accused him of stealing it, to which he replied that if he had he'd be hiding it. D himself was delighted, both at the sight of his employee in his shirt, and by his defence. Then Long misplaced the safe key, always kept under his pillow at night. He finally obtained a duplicate from the bank to unlock the safe, and found 900 rupees missing. Certain it was Lakamyunay, Long placed some marked banknotes in the safe. They duly vanished and the police later traced them in Nakuru but found no culprit. Years later Long was talking to D about Lakamyunay.

'Do you remember how he robbed the safe?' smiled D.

'How do you know?'

'Oh, I got the key back from him, but I did not like to say anything to you.'

Cranworth also remembered Lakamyunay. He'd meet him at the station in the old Ford, motorcars being a new luxury in East Africa, "with a yard-long spear at his side, and remarkably badly he drove too," he writes. When Lakamyunay went too far, using D's car in his absence, getting drunk in Nakuru and driving into a tree on the way home, killing several friends, D dismissed him. Long would tell Huxley many years later that D practised tribal favouritism: he could be 'very truculent, he rowed with the Kukes and they would go on strike.' Long was referring to the Kikuyu, adding that in D's eyes the Maasai could do no wrong.

Maasai thefts paled into insignificance beside predators regularly breaking into *bomas*, learning to avoid traps and poisoned carcasses. Long often encountered lions at night when walking between his hut and the store. Carry a lamp, D advised. One night, feeling unwell, D went to bed unusually early. When the dogs rushed into his hut and cowered under his camp bed, the bull-terrier bitch barking frantically as a large paw came through the half-open corrugated iron door, D sat up and fired his revolver repeatedly at the roof. The lion withdrew, prowled around, then tried again. This went on all night. By morning the roof had been shot to pieces and the hut stank of gun powder. An exhausted Long had slept throughout.

Long wrote about one Sunday when six lions stampeded the cattle, killing three heifers. Armed with D's rifle he sat up all night and wounded one. Two herdsmen, Mesubio and Maramosho, helped him track it, whereupon Long fired but missed. Armed only with a spear, Mesubio dashed after it, getting between Long and the target. "He let go his spear and got the lion," Long writes admiringly, "seized it by the tail without getting a scratch, and started yelling and screaming until the other man Maramosho came up and finished it off."

Not wanting his herdsmen to suffer injuries from such adrenalin-fuelled activities, D invited an American, Paul Rainey, to Soysambu with his pack of bear-hounds to hunt lions. Two weeks passed without significant success, during which Lord Cranworth visited and wrote about one evening after another lion hunt, when D - unusually - had too much to drink. A lady who bred dogs was another guest. 'I can't stand women who breed dogs,' D said repeatedly throughout dinner. 'It oughtn't to be allowed.'

***

Just over a century later, when Soysambu hadn't had resident lions for a considerable period, two pregnant lionesses escaped through the electric fences of neighbouring Nakuru National Park. They each produced three cubs, and a year later eight lions were doing their best to cull the overpopulation of zebra, although unfortunately they also developed a taste for Delamere beef. In late 2015 I was at Sleeping Warrior Lodge, a tourist venue on the southeastern corner of Soysambu, with Hugh and Ann, lunching on beef fillet and admiring the sweeping view. Looking out over leleshwa-speckled hills, Hugh rested his gaze on the dot that was a cattle boma where lions had killed two heifers the previous night. Far below us in the rocky terrain we could make out a Kenya Wildlife Service vehicle searching for lions to dart and collar, in order to regain some measure of control. Hugh launched into his favourite line: 'You know my grandfather was terribly proud…'

'I don't think you ought to be shouting about this,' put in Ann.

Hugh ignored her: '…that by 1911 they'd shot 286 lions on this farm.'

'No,' Ann asserted, 'that was in the whole Rift Valley.' She had a soft spot for Soysambu's new lions; on their mantlepiece at home were two lionesses, painted by Simon Combes, which she fondly called Afterglow and Aftermath.

Finally, on Valentine's day 2016, the two lionesses were collared, one named Valentine, the other Flir, after the nightscope vision glasses that assisted with her capture. Some of the males were later captured by KWS and moved to Nakuru, but returned immediately so had to be translocated further, to Tsavo. Time moved on and Valentine, who'd lost a litter of cubs to predators, revisited Nakuru to find a mate. KWS then mended the hole in the fence. Unable to return, Valentine paced up and down for weeks, growing thinner by the day, oblivious to jeering, stone-throwing passers-by. Eventually KWS allowed Rowena White, Soysambu's volunteer lion researcher, to feed her. Hugh even consented to donating beef from the Soysambu slaughterhouse. When she'd finally been captured and returned, we watched a desperately emaciated Valentine shadow Flir and the half-grown cubs, still an outcast, keeping her distance. As darkness dropped, we heard the last bleat of an antelope Flir had caught in a nearby thicket, which she then consented to share with Valentine. As we told the story the following day at Main House, Hugh surprised me by sharing Ann's delight. The challenges of farming versus conservation temporarily shelved, we raised our glasses: 'To Valentine!'

***

When Florence was due to return, D imported three prefabricated houses from Norway. These came in panels, transported by ship, train, then finally lugged to their chosen sites by ox-wagon. The largest, erected near the Meroroni river, was for Florence, a concession to her health, although D stayed put in his hut. McCall was given another one, although better accommodation didn't prove enough to keep him; in 1912 he finally left. D remained generous to the end, McCall departing wealthy enough to start his own sheep farm. Over a century later the three prefabs still survived. The smallest, formerly McCall's, had originally been on a ridge, southwest of the lake, but had at some point been moved closer to today's offices, where it now housed a manager and several tenacious swarms of bees.

A new Governor, Sir Henry Belfield, arrived towards the end of 1912, and D wasted no time telling him of his determination to see settlers electing representatives to the Legislative Council, an important step towards self-government. East Africa's white population was now almost 6,000 and government systems were inadequate. In a speech to the Convention of Associations he further attacked land policies, capital 'laid out in the wrong place and in the wrong way,' the vacillations of the Indian land policy, the breakdown of the railway, native taxation, 'feudal' game laws and 'a form of administration under which it is impossible for the official and unofficial elements of the population to live together in unity.' Behind Belfield's back D called him, 'that very admirable servant of the crown,' while Belfield claimed that D's attitude was akin to putting a pistol to his head. Once again D and his fellow-farmer and colleague, Arthur Baillie, were dismissed from the Legislative Council.

D laid a 20-mile pipeline running down from a dam he'd constructed at the confluence of the Mereroni and Mbaruk rivers, Soysambu's only water source. The river then drained away into Lake Elmenteita, but the rest of the farm, which was almost all of it, was bone dry, so D's creation of this first pipeline would be transformative, enabling great leaps in development. He insisted on night shifts, although after close encounters with lions the workers went on strike. Finally the pipeline reached its destination. At the news, D left his dinner, summoned Long, and drove his Ford six miles up the rough stone track. They lost their way repeatedly, but eventually got to turn on the water, and drove home, where D slept briefly. Before dawn he drove to the far end of the pipeline, where it filled a large concrete tank. He measured the speed the water was coming through, using his watch and a four gallon petrol can.

'67,000 gallons a day!' he announced triumphantly. ('The pipeline started off right up at the dam at four-inch,' Hugh told me, 'which was rather expensive, then it went down to three-inch, and grew smaller and smaller as it went right across the farm, until it got down to half an inch. Water flowed day and night.')

The first pipe dream realised, a two-storey barn was built from pumice and cement with cedar floors, and a stable yard - "about forty boxes for bulls and horses," Long recorded. Dips, stores and offices were also built, then a stone house at the top of the bluff overlooking the lake, facing Galbraith's Kekopey. The stone had to be brought by rail from Nakuru, then ox-cart. It was a simple affair; a small living area, veranda, two bedrooms tacked onto the side, and a separate building for the kitchen. By 1913 it was ready, but as D didn't plan on leaving his hut, Long moved in. Early photos show this bleak and featureless building on a treeless bluff.

***

'I planted most of these trees,' said Hugh, indicating their well-shaded garden. Later on, he added, his grandfather built the outhouse, still known as the Bull Box, 'room for two bulls.'

'Now a large bedroom,' added Ann.

'And a room for a herdsman.'

'Now another little bedroom and a bathroom.'

***

Fifteen imported Shorthorn bulls arrived at Elmenteita station. Sinbad the Sailor had died of heatstroke on the way; the rest were half-dead when they were herded through the darkness by the guttering light of hurricane lamps, followed by whooping hyenas. After a mile, Linedraw Rake lay down and refused to get up.

'If the bull will not go to the stable, then the stable must go to the bull,' D said. 'We must build a grass shelter.'

"It took us the whole night to get the other nine home," wrote Long. "The worst part of all was that they had contracted mange on the boat, and most of them were hairless and looked more like rhinos." Linedraw Rake lay resting in state for two weeks, finally joining his friends, apart from Lucky Jim, who'd fallen victim to a deadly puff-adder. At the same time two Somali men arrived with 600 Boran cows. Their average yield was less than 200 gallons a year, but breeding them with the new bulls raised this to 700 gallons.

D's heart had been troubling him, but he continued running Soysambu from his bed until the beginning of 1914, when bad health forced him to return to England. Florence, whose heart wasn't strong either, stayed at Soysambu to supervise, growing so weak she could barely walk.

CHAPTER 6

Taking the Strain

D r Atkinson hastened to Soysambu, where, he told Huxley, he finally persuaded Florence to go to Nairobi. D returned to East Africa, but two days later, on 12 May 1914, Florence died in the arms of her good friend, Mrs Milne. She was 36. The cause of death was given as heart failure. It might have been congenital (her brother Berkeley would also die prematurely), but there were various other theories about contributory factors. Exhaustion. Depression. Stress. Some long-term undiagnosed tropical disease?

"Her courage and gaiety in the face of many troubles and disappointments had won the admiration of all who knew her, and her death was a very real sorrow to all East Africans," Huxley writes, adding sagely that D "gave more of his heart to his dreams and schemes for the growth of his adopted land than to his wife's happiness." Florence had been closer to her brother, especially Berkeley, whose charm and wit, Cranworth wrote, matched his sister's. "When the two of them were in Nairobi for a week or a night there could hardly be a dull moment."

Beryl was devastated. Florence had been more of a mother to her than Clara Clutterbuck, who'd left her so young, taking away Beryl's brother. At the end of 1914 Clara would marry Sir Henry Kirkpatrick, although she most likely had no idea that her estranged daughter would now have a half-Somali stepbrother; Abdullah was the son of Kirkpatrick's Somali wife, born in 1907, as recorded in Terence Gavaghan's *Of Lions and Dung Beetles*. Having married according to Muslim tradition, and likely keeping that quiet when he undertook a Christian marriage in England, Kirkpatrick then had an English son, who would inherit the Baronetcy after substantial settlement had been made to Abdullah. The latter grew up to become a prominent merchant in Isiolo, where he would be fondly referred to as 'the bastard baronet.'

***

A century later Abdullah's elderly grandson told my friend, Tom Lawrence, that when Kirkpatrick had left East Africa in about 1910, D had looked after Abdullah and his mother on Soysambu, a story which surprised Hugh. Neither was there mention of this in anything I'd read, nor indication if Beryl knew anything.

***

Atkinson was also heart-broken. It seems that he never married and Huxley's unused interview notes suggest that he'd been waiting and hoping. He told Huxley that although Florence was 'very fond' of D she was not in love. When he once told Florence how beautiful she was she replied, 'No, I'm not beautiful, but I'm clever, because if I wasn't clever you wouldn't think me beautiful.' Before her death, he said, she was 'smoking incessantly,' although she couldn't walk 20 yards without panting. He listened to her heart and knew she wouldn't survive. 'She was excitedly waiting for D to come out to tell him she was leaving him,' Atkinson insisted. 'He used to lose his temper terribly with her and abuse her...a loose pig was the end of the world, even when he'd spent £500 on some useless implement.' At these outbursts Florence would calmly send for Atkinson to come and Atkinson would distract D, for he was, Atkinson said, 'never logical unless you made him see it.'

It's hard to know how reliable a witness Atkinson was. He wasn't widely popular, described as a "blackguard" and a "blustering bully" by Sir Frederick Jackson, a veteran of the Imperial British East Africa Company. Stephen North in *Europeans in British Administered East Africa* records Atkinson- known as "El Hakim, Arabic for a wise or learned man, notorious for his dubious ivory dealings- being acquitted for murder after he had blown up some tribesmen in the north of Kenya. However, Florence's remark about Sir Lancelot suggests that they were in love.

There's little about Florence in *White Man's Country* - in fact remarkably little has been written at all about her. Any desire to leave D had been kept secret. Cranworth makes a throwaway remark when writing about D's second marriage, that his first had "also" been one of "great happiness." But it would hardly be surprising if Florence's unhappiness had spilled out in other ways, notably seeking attention from other men. There'd been a rumour that Clutterbuck had fallen out with D back in 1905 because of his feelings for Florence. The former Governor's wife, Gwendoline Girouard, gossiped about Florence's alleged antics during race week. "After all the other ladies had gone to bed," Gwendoline wrote in a letter, "dressed...up in motor-scarves (nothing else), she came downstairs and danced the Salome dance to the men!"

Cranworth, in spite of acknowledging Lady Girouard's charm, is quick to point out in his memoir that she was considerably younger than Sir Percy, wasn't always tactful, and was prone to inaccuracy. But if Florence had occasionally spread her wings, indulging in a little wild behaviour, she could hardly be judged for it, considering that most of her life was a daily drudge, living with a volatile, bullying husband with whom she'd likely fallen out of love. Busy as he was with the affairs of farming and the country, it's unlikely D gave his attractive, cultured and clever wife the attention or credit she deserved. Her role, as wife of such an important figure, coupled with her upbringing, would have obliged her to grit her teeth and get on with being Lady Delamere, assisting with D's endless experiments and schemes which he continued in spite of his mounting financial problems. And all this while living impossibly far from her son, now 13, but a long ship's voyage away because there were no schools for European children in East Africa.

It's no surprise that Florence died young of an illness likely to have been exacerbated by so much stress.

***

To add to Florence's brief and puzzling story, mysterious circumstances would later surround her removal from Nairobi South Cemetery and reburial. Walled, sheltered from Nairobi's adjacent industrial area by vast trees, the cemetery dated back to 1900, the adjacent Jewish cemetery to 1909, followed by the 1914-1918 War Graves that remained under the good care of the Commonwealth War Graves Commission. By 2005, when I visited, everything else had fallen into overgrown, broken neglect, until a trio of unsung heroes stepped in, led by Monty Brown, an avid historian who regularly drove from his home north of Nanyuki as part of this voluntary Sunday mission. They removed fallen trees, winched back toppled gravestones and repaired broken ones, replaced stolen plaques, studied the original Railway Register of Graves to create an accurate plan, and Monty wrote a guide book.

Monty pointed with a wry smile to the grave of Reverend Peter Cameron Scott, founder of the Africa Inland Mission at Nzaui in 1895, who died of fever a year later and was buried there, then moved. Whoever dug him up found two skeletons, so compromised and took half of each. A large triple grave was reserved for the Delamere family. The stone read: "Sacred to the memory of Florence AMB the beloved wife of Hugh Cholmondeley 3rd Baron Delamere who died in Nairobi May 12th."

'She was the only Delamere to be buried here,' Monty explained. 'She was exhumed in 1950 and moved by the family, leaving the stone upside down for 58 years, until we came along.'

So where was she buried now - on Soysambu?

'No,' said Hugh, 'although I wasn't here in 1950. I was at Cambridge.'

I asked 87-year old Tobina Cole, who'd been married to Florence's nephew.

'I should think they took her back to Ireland,' she said.

But no, Florence wasn't in the family cemetery in Ireland.

Florence, who'd once sat for a portrait by Lafayette (now in the London archives of the National Portrait Gallery), didn't seem to have been the subject of any photos in the protectorate, though Ann had a large brown leather-brown album that had belonged to her. She'd painted the Delamere family crest carefully into its opening page, writing on the page opposite in a large sloping hand, The Book of Thomas Cholmondeley 1900.

The half-filled book, Florence's precious record of her son as he grew up far away in England, contained photos up to 1912. Their young subject is ultra-serious; initially a baby dressed in impractical regalia, then a toddler, dolled up as a little girl, as was fashionable. ('I suppose it makes it easier to change a nappy if you're dressed like that,' observed Hugh as we looked at a photo of his chubby-faced father in dress, bonnet, girls' shoes and white socks). As he grows up, Thomas sits astride a pony or holds a fishing rod. His age is pencilled in, sometimes the place; Miss Pincoff's school, Heatherdown Preparatory School. He is easily recognisable from group photos as his great-grandson, Hugh Cholmondeley, bears a striking resemblance. In one photo 12-year-old Thomas is with the Cranworths and their son, leaning against Lady Cranworth, a position striking a poignant reminder of the absence of his own mother. As his godparents, they provided him with a home during his school holidays. And to Thomas, Lord and Lady Cranworth must have been a more significant influence than his parents, far away in East Africa.

I closed the album, saddened by Florence's short life, her separation from her only child and her difficult marriage. A century later, nobody seemed to know - or even care - where she lay.

CHAPTER 7

No Peace

Burying any grief or other disturbing thoughts, D kept busy, drawing up plans for the subdivision of his 100,000 acres at Njoro into farms sized between 300 and 3,000 acres. A pipeline was surveyed to provide water to these plots from the Rongai river.

A 28-year old Danish woman, Karen Dinesen, had arrived in East Africa in early January, marrying her Swedish cousin, Baron Bror Blixen-Finecke, on arrival in Mombasa. In spite of Karen Blixen's stay in East Africa only lasting a decade and a half, she would become far better known internationally than Florence Delamere, notably for her famed memoir *Out of Africa*, also made into a film in which Karen was played by Meryl Streep. While Blixen went on hunting safaris, Karen ran their farm on the outskirts of Nairobi, an area still called Karen, and where her former home is now the Karen Blixen Museum. From the outset Karen Blixen had great respect for D, with whom she would forge a firm friendship.

In the middle of that summer the weekly paper printed a cable about the murder of an Archduke in the Balkans, but D ignored the rumours of war. More relevant was news of the Indian railway workers and Public Works employees striking because of poll tax. On the morning of 4th August 1914, however, D went to Elmenteita station to arrange cattle transport. Major Ross, a game ranger, was heading to Nairobi. The Empire was at war, he announced. D strode up and down the platform swearing; the timing couldn't have been worse - just as things were beginning to improve...

British and German East Africa shared a 300-mile border, from Lake Victoria to the Indian Ocean and dividing Maasai country. At this stage it was uncertain whether this war would affect the protectorate, but armed settlers flocked to Nairobi to sign up at the volunteer enlistment office. Meanwhile the Indians went on striking, Germans were arrested, and 800 Somalis marched to Nairobi House to offer their services. Florence's brother, Berkeley Cole, organised them into a troop of mounted scouts.

Berkeley had initially farmed at Njoro, then moved to Naro Moru, where he had a Somali mistress, not unusual for men in remote parts of the protectorate, but nonetheless frowned upon by other settlers. Karen Blixen deemed Berkeley "a typical Englishman of a certain class and period, - whom I like a great deal, but whose limitations in their view of life and humanity is almost comical... they enjoy wine, hunting, a certain kind of love with sincere understanding, but anything other than this is a closed book to them. And yet all the same time they think they can rule the world, - and the odd thing is that they are not at all bad at it!"

Cole's Scouts would become a somewhat unorthodox sector of the East African Mounted Rifles, the latter starting up on 5th August with a motley mix of over 400 settler volunteers, most of them expert riders and crack shots who knew the country well and spoke Kiswahili. In spite of their surprise at being issued with regulation uniforms and obligation for formal training, these men would prove invaluable. Among its officers were Cranworth and professional hunter, Denys Finch Hatton, another old Etonian with whom both Karen Blixen and Beryl Markham would fall deeply in love.

A camp was formed at the racecourse, racing having been suspended, although many troopers stayed with friends in Nairobi, in hotels or the recently opened Muthaiga Country Club - D was its first President - which was now obliged to close. D himself wasn't soldier material, Cranworth points out: "The discipline would have killed him, or led direct to a court martial." However, D did send a telegraph from Elmenteita to the chief staff officer of volunteers, offering his services as Intelligence, aware that the Uganda Railway was less than 50 miles from their unprotected borders, lying in country only known to the Maasai. He was appointed O.C. Intelligence on the border, leaving Long, to his chagrin, to look after the farms. D rode off into the bush on a mule with some Maasai companions, blankets and rations, to organise scouts and border patrols. "All news of the movements of the enemy had to pass through Lord Delamere's camp," wrote Karen Blixen in *Out of Africa*, "but Lord Delamere was moving all over the Reserve in such incredibly swift marches that nobody ever knew where his camp was to be found." Bror, Karen's husband, was also stationed along the border, with Karen busy arranging and delivering his supplies, always carrying a photograph of her friend, German General Paul von Lettow Vorbeck, with her in case of arrest by the Germans. "Once my way took me within a couple of miles of Lord Delamere's camp, and I rode over with Farah and had tea with him," she continues. "The place, although he was to break camp next day, was like a city, swarming with Masai. For he was always very friendly with them, and in his camp they were so well regaled that it had become like the lion's den of the fable: all footsteps turning in and none out...Lord Delamere in the centre of the stir, small, and exceedingly polite and courteous as ever, his white hair down on his shoulders, seemed eminently at ease here, told me everything about the war, and offered me tea with smoked milk in it, after the Maasai fashion."

Meanwhile the Germans had taken the offensive early on, a clever policy that would be successful in deploying British Allied troops away from the Western Front. Taveta, the border town on the British side of Kilimanjaro, had been taken by Von Lettow Vorbeck by mid-August, thus controlling an important corridor into German East Africa. The German border lay dangerously close to the Uganda Railway where it passed through Tsavo and the Taru Desert, and the Germans were able to sabotage trains. The EAMR were moved to the borders, getting off the train at Kajiado and marching through the bush with no transport or food, killing game for meat, fending off lions and rhino. By September troops were arriving from India, and the Germans had occupied Kurungu Bay on Lake Victoria. One of the EAMR squadrons was rushed back to drive them out. As well as tsetse flies, wild animals and Germans to worry about there was dysentery, sunstroke, malaria and blackwater fever. On November 2nd the British failed to remove the Germans from their posts on Longido, a sharp volcanic hill just beyond the Namanga border. ('The Germans had very little artillery, but they used it to great effect,' Hugh told me. 'They could see the British troops miles away, and shot them down like flies.')

The British, now supplemented by the Royal North Lancs, then failed to capture the port of Tanga after a disastrous three-day battle. Other defeats followed, although there was a small victory for the British at Kisii in south western Kenya.

Most settlers, who'd left their farms under the control of wives or headmen, were finally given leave in early 1915, although they were still much in demand. By April Nairobi was full of Indian troops, while British warships patrolled the coast. In spite of a weak heart, D had endured six months of long days riding through the bush, uncomfortable nights in the open and a limited diet supplemented by quinine. He'd been sending runners and pigeons (some of which were intercepted by hawks) to Nairobi with information brought in by Maasai scouts. Finally, running up a hill to an observation post at midday, he collapsed. An ox-cart took him to Nairobi, where he boarded a train, arriving back at Elmenteita with diarrhoea, heart pains and malaria. In spite of D's protests, Long wired the doctor, who instructed him to dose D intravenously, alternately with arsenic and distilled water, administered by Long standing on a chair holding a cup. When D finally saw a doctor, his heart was found to be severely strained, and he was confined to Nairobi's Scott Sanatorium for several months.

By mid-1915, after the arrival of the 25th Battalion of Royal Fusiliers, South African and Rhodesian battalions were then deployed, finally destroying the German ship, the *Koenigsberg*, in July. The crew escaped, most of them armed, and joined Von Lettow Vorbeck.

September saw the largest ever meeting of settlers, urged on by a still ailing D, to urge the government to adopt a definite line of action to replace the incompetent running of the civil side of the military – emphasising that if it wanted more help, then settlers must have more say in running the country. The government formed a War Council, and finally the country was divided into three areas, with a representative from each elected by the settlers.

At the beginning of 1916 General Jan Smuts arrived from South Africa, and many of the EAMR were appointed staff officers; within a few months these men had proved themselves too valuable to be troopers and many had already been transferred to other units. After their defeat at Salaita near Taveta, Smuts took the offensive, starting from Longido, capturing Taveta, Moshi and Tanga, pushing Von Lettow Vorbeck south. Some of the remaining EAMR men helped to dislodge the Germans from the Usambara Mountains but, weakened by malaria and forced to eat rats, only a major, sergeant and two troopers survived. And thus the regiment died out.

Towards the end of the year, barely able to walk, D was forced to return to England to spend six months in a London nursing home. With a strained heart valve, the doctor made it clear he shouldn't live at altitude for more than a few months a year. Dempster was still renting Vale Royal, where the last of the pigeons had been made into pies to save the corn for the Belgian refugees living above the stables. He gave D a leatherbound photo album of Vale Royal, with photographs of the house, interior and gardens taken in 1915 by a professional photographer in Northwich.

Thomas, known to friends as Tom, was now at Eton, but D was too preoccupied with financial worries to give him much time. Growing increasingly angry and impatient with his father's financial dealings, Tom had learned about money the hard way. Having spent his entire over-generous allowance the previous year on two horses, amongst other things, he was now £400 in debt. The Cranworths had cut his allowance down to half a crown a week, which only kept him in illicit tuck - three pots of marmalade a week.

After six months, not having grown any closer to his son, D returned to his farms, joking that he couldn't afford to die yet. Long finally went to fight in France, while D struggled on with 23,000 sheep. It was impossible to ship wool to England, but he could provide meat for troops. According to Huxley, during one fortnight he sent 1,200 Thomson's gazelle carcasses to Nairobi. With the veterinary department struggling to keep transport animals alive, disease was spreading. "I have nearly 9,000 good ewes just starting to lamb and my cows calve in September-

October-November," wrote D in October 1916. "And now the rinderpest. I have been seruming myself, but am now going in for the double inoculation." This was a new method, but eventually it simply spread redwater throughout the high-grade herds. In 1917, a very wet year, threadworms caused 25 percent mortality in lambs. A cattle disease called streptotricosis struck too. Soysambu only had 1,600 cattle left. D tried to buy more, but even the Somalis couldn't purchase any, and when he finally managed to buy 1,300 cows from a Greek at Mwanza, the military took them before they were delivered.

He struggled on, counting sheep weekly, supervising dosing, marking and biannual shearing (to deal with scab), ignoring his severe headaches. Some elderly Africans who'd been taught by McCall were paid three shillings per 100 sheep. D finally managed to get six shorthorns from Australia to continue with upgrading stock, but the government laboratory near Nairobi managed to kill them while inoculating them.

Galbraith Cole had returned from his period of exile in Britain, disguised as a Somali. The government turned a blind eye: Galbraith had suffered many years of rheumatoid arthritis and was now almost crippled. Lonely without Florence or Long, D regularly visited him, grateful for Cole's assistance with his rams, in spite of his criticism of D's complicated method of ear marking. "He's a very interesting man to talk to when he's by himself, full of original ideas," wrote Cole. "Sometimes I think he's the most brilliantly clever person I know. Marvellously quick to understand things, but he shuts his mind to all the things except those which actually have to do with the material side of life..." This, Cole felt, left "a sort of gap, a something rather hollow in his company."

"Pioneers like Delamere often seem to have a dead side to their natures," explains Elspeth Huxley. "They seldom appear to take any interest in music or art, or to look for beauty in existence. They cannot afford to do so. They must not admit the need for such spiritual stimulants in the midst of the raw, prosaic realities which surround them..."

Karen Blixen also tried to analyse men like D, writing to her mother that "...in a completely simple and straightforward way" they were "looking for the primordial values of life..." She didn't always praise the British, but she admired them "for their clear, almost inspired and simple understanding of their own nature and the completely unperturbed way they live in accordance with it." Galbraith Cole, she writes, had "aplomb or faith in the rights of his own nature that leads Lord Delamere, for instance, to turn his back on everything in England and live among the Masai...I believe that they are some of the happiest people in the world."

"You never really get to know him," reflected Cole of D. "I doubt if anybody ever has. He won't be known, but he likes to know others." He felt D's attitude was "take all and give nothing," while for him Soysambu was a "dreary place...There's something about it that always depresses me and somehow there's a sort of bareness about Delamere's surroundings that I can't explain." Edward Powys Cobb, whose farm lay above Soysambu, near Mau Narok, would later tell Huxley that D had 'absolutely no artistic sense at all. All that side was dead. He lived in a mess and had no feeling for colour.' Eleanor Cole, who married Galbraith towards the end of the war, would later write in her memoir that D "banished out of his existence everything that wasn't intensely materialistic." And yet, she acknowledged, "He was in reality intensely sensitive and this gave him the power to hurt as well as to sympathise. He had a secret dread of going mad - it was in the family. He couldn't stand the dark and always slept with a light in his room. He was really an intense physical coward and forced himself to be brave. He was pea-green with fear before going out hunting, but shot more lions than anyone else."

Meanwhile the war continued in deteriorating conditions. The final advance on the Germans had been launched on New Year's Day, followed by one of the wettest rainy seasons ever recorded. The Maasai continued to boycott the war, with D always quick to defend them. Early in 1917 he was elected to the War Council, while he was also spending considerable time touring the country with the Economic Commission appointed by Belfield, taking stock of resources and aiming to suggest an economic policy for post-war reconstruction.

1918 brought severe drought. Coffee crops failed. Tinder-dry Soysambu had its own battle against a huge bush fire. Eleanor Cole wrote to her mother about D's lucky escape: "He had to turn out all his stock - bulls and rams and horses - and himself got caught in a corner so he had to drive the car he was in up on to the verandah of his house!" Karen Blixen wrote to her mother about the ensuing famine: "I have been speaking to Lord Delamere, because he is trying to shoot down all the zebra on his farm just now, - for fear of epidemics, - and sending them down to Nairobi." She questioned whether "natives" would eat it: "White people cannot eat zebra..."

***

'Grandfather sent 26,000 zebra off this farm in the war,' Hugh told me, a note of envy in his voice, as Soysambu's zebra continued multiplying, consuming the limited water and diminishing grass. 'Grandfather and Gilbert Colvile, who were great muckers, did their bit for the war effort. Their idea of supporting it was to get the Kenya Maasai to steal cattle off the Tanganyika Maasai, which of course Kenya Maasai were very expert at. Well, of course you had to give half of what had been stolen to the Maasai, who stole it. Gilbert Colvile gave up his half, which, say, was a quarter, which he sold to the British Government to help feed the troops, and a quarter he kept for himself, which was why his cattle always had shorter legs than the Borans - Maasai cattle always have short legs. My grandfather, of course, had to give half to the Maasai, and he gave, not sold, the whole of his other half, to the British Government to help feed the troops. That's why Gilbert Colvile died rich and my grandfather died poor.'

***

By now the King's African Rifles had drawn up a scheme for the conscription of 300 Maasai, but when a company of armed KAR arrived in Narok the warriors hid in the forest, having made it clear they would fight, but not carry packs. The KAR surrounded a village to arrest some rebellious *morans*, the term used for unmarried

Maasai warriors, and opened fire, killing two women, ten cattle and wounding four others. D immediately wired his protest to the Commandant and Chief Secretary. The government, terrified of repercussions, accepted his offer to negotiate. Meanwhile a large force of fierce *morans* from the Purko clan stormed a KAR camp, spears held aloft, killing 14 and wounding many more; pillaging and burning shops, murdering Indian shop owners. The telegraph line had been cut from Narok to Elmenteita, so D rode off before dawn with some of his herdsmen, including Mesebero.

As the sun began to light the eastern horizon, a band of *morans* accosted them. When D spoke in Maasai, they lowered their spears. 'That is Delamere,' said one. A long discussion ensued. As the sun rose they moved beneath the shade of a spreading acacia. Blood must be avenged by blood, the Maasai said, and they would fight the government until they'd done so. At some point during this long, hot discussion, Mesebero heard the news that his brother had been amongst those *morans* killed by the government. As he fell to the ground in a fit, the situation deteriorated, and D had to exercise all his powers of diplomacy until late that night. He then carried on to Narok, where he made it clear to KAR officers that they should not carry out their plans to inflict a lesson on the *morans*.

'...You, Delamere,' said the Maasai's spokesman when he was back with them, 'are our friend and you have always taken our side against the government.' They agreed to let him to speak to Parsaloi Ole Gilisho, their rebellious spokesman who had opposed the Maasai move. Although still furious about the shooting of their women and cattle, accepting D's sympathy, he agreed that the *morans* would stop their attacks. Ten days later D was able to persuade a contingent of *morans* to join KAR, although in reality this didn't actually happen. They simply continued their policy of passive resistance, avoiding government officers until the end of the War.

"Lord Delamere then disappeared without a trace into the Reserve," Karen Blixen wrote to her mother, not impressed by the mess the government had made of the situation, "and as far as I know has not yet turned up again, but no doubt he has thrown oil on the troubled waters by his sheer presence." D she described as "the 'Little

Father' of the Maasai…I can imagine that it is a relief for him to go down and sit and talk with his old Maasai chiefs, so they won't get him back too quickly; he has to tear about up here between his farms and a whole lot of committees and counsils [sic] for which he most probably has a hearty distaste."

In another letter she wrote that D was "one of the old 'Masai people' who have lived among and grown to know the Masai thoroughly, and have a great interest and sympathy for this ill-fated race, - dying, as I believe, like the Indians in America, of a shortage of living space; there is little doubt at all that they have been treated with gross injustice and that this is still continuing to this day."

She was acutely aware of the rift between older and newer settlers. Her lover, Denys Finch Hatton, was one of the former set, "like Delamere, Galbraith Cole and van de Weyer; they are a much better type than the later ones. Society here," she went on, "is divided up by a strictly defined order of precedence which rests almost solely on the length of time one has been out here." Old settlers were, she claims, "the people who really mean something here." Late in 1917 the British finally took control of German East Africa after East Africa's last combat in a four-day battle, and the surrender of most of Von Lettow Vorbeck's forces, although he managed to escape south into Portuguese territory and return with reinforcements. He finally surrendered on November 25th 1918, in Abercorn, Northern Rhodesia, twelve days after the Armistice.

The East African Campaign had been fought over 750,000 square miles with 150,000 Allied troops battling against only 25,000 German ones. The British Carrier Corps, formed in 1916, consisting of Africans who faced the logistical challenge of transporting food, water, medical supplies and munitions to troops, saw a huge loss of life. "I have always thought that a more generous recognition of their immense services might be forthcoming," writes Cranworth, pointing out that the East African Campaign had cost "more money and three times as many lives, if deaths from disease involving porters as well as combatants are included, than the whole South African War," and the Protectorate was "the only part of the British Empire to know invasion, and, partially no doubt from this cause, the response of her white population and the casualties they suffered were in proportion to her numbers greater than those of any other colony."

"Among African soldiers and military carriers recruited from British East Africa alone," writes Edward Paice in his article 'How The Great War Razed East Africa,' "more than 45,000 men lost their lives. This equated to about one in eight of the country's total adult male population." The true figures, however, were undoubtedly higher. "As many a British official admitted, the full tale of mortality among native carriers will never be told."

CHAPTER 8

Settling Soldiers

War, drought and famine had left the protectorate in a bad way. There'd been no Governor since Belfield's retirement in 1917. When Sir Edward Northey arrived in January 1919, he set up a new Legislative Council, reorganised the railway and civil service, raised loans and balanced the budget. He appointed D and Tommy Wood to be on the Executive Council to represent settlers' and commercial interests respectively, and launched the soldier-settler scheme, dividing the country into settled and native areas. According to Huxley, the plan was less about patriotism or economics and more about strategy; fears that the white man's exposed vulnerability during the war could generate a safety issue, best addressed by increasing the white population. Belfield's Land Commission (of which D was a member) now recommended all surveyed land be offered to soldiers on 999-year leases at an annual 10 cents per acre. Northey adjusted this: settlers taking up larger blocks (over 160 acres) must buy the land on easy terms. Land would be allotted by ballot to settlers considered suitable, approved by selection boards in London and Nairobi.

In June the first draw took place at Nairobi's Theatre Royal. A few weeks later there was another at London's Colonial Office. In November around 1,500 prospective settlers left England. The government wasn't overly generous; they were obliged to pay duty on household goods, and some of their farms turned out to be waterless or otherwise useless, but around 75% eventually stayed.

D had sold a third of Equator Farm in two large blocks immediately the war was over, purchasing 400 acres of land at Loresho, just northwest of Nairobi, where the red-soiled ridges seemed ideal for growing coffee, recalling how the White Fathers' mission had started off coffee in East Africa with Arabian seed in 1898, the first plantation taking root in 1900. Now, to keep Soysambu going, he needed to sell the 500-acre farms into which the remaining two thirds of Equator Farm had been divided. But to be marketable these required access to water, so he built the pipeline he'd surveyed before the war; 16 miles of it with 39 water tanks along the way to serve the new 500-acre farms, costing him about £12,000. Though he badly needed funds, he made it easy for buyers by allowing gradual payment. Clutterbuck bought 1,000 acres. A new arrival, Gerald Sladen, also bought a farm, although this turned out to be dense forest and bush. Unable to cross the Molo River to Rongai, the Sladens spent their first year in a cedar house at Njoro until they'd built a bridge. His wife Mabel kept diaries, describing their two-day road trip to Nairobi from Rongai in August 1920, stopping for lunch with D before thoroughly losing their way. "The road is a bit puzzling," she noted, "as so often what looks like a main road is merely a farm road and the grass track is the main road."

Boy Long returned from the battlefields, having married Mary Millicent Erskine-Wemyss two years previously, while he was a Lieutenant in the Grenadier Guards, a marriage that hadn't lasted. There'd been dramatic change back home: "Parties and plenty of good food and wine, people always coming and going; Soysambu was a sort of club," he wrote - although some things hadn't improved; D had lost about 25,000 sheep to heartwater and streptotricosis, the pastures now so contaminated that those remaining needed to be moved. Boy Long and Mesubero walked them to Ndaragwa. This proved too high and cold for sheep, but below yawned the Laikipia plateau, some of it allocated to soldier-settlers, but most of it lying empty after the second Maasai move, so Long walked the sheep there.

That Christmas of 1918, Alexander William Rooken-Smith, a settler who'd come from South Africa in the early 1900s, offered D £10,000 for his 20,000 acres at Ndaragwa, and was surprised at his refusal, as he felt the sale would have benefitted D, rather than having Long, described in Rooken-Smith's diaries as "often neglectful and wasteful," racing around the country. Rooken-Smith was camping on his own 10,281 acres above Elmenteita, land that included a forested spring. D asked for first refusal should Rooken-Smith ever want to sell this, and Rooken-Smith would later offer it to D at £2 an acre. D would put down £5,000 cash, to pay the remainder over 10 years at 6% interest - a payment Rooken-Smith claimed D never completed. Meanwhile things were changing in Laikipia as soldier-settlers began to arrive, throwing Long and D's sheep off their new farms. "I was left with only the land that they did not want because it was bad or because it was waterless," Long writes, "and I got Tarlton to let me have his farm, Soleo (sic), as my headquarters. When I had proved this the best sheep land on Laikipia he sold it to Galbraith Cole."

Hugh Martin, the Commissioner for Lands, toured Laikipia, pointing out that so many sheep couldn't continue to roam the area indefinitely. He proposed that D give up his Ndaragwa land and take up some of the abandoned soldier-settler farms instead. As D was in England, Long negotiated with the government on his behalf for 63,000 acres of sheep land in exchange for 21,400 acres of agricultural land at Ndaragwa, which could be sold as small farms for more than three times the price, securing double the annual rent for the government. This prompted some British politicians to accuse D of wangling three times the amount of land for nothing from the government, even of stealing it from the Maasai. In response the local government sent a delegation, who found the 63,000 acres empty apart from a handful of settlers' sheep and herdsmen. D offered to withdraw if the government could sell it in smaller blocks. They couldn't, and the land exchange went ahead. D then spent another £18,000 purchasing land with river frontage in order to water the rest with a pipeline. In a few years this had been completed and D was successfully farming over 30,000 sheep on his new Laikipia farm, employing 100 herdsmen, mainly Maasai, and - to the chagrin of other settlers - paying them handsomely.

***

I asked Hugh about this farm in Laikipia, a story which Hugh firmly began at the beginning. 'They dished out chunks of 5,000

74

acres of Laikipia to all sort of soldiers, but with no reference to whether there was any water or anything like that. I think you had to show that you'd got some money, enough to build a house on it and develop it; it wasn't very much - maybe 200 pounds.' But he had a different take on D's acquisition of the abandoned soldier-settler land. 'Well, running along one boundary was the Ewaso Nyiro, which was quite a useful permanent year-round river, but on all the rest of it there was not a drop of water at all, unless you drilled a few boreholes, which was way beyond the capacity of the settlers. My grandfather felt sorry for these people. He bought fourteen of the 5,000-acre plots, I think.'

'Boy Long ran his sheep there and did extremely well,' Ann pointed out.

'But it's all black cotton soil or solid rock - these sort of ridges of bare rock with nothing on it except whistling thorn, then in the hollows you've got quite deep black cotton and grass.'

'Sheep did better there than in the Rift Valley.' The White-browed Robin Chat was singing at full pelt in the nearby shrub and I had to lean forward to hear Ann.

'What did the farm's name - Ol Pejeta – mean?' I asked Hugh.

'Ol Pejeta means the bald man in Maa, as there's a hill, a sort of volcanic dome, that looks like a man's head.'   'Did your grandfather name it?'

'No, the Maasai did!'

(I later discovered that in Maa, Ol Pejeta actually refers to a place for roasting meat.)

***

Soysambu's stone house now empty, D briefly moved in. Fawcus told Huxley he'd been a guest there "in about 1920," praising D's "outstanding range of knowledge about every subject on earth," adding that "he carried masses of figures in his head." Fawcus remembered sitting up over a brandy until 3 a.m. arguing with D, who then allowed his guest two hours' sleep, coming into the guest room before dawn "to continue the argument."

D had also bought land on the volcanic Eburru mountains

bordering Soysambu, and now he installed another pipeline. The first attempt, a cedar flume, was abortive, but the second, galvanised iron, was a success. Soysambu now had 30 miles of pipeline (worth £25,000) and fifteen sets of water tanks. Not that this guaranteed water: baboons had learned to jump up and down on the ball-cocks, and a portly hippo tried to climb into a water trough, cracking the concrete. An armed guard was dispatched to each tank to inflict the death penalty.

***

Hugh's story about one of the water tanks his grandfather built is told in his irascible collection of stories *Not in the History Books*. His grandfather saw an advertisement in the South African Farmers' Weekly for Mauser rifles confiscated after the Boer War, now rusted solid. "My grandfather was looking around for some cheap steel," writes Hugh, "to reinforce the walls of some concrete water tanks." D purchased all one thousand rifles, which were then bricked into the tank. About a year later, the Foreign and Colonial Office, alarmed by a half-sent telegram from a ship (Help Urgently required–) suspected Delamere, and then discovered that the previous year he'd imported a thousand Mauser rifles. According to Hugh a battalion was dispatched from India by ship, but then halfway into the voyage the rest of the telegram arrived: –for famine in Turkana. People dying. Send grain." So the battalion returned to India," concludes Hugh. "The rifle barrels are still embedded safely in the concrete tank."

In 2018 the cattle still drank at the trough beside the reinforced tank, where Hugh was obliged to employ someone to chase off the zebra until the cattle had replenished themselves. The zebra also enjoyed the mineral salts provided for the cows to compensate for the deficient soil, which was the reason elephant had never, to Hugh's knowledge, come here. 'Nor did the Maasai allow their cattle to calve here as they'd be born with swayback disease.'

'The Maasai burned the grass every couple of years to get rid of the ticks,' Ann added.

'Yes, that's why there were no trees either.'

At lunch one day D found himself on the left of the hostess, wife of a dairy farmer.

'There are two streams running through our farm of two different colours,' she explained to the Governor, seated on her right. 'One we call the Blue Nile, the other the White Nile.'

'I take it that it is the latter you use for watering your milk,' D commented.

He'd already decided dairy farming was to be his next project, with the aim of improving milk quality. He bought - on overdraft - 2,265 acres of excellent pasture beside Lake Naivasha, stocking it with pedigree Friesians and the best heifers from Soysambu, shipping out more Friesians and Shorthorns from England, and an experienced cattle man. D's temper quickly became the talk of Naivasha: Powys Cobb told Huxley about D's 'fearful row' with the auctioneer at a cattle sale, although afterwards he remorsefully gave the man a pure-bred bull.

Labour remained a challenge - the government had taken many men to build the new Uasin Gishu railway, which branched away from the original Mombasa-Kisumu line at Nakuru to pass through the farming areas of Rongai, Molo, Eldoret and on into cotton-rich Uganda - but the poor economic state of the country meant that exports urgently needed to be increased. Although there was never legal compulsion for Africans to work for European farmers, there was a clause in the Native Ordinance of 1912 which entitled the government to call out young labourers for six days of every three months for communal works - changed in 1920 to up to sixty days a year - unless employed for three months in any other occupation. A year later the white paper would be modified by Churchill, avoiding compulsory labour "except where absolutely necessary for essential services."

In 1920 Kenya became a British Colony, flanked by Italian Somaliland, Abyssinia, Anglo-Egyptian Sudan, the Uganda Protectorate and Tanganyika Territory. The economy was recovering, although the government's decision to stabilise the East African rupee at two shillings resulted in all producers' debts and developers' overdrafts increasing overnight by 50 per cent. D was even compelled to find extra money to pay annual interest on a further sum he'd never borrowed. He was still owed money from the sale of about a third of his Njoro land; as flax prices slumped, instalments weren't paid. He waived them for several years, then reduced them, and eventually gave up on about a third of the money he was owed.

In 1919 eleven electoral areas had been established. D had also been one of two settlers appointed to the Executive Council. In February the following year, the Protectorate had seen its first election, with D elected unopposed for the Rift Valley constituency. While he proposed the eventual merging of Kenya, Uganda and Tanganyika, he felt Kenya should stand alone until it was a self-governing colony. His controversial views earned him enemies, but only bold men opposed him. Resignation continued to be his response if his protests were ignored, and within six months he'd resigned from both the Legislative and Executive Councils.

In 1919, aged only 16, Beryl Clutterbuck had married Captain Purves. Frequently escaping her older husband, whom she found a drunken bore, and riding away into the night on her horse Pegasus, she often headed to Soysambu. Tom was home for Christmas 1920. He was a few years older, although still a virgin, according to Beryl's biographer Errol Trzebinski. This changed after a roll in the hay with Beryl in the pumice building beside the stables. Some months later Purves allegedly turned up at Soysambu and gave D a black eye in revenge for his son's attempts to steal his wife. While her husband punched her surrogate father, Beryl rode Pegasus for a perilous sixty miles over the Aberdares, at night, to Solio and her "uncle" Berkeley, where she failed to find Denys Finch Hatton, on whom she'd set her sights, so she resignedly returned to her husband.

Beryl and Tom shared a love of horses. Although D and Tom seldom agreed, especially when it came to money, Tom redeemed himself slightly with his racing skills, sometimes riding D's horses, often winning.

***

'My grandfather had two horses in a race,' Hugh told me, warming up to a story. 'One was a dreadful broken-down old nag with odds at 100-1. The other was a decent racehorse with odds at 5-1. It was going to win and Father, who was light and small, was riding it. But the girths weren't done up. So the saddle slipped and Father fell off. He was fourteen lengths ahead. The horse stopped, the white cloth had fallen up. So Father picked it up, put back the saddle, and remounted, but got beaten. Only by a short head.' Hugh was interrupted by Easter the donkey, who'd formerly belonged to their son Tom. Now she clopped onto my veranda, appearing to be following the conversation with interest, although she was probably more interested in the carrot cake.

'Hello, lovey - could you manage a carrot?' Hugh said, fumbling in his pocket.

***

Ignoring his health, D became further embroiled in local politics, remaining a thorn in the side of the British. In May 1921 he formed the Reform party, resuming his place on the Legislative Council that August. An Economic and Finance Committee was later formed, with D sitting on it. In between he rushed back to Soysambu at weekends, jolting around the farm in his elderly Ford, departing again before dawn to Nairobi for the next Monday meeting.

There was now a financial crisis. Africans were only exporting a few hides, Indians contributed relatively little wealth, and the settlers - all 1,339 of them - were in debt to their banks, while accounting for nearly all the exports, mainly coffee and sisal. The money from unproductive government expenditure, D pointed out, came partly from the pockets of Africans paying hut tax and would be better spent on agricultural instructors and technical schools: 'I look upon education and medical services as insurance,' he said. 'As much money as can be afforded should be spent on African health and education... At present the money which should be building factories for meat canning and creameries and for putting more land under cultivation is being used to pay for an extravagant administration completely out of keeping with the finances of the country.'

There was another issue: what had become known as "the Indian question." Back in 1907 Churchill had also realised that overshadowing this promising land was the difficult question of the future status of the Indians, and D had remained adamant that the government should not allow unchecked immigration of Asiatics. The Economic Commission's 1919 report had not been accommodating, and by 1921, with 22,822 Indians (to 9,651 Europeans and around three million Africans) in the colony, the Indian Association in Nairobi was demanding, among other things, their equal representation on the Executive, Legislative and municipal councils, no segregation in towns, rights to buy land in the best farming areas – which had become known as the White Highlands due to their exclusivity - and a continuation of unrestricted immigration. "Our people will either create a civilisation for all - themselves and the indigenous peoples - or in the far future the indigenous peoples may oust them - who knows?" wrote D, his views concurring with most settlers. "No man today knows what the ultimate future holds between ourselves and the indigenous peoples of Africa." However, he added, "an unchecked flow of Asiatic immigration into Africa, and a state of affairs is created which no man can control at all."

"It would be fatal to give India the government here when our native races were beginning to realise that they had a future before them," the Bishop of Zanzibar wrote. Kikuyu elders wrote to Northey, making it clear they didn't want Indians in positions of authority, although Harry Thuku of the Young Kikuyu Association organised a meeting at which resolutions were made supporting the Indians' claims, then forwarded them to the Prime Minister. Indian spokesmen were making it clear that an overcrowded India was looking to expand into other parts of the British Empire, as was its right, and Alibhai Mulla Jevanjee, leader of Kenyan Indians, was in London presenting their case. Kenya, he affirmed, could become 'a second India.'

The Convention of Associations had formed a five-member Vigilance committee, of which D was one, meeting in secret to form a plan. 'People in England apparently think that by handing Kenya over to be dominated by India they are doing something towards solving unrest in India,' D raged, adding that placing the Indians in a position to govern 'would probably be the most unstatesmanlike and wanton concession to clamour and the forces of disaffection in our history.' The Convention sent D and another representative to England.

Just before he left, D was having breakfast with his Soysambu manager, Bobby Roberts, at Muthaiga Club. 'I woke up early and started thinking about that land in Loresho,' he said to Roberts. He took his menu card and began to draw on the back. 'I think I would like a house built...of stone, like this...'

'Where is the money going to come from?' inquired Roberts.

'Borrow it,' replied D, abruptly changing the subject.

D arrived in London with dysentery, scruffy and under-clad because his luggage had been left in Genoa. Churchill, now Secretary of the State for the Colonies, listened and pledged, amongst other things, to reserve the Kenya highlands for Europeans, and that future immigration of Indians would be regulated, even going so far as to say that the country might look forward to becoming a self-governing colony. But he was replaced in November, and two under-secretaries drew up a report that stated, amongst other things, that Indian immigration would remain unrestricted. Northey was "recalled" and Sir Robert Coryndon, a South African, arrived from Uganda. 'Have accepted Governorship of Kenya: no more peace,' he wired to a friend. He was summoned to London in March 1923, with selected European and Indian delegates. D led the former, and Mr Srinivasa Sastri, who hadn't yet visited East-Africa, was the principal Indian spokesman. Aware he had to appeal to the British public, and as usual ready to fund the cause, D rented a well-staffed house in Grosvenor Place. The butler took one look at his torn coat and khaki shirt and refused to admit him. His eyebrows shot up further at the sight of two young Somali men who'd accompanied D.

D spent three expensive months battling the issue, inviting the press to lunches and dinners, giving interviews and writing letters.

He was by now, says, Cranworth, a more moderate man, and took a "statesmanlike course." The Indians wanted complete equality, including common citizenship of the Empire, while D's framework for a new Kenya constitution was predicated on immediate legislation to restrict immigrants on economic criteria. Coryndon sided with the settlers. The Colonial Office dithered before giving in to their concern about the possibility of armed settler rebellion in Kenya.

A white paper was finally produced, giving settlers the White Highlands and political superiority. Segregation in towns was to be abandoned, but immigration remained a grey area. D and his delegates accepted these terms, although they protested at five Indian seats on the Legislative Council. For a tense few days the Colonial Office tried and failed to establish telegraphic communication with Kenya. D decided against telling them it was actually a storm that had disabled the telegraph system, suggesting that the Secretary of State cable reassurance to the colony that the government genuinely intended to bring in new immigration laws, and assisted in drafting the cable. The perceived problem might have been averted, but it took D's fellow settlers some time to accept what they saw as a non-victory when D arrived home. The Indian community weren't happy either, engaging in campaigns of non-cooperation.

CHAPTER 9

Aside from Happy Valley

The 1920s heralded plenty of fun in Kenya, notably for the wealthy white settlers, with one small but dissolute group of settlers tarnishing the name of the colony. The homes of the so-called Happy Valley set were tucked away below the Aberdare mountains in the Wanjohi Valley, prime farming land 150 kilometres north of Nairobi. The indigo hulks of the Kinangop, Aberdare and Kipipiri mountains encircling Happy Valley were visible from Soysambu on the eastern horizon, but it took more than a day to drive the 33 rough kilometres. By strange coincidence, long before I thought of writing about the Delamere family, when researching my previous book on Kenya, *The Ghosts of Happy Valley*, I'd acquired some anonymous typed notes that had somehow passed into the hands of an impoverished caretaker living in a crumbling red-brick dairy that was the only surviving part of Slains, the house where Happy Valley's infamous doyenne, Lady Idina, had lived when married to Hon. Josslyn Hay, the future Earl of Erroll.

'This is the story of Lord Malcolm,' said the caretaker, 'son of Lord Erroll.'

Erroll never had a son, but I eventually identified the writer as Malcolm Watson, who'd worked for D. His notes recall going for a job interview in Loresho, where D had based himself, no longer having use of the prefab house; this was occupied from 1921 by Jim Elkington, the early settler renowned for his racing and hunting stables. He'd left his wife on his Nairobi coffee farm and come to attend to his Elmenteita farm, Bussilunhun, bringing his lion, Paddy, now confined to a cage since he'd attacked a younger Beryl. At Loresho, Watson admired the bougainvillea and golden shower that scaled the roof and trellises - "A far cry from English manors but really more attractive in my view," he wrote. D met him with "an engaging half smile."

'I know your father,' D said. 'Met him when he came to Nairobi to recuperate from his wounds…You want to learn all about cattle ranching?'

Malcolm accepted D's offer of a position at Naivasha, on the farm he'd named Manera, working under D's highly-strung manager Roy Homewood: no pay, but food and a sparsely furnished converted stable to sleep in, the gaps in the walls letting in the relentless dust that blew into everything. "The place was very bleak," Malcolm wrote, surprised at the numbers of visitors who turned up, mainly to shoot duck, taking advantage of D's limitless hospitality. Some were "not so welcome" Malcolm writes: the "remittance people" from Happy Valley, listing them as Josslyn and Idina Hay, Alice and Frederic de Janze and Kiki Preston. "The capers of this group were notorious for their utter immorality. Africans were afraid of working for them and Europeans avoided working for them if they could." Malcolm's view of his boss's involvement with such people was unequivocal: "Lord Delamere…had little in common with any of them."

Beryl, who'd been living in various places, including a tent beside Nakuru racetrack, returned to Soysambu, where D offered her some stables for her horses and a converted horse box to live in. A few days after she'd enjoyed Christmas dinner of 1922 at Kekopey with D and Tom, her aggrieved husband, Jock Purves, stopped D on the steps of his Nakuru hotel. He'd intended to hit Tom, but as he wasn't there he went for D, drunkenly pursuing him to his car, climbing in and refusing to get out. Purves then turned violent, throwing punches for Tom as well as Boy Long, as Beryl had moved on from Tom by then and was enjoying an affair with Long. Mary Lovell, Beryl's biographer, writes that Purves broke bones in D's arm, jaw and neck, resulting in further forced convalescence. The incident was the talk of the colony. "They say Delamere is very worried and depressed," Karen Blixen wrote to her mother, "and of course it is very damaging for the whole country," adding that Boy Long had left the country after Purves had threatened to shoot him.

At Soysambu Beryl produced many winners on the racecourse, while D helped her to dissolve her marriage. Many years later she would tell Mary Lovell about the constant bickering between Tom and his father, including an occasion during afternoon tea when an exasperated Tom got up to leave and D threw a pot of hot tea after him, remarking, "How did I ever come to father that?" Tom, it seems, didn't share his aspirations for the colony, or condone his extravagant funding of it. In a rare moment D confided to the Chairman of the East African Commission and Under-Secretary of State for the Colonies, William Ormsby-Gore (who later told Huxley), 'that his son's dislike of Kenya was a very great sorrow to him. He wanted his work to be carried on.'

Tom had endured enough, and returned to England, where he joined the Grenadier Guards.

***

'They didn't really want him,' pointed out Hugh.
'He was too small,' added Ann.
So Tom was posted to the Welsh Guards as a junior subaltern.

***

Meanwhile, Coryndon the Governor and his colleagues were obligingly holding meetings at Loresho, where D was incapacitated on his sofa. Suddenly his land-dealings were a public controversy, thanks to the publication of a book, *Kenya*, by Norman Leys, which quoted a letter from an early settler and political opponent of D's, Robert Chamberlain, to the *East African Standard* in 1920: "As long as the Land office would yield juice, his Lordship was there with insatiable powers of suction." Leys further alleged that Kenya's 100% duty on imported wheat and flour was "to protect an infant industry largely conducted on a single immense estate." Huxley points out that the duty was 30% and D was no longer growing wheat. Although he still had Unga Ltd, having bought most of his shareholders out because no money was being made, it never paid a dividend after the duty was imposed. The manager of Unga Ltd later verified the fact that during the 18 years up until then D's sole concern was in fostering the wheat industry. The Secretary of State ordered a full report which concluded, "It would not, I think, be too much to add that no better settler ever spent his all in such a difficult colony...and that any suggestion of underhand dealing in respect of his land or any other transactions with the government is not only cruel and malicious but conveys the precise opposite of the plainly evident truth."

In early 1923 D became Chairman of the European and African Trades Organisation, started partly to enforce a boycott against Indian artisans, as well as to act as an employment agency for Africans. Along with Sir Northrup McMillan, D pledged support to trading centres and lent money to interested Africans. Education largely remained in the hands of the missionaries, but D's views were finally endorsed by a commission advocating more practical and technical education, resulting in the opening of a teacher-training school for Africans at Kabete, the first of its kind in East Africa, which also aimed to train them to be community leaders.

Boy Long had returned and got married again, this time to Mrs Genesta Farquhar, a wealthy and elegant divorcee who'd travelled widely and alone, including through Somaliland, where she claimed to have met an old man who remembered D. She joined Long, whom she described as the handsomest man she'd ever seen, in the stone house, later writing in her memoir, *A Stone's Throw*, "The best times were when we went to the sheep farm at Laikipia, which was run rather haphazardly. There was always trouble - sheep stolen or missing or sick or dead." She described D as wise, brave, and very charming, although apparently he disliked her, limiting his stays on Soysambu, preferring his Loresho home with its veranda looking over forested ridges to Mt Kenya.

D was now less reclusive, taking up golf, even gracing the dance floor, and proud owner of a small fleet of cars, mainly for the use of his guests. Cranworth was somewhat surprised when his recommendation of "a rather expensive American brand" as better suited to the terrain saw D buy six. As if this wasn't enough, D wrote to Boy Long instructing him to purchase a bright yellow Packard.

The bank refused to increase the overdraft. "You can give the bank the security of that farm on the Mau, the one they haven't got yet," he wrote. He didn't actually have a farm on the Mau, although he was possibly referring to the land on Eburru, extending sideways from the Mau escarpment.

That October D hosted dinner at Muthaiga Club for Coryndon, Sir Geoffrey Archer, Governor of Uganda, and about 50 guests.

***

'He was the biggest family disaster in generations,' Hugh complained. All this largesse had been funded by selling off Vale Royal's estate. 'The last of the land went in 1923.' Tom had argued constantly against selling the good arable land. 'You silly boy,' D would respond, 'You know nothing.'

Hugh's grandfather's generosity had been reborn in him, it seemed, as he went on to tell me he'd just sent some relation three airfares to come and stay in Kenya - 'Everybody in Britain is broke, aren't they?' When I challenged this, Hugh simply shrugged: 'My money tree didn't flower this year.' I'd learned by now that Hugh and Ann's courtesy and kindness often resulted in over-use of their hospitality. Yes really meant no, but in what seemed a case of *noblesse oblige*, unheeding visitors poured in, not all of them beloved enough to warrant their staying a week - or even half a day.

***

Determined to make southern Africa more East Africa conscious, and to talk about the possibility of federation, D persuaded the South African Trade Commissioner to accompany him to South Africa in mid-1924. In Durban he finally had a haircut after street kids followed him, laughing and pointing. After meeting Smuts, then visiting Salisbury and Victoria Falls, a new commission was formed and invited to Kenya, where D duly entertained over 80 people to dinner at Muthaiga Club. The settlers' efforts were much praised afterwards, both by the Labour member and the official report, which stated: "We wish to record our opinion that

Kenya has been fortunate in the type of settler she has attracted. In fact, few of Britain's overseas colonies at their commencement have attracted a better type. They are men and women of energy and goodwill."

Back in England, Tom became engaged to 20-year-old Phyllis Anne Montagu Douglas Scott, daughter of Lord George William Montagu Douglas Scott, son of The 6th Duke of Buccleuch and Lady Elizabeth Emily Manners, daughter of The 7th Duke of Rutland.

In their wedding photograph (D didn't attend, visiting southern Africa instead) Phyllis, wearing the streamlined fashions popular in 1924, is seated so as not to accentuate her height, her long train pooling in front of her. Surrounded by bridesmaids and flowers, she looks bored. Presumably she realised her new husband was broke. As Elspeth Huxley's notes indicate, Tom was now extremely worried about his father's financial affairs - the latest development being the liquidation of the wattle bark factory. It was around this time, Mary Hopkirk recalled, that the Romney portrait of the Countess of Londonderry hanging at Vale Royal fell off the wall. When this happened, an old prophesy had claimed, the end of the family - or Vale Royal - was nigh.

In January 1925 Jim Elkington shot himself in the prefab house. It was rumoured not to have been an accident; he'd been devastated when the married Kathleen Tatham-Warter had refused to leave her husband, in spite of having an illegitimate daughter with Elkington. As an executor and trustee of his will, D instructed Long to shoot Paddy the lion.

Now living in London, Tom brought Phyllis to Soysambu, staying in the wooden prefab.

***

'Mother complained that it was built like a railway carriage and you could hear whatever was happening in the next-door room,' said Hugh. 'While she was there, there was an earthquake and she thought it was a dog scratching under the table, but eventually when the paraffin lamps, which were hung up, started swaying, she realised.'

Phyllis was even more startled by her father-in-law: 'A very tiresome man he was. My mother had a lot of gramophone records, and she put them down beside his and she came in one evening and found him breaking them and putting them in the fire, saying, "What is all this rubbish?"' Hugh paused to swat at a mosquito. 'My parents met at a ball. Father was always gadding about at balls...! Do you know she was very much taller than he was? With her high heels on she must have been six foot three? She always wore heels to show off her rather good legs.'

***

By the end of 1924 the new railway had reached Eldoret. Coryndon, with his enthusiasm for Kenya's development, was popular. Following D's direction, money was directed to African agriculture and benefits, a school of dairying opened in Maasailand and local native councils established. Then there was a spate of deaths: Coryndon died suddenly in early 1925. Berkeley Cole died that April. Then back in Cheshire Robert Dempster died, so D was once again saddled with the unwelcome expense of Vale Royal. He also had a new granddaughter, born on Boxing Day: the Hon. Elizabeth Florence Marion.

There was still big talk of amalgamating British territories from Nimule on the Nile, stretching south for 1,600 miles to Livingstone on the Zambesi, with D promoting the idea of Nairobi as the ideal federal capital. The new Governor, Sir Edward Grigg, was also a fan of federation. Joining D in his enthusiastic pursuit of this dream, he agreed to the upgrading of Nairobi's and Mombasa's Government Houses, at a cost of £80,000, designed by Herbert Baker, overseen by D. Karen Blixen took a dim view of this: "The English," she wrote to her brother in early 1926, "were a shameless race - raising native taxes and building a new Government House while the Africans were starving...the champagne flows in torrents at their races and so on...Lord Delamere recently held a dinner for 250 people at which they drank 600 bottles,...and they just do not see it; the ladies here are quite capable of asking, when they hear that the natives cannot get posho, why they do not eat wheat or rice instead..." Karen asked her brother to take up the question of native interests with the League of Nations.

D was all in favour of the persuasive powers of champagne. He'd formed a small non-profit company, Colonists Ltd, to open up the southern highlands of Tanganyika, raising £6,000 capital in partnership with Lord Egerton of Tatton and Sir John Ramsden, both Kenya settlers. Now, D decided, was the time to have an unofficial conference with leading settlers from Kenya, Tanganyika, Uganda, Northern Rhodesia and Nyasaland. He chaired it at an unused mission house in the southern highlands of Tanganyika, approximately 1,000 miles from both Nairobi and Livingstone, serving champagne by the tumbler. A resounding success, it cost him £1,600 (almost £100,000 today). When the second conference was held in Livingstone in September 1926, South African newspapers dubbed him "the Rhodes of East Africa," although D was forced to realise that the time wasn't ripe for closer unification. He hurried back to Kenya where he was elected unopposed for the Rift Valley.

D was busy developing Manera, stocking it with high-grade Friesians, introducing milk-recording, growing lucerne for feed and setting out to rear calves on a more scientific basis. Malcolm Watson writes that D believed in "the shotgun method" - crossing many British breeds of bull with local Zebu cattle - the latter more disease-resistant, but producing less milk, although it was higher in fat. But as they'd been "all mixed up by the various managers" there was little knowing which bull had sired which calf. However, a combination of good star grass and lucerne fattened them up, the milk yield improved, and the 40% calf mortality rate dropped as Watson sterilised their feeding equipment to prevent white scour. Lucerne production also improved as he worked on improving the soil. When Watson was digging a well to pump water for troughs and cattle dips using a windmill, he was intrigued to find prehistoric flint hand tools amongst all the layers of volcanic soils left by eruptions from nearby Longonot crater. He persuaded D to order a Holt Caterpillar Tractor to assist in pumice breaking.

The labourers were having literacy classes in the stables, and hay was fetching seven shillings a bale. Meanwhile D started a Co-operative Creamery, which he'd planned since buying Manera. It was the second in Kenya, with D aiming to encourage the expansion of Kenya's dairy industry, engaging support from Naivasha farmers, donating a portion of Manera for the factory, providing capital, importing an expert from Australia and waiving payment for his own cream for six months. When another creamery started up, D then dedicated much time to amalgamating them into a precursor to Kenya Co-operative Creameries. He was also promoting mixed farming to encourage soil fertility, assembling a team of scientists and trying to persuade African cattle owners to sell their surplus stock for money to combat overstocking and erosion. He became a director and funder for a trial meat factory at Mwanza in Tanganyika.

Meanwhile, Beryl was giving marriage another go, marrying Mansfield Markham, second son of Sir Arthur Basil Markham, British industrialist and politician. D gave her away and made a speech at their Muthaiga Club reception.

Long left D's employment; he'd been exceptionally well treated and paid, he writes, but he and D had fallen out over his marriage. Genesta had bought Nderit, a farm neighbouring Soysambu to its northwest, and encompassing part of the shoreline of Lake Nakuru. Boy and Genesta had already moved to the house and garden Genesta had designed overlooking Lake Nakuru. According to Frances Osborne in *The Bolter*, Boy was, by 1926, involved with the Happy Valley set and having an affair with Lady Idina Hay (whose countless lovers included Oswald Mosley) while Genesta was off on her travels. Idina detested Genesta, and the sentiment was returned. It would be at one of Idina's infamous parties that her equally scandalous neighbour, Alice de Janze, introduced Boy to Paula Gellibrand, a fashion icon of the 1920s who'd already discarded two husbands. Paula's affair with Boy Long began in 1928, according to Paul Spicer in *The Temptress*, although Genesta doesn't refer to an affair with "someone else's wife" until 1939, when their marriage would finally fall apart.

Long's departure left D running Soysambu as well as his Laikipia farm, where home was another hut, a piece of sacking serving as a door. Juggling life as farmer and politician, surviving on minimal sleep, D managed to periodically entertain huge numbers of guests at Loresho, dance all night, then eat breakfast at sunrise in preparation for a busy working day.

In September 1927 Tom and Phyllis had a second daughter, the Hon. Anne Jeannetta Essex. The wheat industry now firmly established, D was busy disposing of his controlling interest in Unga Limited to the Wheat Growers' Association, which would join up with the Kenya Farmers' Association three decades later.

At Manera the flood of guests continued, Malcolm Watson finding some of them a great deal more interesting than the Happy Valley clique, such as the Argentinian rancher who'd ridden from Patagonia to New York. D continued to host elaborate duck shoots in the Manera wetlands, providing fine wines including 1915 Pol Roger Champagne. All this while Watson wasn't actually paid, although his resignation prompted D to persuade him to remain for £40 a month. But although D's farms were finally making profits - in 1926 his wool alone fetched £34,000 - it all belonged to the banks.

By now nearly five million acres of Kenya had been settled by Europeans. Kilindini harbour had four new deep-water berths, and the railway line to Uganda was complete, along with the extension of the Thika line to Nyeri. Determined Kenya must avoid the intellectual poverty he felt afflicted Europeans in countries like South Africa, D proposed a new European boys' secondary school, insisting there'd be a waiting list within two years. Wealthier settlers had always sent their children to England, while others attended the overcrowded Nairobi School (for Europeans) that had been founded in 1902 and divided in 1925 by D and Grigg into a senior boys' school (later named the Prince of Wales), a senior girls' school (Kenya High) and a junior school (Nairobi Primary). The first stone of the Francis Scott High School (later Nakuru School), majestically situated on the lower slopes of Menengai Crater, was laid by Grigg in 1927. Within two years there was indeed a waiting list, and by 1931 Eldoret and Kitale would also see new schools, all with elegant buildings designed by Herbert Baker. European and Indian education continued to be supported by their own communities, with African education financed out of central funds.

Cranworth noted of his friend that "the personal element and the idea of profit became submerged in an ever-growing passion for the country itself, which intensified with every year of his life. Certainly in his latter years he gave ten hours at least to fighting for Kenya's future to one in connection with his own affairs. He forgot his history and his erudition, and to that extent, perhaps, became a less engrossing companion for a stranger."

However, it seemed that D's courtesy still defined him. He was 'the last of his race,' Eric Dutton, PS to Grigg, told Huxley, 'a true British gentleman...He would pace the room, snapping his fingers, but he never swore, hardly ever said damn, and he never said anything against a woman.' And now, D was about to prove that he could still charm the opposite sex.

CHAPTER 10

New Love

Tom was in Kenya when his father announced that he was marrying Gwladys Markham, whom he'd met while she was staying at Government House. "Lord Delamere forthcoming marriage with Lady Markham," reported the *Western Morning News* on 16 May 1928. Born Gwladys Beckett, daughter of the Hon. Rupert Beckett, granddaughter of the 2nd Marquess of Anglesey, she'd become a society girl at the age of four when her photograph graced the pages of *Tatler*. Her marriage to Sir Charles Markham, older brother of Beryl's husband Mansfield, had ended unhappily in 1927.

The 31-year-old Gwladys now married a father-figure 27 years her senior, bringing three children into their marriage. Unlike Florence, Gwladys was eye-catching rather than beautiful, with her black hair, dark eyes and very pale skin. Although like Florence, Gwladys was intelligent and vivacious, she was more highly-strung. After a brief engagement their marriage took place at St Andrew's Church, with a reception at Muthaiga Club, which gifted them £165 in subscription, in recognition of D's being President for almost 30 years. Tom attended, along with Beryl, Mansfield, and Karen Blixen, and the newlyweds sailed to England. Afterwards D and Gwladys based themselves mainly at Loresho where, in spite of their new marital bliss, some things didn't change; D still slept wrapped in blankets like a Maasai - 'no sheets,' Hutton (likely to have been Gerald Hutton who farmed in Molo) told Huxley, in 'a little tin hut in the garden...' And he still needed to keep a light burning in case he sleepwalked.

Later that year the Prince of Wales (subsequently Edward VIII) visited. Driven up-country in D's "big American car," according to Charles Hayes in *Oserian: Place of Peace*, he stayed with D and Gwladys on 8th October in the Soysambu prefab, where the neglected plumbing received some hasty attention. They took him to lunch at Nderit, where the Longs had been busy driving off a pack of wild dogs that had eaten nineteen cows. "He is the easiest person in the world to get on with," Genesta wrote, "once he's out of the public eye; cheerful and amusing and apparently entirely unselfconscious." The following day, she continued, they went up the hill to the new Gilgil Club for golf and a reception: "It was in the club dance banda with all Gilgil and Elmenteita standing in stiff clumps against the walls while HRH and Lord D. went round and talked, and what he finds to say to them all I can't imagine. Of course he does it marvellously. Margaret Collier distinguished herself by trying to make him shake hands with her dog."

Before D accompanied the prince and Finch Hatton on a shooting trip, there was a flurry of social activity. Karen Blixen joined them at Government House for dinner, noting that the prince actually stayed at Loresho, attending the native dance or *ngoma* hosted by Karen in her garden, with dinner afterwards. She seated her royal guest between herself and Beryl - who would notch up both Edward and his brother Henry, Duke of Gloucester, among those she seduced. Rumours would multiply as to who fathered Beryl's son, Gervaise Markham. Beryl didn't deny anything, and meanwhile Karen remained blissfully unaware of Beryl's feelings for her lover, Denys. Then there was a dance at Muthaiga Club. "Lady Delamere behaved scandalously at supper, I thought," Karen wrote in a letter. "She bombarded the Prince of Wales with big pieces of bread, and one of them hit me, sitting beside him, in the eye, so I have a black eye today, and finished up by rushing at him, overturning his chair and rolling him around on the floor. I do not find that kind of thing in the least amusing, and stupid to do at a club; as a whole I do not find her particularly likeable, and she looks so odd, exactly like a painted wooden doll..."

Gwladys had met her match, concluded Cranworth. "D liked a rough-house to the end of his days, and he would love to egg people on to start one, though it was an entertainment in which he himself most reluctantly could take but little part. He rather enjoyed being an *enfant terrible*, especially when there was anything of a social function taking place."

There was even talk that Gwladys herself had an affair with the Prince of Wales, a claim substantiated by her granddaughter. Globally, these were times for throwing caps in the air, with women finding new sexual freedom. Anything was possible in Kenya in the roaring twenties, with that lingering Happy Valley altitude-alcohol-adultery ethos that had sprung from a surge of economic prosperity and a touch of post-war euphoria. D has been accused by many journalists of being part of the Happy Valley set, but I firmly believe it was highly unlikely that D ever succumbed to extra-marital dalliances. There was a certain naivety about him, extending into his choice of friends, but perhaps it was merely because his sense of duty was paramount, thus extending a friendly hand to assist all settlers regardless of their moral standing. Moreover, in spite of his sudden displays of unbounded extravagance - invariably aimed at furthering the interests of his country - and even while occasionally maintaining his youthful reputation as a roisterer, D was, as his grandson Hugh repeatedly said, 'far too busy.'

Early in 1929 a critically ill D was told by his doctor to slow down, that any more strain on his heart would kill him. He resigned from the Legislative and Executive Councils and headed to South Africa with Gwladys, but after a few weeks insisted on taking the train to Lourenco Marques, and then a rickety boat back to Kenya to attend to urgent matters. But, try as he might to continue his rigorous work regime, he tired easily and felt less inclined to throw parties. His wife became "his right hand in all his later work," writes Cranworth, "and her assistance to him was invaluable." Gwladys also took over a hotel he'd started at Iringa, in southern Tanganyika, making a little progress with the debts.

Many road trips didn't improve D's health, especially after spending the night in a trench when his car broke down. He managed to drive to Livingstone, in spite of lumbago, composing a very long telegram on the way, outlining a complete agricultural policy for Kenya, sending it to a commission in Nairobi. He spent huge amounts on his telegrams, Dutton told Huxley, and yet he 'never opened letters - they used to lie around for weeks.' Figures 'bored him to tears,' Ormsby-Gore, added: D preferred not to have to do accounts.

Galbraith Cole, still only 48, was now afflicted with unbearable arthritic pain. Eleanor Cole's memoir merely records that on 6th October, 1929 he died. Elspeth Huxley tells the full story. At Galbraith's request Eleanor loaded his revolver, then took the dogs for a walk, while Cole's faithful Somali servant accompanied him to his favourite spot overlooking the lake, holding the weapon so Cole could pull the trigger. Eleanor built a stone cairn at his resting place, on a hill above the lake. It was another blow to D to lose his old friend.

In the 1930 New Year's honours list D became the first Kenya settler to be awarded a KCMG. Gwladys went to England that March where D wrote to her daily, his large writing scrawling restlessly across blue paper, revealing a very different side to him, his adoration for Gwladys spilling over every page. As I read them in the Weston Library I realised he had deep insecurities, not least his fear of losing his younger wife, coupled with enormous guilt about his financial mistakes.

Like her friends, he called her Glady, although his letters begin with "Darling," signed off "Yours D," sometimes with extra endearments; "Goodbye my sweetheart, all my love..." Already devoted to his three step-children, Charles, Mary and Rose, he sent the nanny off to buy Easter eggs, ending one letter, "Darling, don't worry, the children will be quite alright and D will look after himself and will never give you a moment's anxiety. Promise." He grew increasingly worried when he didn't hear back, expressing fears she'd "get bored" with him.

"I can never forget the day we were engaged to each other," he writes on 27th April. "I can only hope and pray you still feel the same. You have made me the happiest man in the world. Don't slip away from me sweet. I get so nervous when you are away and I don't hear from you...Do you miss me Glady as I miss you?...You are the complement of my life. Without you I am only half alive."

He recalls their trips to Laikipia - "how delicious those trips were" - adding that even their dog Simba (Kiswahili for lion) missed her, howling at night. (On one such safari they had stayed at The Outspan Hotel in Nyeri, which prided itself as "the only up country comfortable hotel with private bathrooms, and hot and cold running water, and their own W.C." according to Lady Victoria Fletcher's autobiography, *From Castle to Caravan*. Her brother-in-law, Eric Sherbrooke Walker, owned the hotel, so when it was discovered that these honourable guests didn't share a bedroom, Lady Fletcher happily moved out of her single one to make space for Lord Delamere. When D discovered this, however, he was mortified and moved back into their double room where he slept the night in the bath.)

"I simply look forward to seeing you again," D writes in another letter to Gwladys. "That and the future of Kenya are the only two things I ever think about. I am just as serious as ever about the latter but I don't enjoy even planning those things without you."

After a month of no response since Aden, D writes, "Only a month to the anniversary of our engagement and two to our marriage. The best day's work that I ever did. And I hope that my sweetheart does not regret it all the time." He misses her "terribly," her absence "a sort of horrid vacuum," increasingly become "an obsession."

"Knowing you and knowing that you would never say anything unless you meant it I feel happy and secure again," he wrote after Gwladys remembered to cable on his birthday. "After two years with you, I cannot tell you how dull and wretched life is alone." Doubts creep back; having not heard from her since Genoa, D writes, "I get jealous of anyone you speak to or see or anything. Only on the surface. Really I am delighted that you are having a holiday and seeing people and enjoying yourself." At the same time he hopes that being in England hasn't made her regret her marriage.

D's letters are also revealing about Gwladys: her fear of thunderstorms, people she disliked, her jealousy. "None of your enemies seem to frequent Muthaiga now except Mrs Frank Williams who meanders about in a semi-conscious condition half the time," he writes. Frank Greswolde Williams was notorious as the supplier of drugs to the Happy Valley set, even more so for offering the Prince of Wales cocaine at Muthaiga Club. On 21st May D mentions that, while staying at Nderit with the Longs, "Lafone" appeared, so he went off to bed promptly. "I heard they (the Ps) were leaving in a few days through Dempster when they wrote about the Naivasha land. Perhaps they have left."

Michael Lafone was part of the Happy Valley set, as was "Mrs P," who is likely to have been the wealthy Alice (Kiki) Preston, notorious for publicly injecting her heroin with a silver syringe, her many lovers including Prince George, Duke of Kent. Amongst the guests she entertained at her Naivasha home, Mundui, was Evelyn Waugh, who described her as "a lovely American" who slept all day, appearing for dinner. Kiki continued to waft between Mundui and Paris until her suicide in London in 1938 from an overdose of heroin. As D did fraternise with this insalubrious clique, perhaps she hoped to add him to her list of conquests, although it's unlikely she succeeded. There's a photograph in Errol Trzebinksi's *Life and Death of Lord Erroll*, taken at Loresho in 1926 of a reluctant-looking D beside three jauntily posed Happy Valley-ites: Raymund de Trafford, Frederic de Janze and his wife Alice (who later married de Trafford). Another undated photo shows D, again at Loresho, with Kiki Preston, taller than him in killer heels, smiling triumphantly as she clasps him around the neck with both arms. Topee in hand, head bowed, right foot forward, he appears to be trying to escape. Unfortunately many writers continue to seize upon such images, imagining them photographic evidence of D's involvement in Happy Valley, although such snaps wouldn't have been something he initiated, or even kept.

Whatever his relationship with "Mrs P," it had aroused Gwladys's suspicions. "You say you heard Mrs P had sent me a letter," he insists. "Have had no communication direct or indirect with her. Don't believe anything of that sort." Later he writes that in Muthaiga Club he'd pulled aside a curtain and found himself a foot away from "the Ps," at which point he'd hastily withdrawn.

But amidst the social trivia were constant financial worries. D's Kenyan estates were now in receivership. Two years of drought and locust infestations had decimated his farms and D's overdrafts had mounted. Hugh Dempster, the new manager appointed by the bank had moved to Soysambu with his wife Lorna, living in the stone house, where D now avoided staying, preferring not to stay at the prefab house in Gwladys's absence, but usually seeking out the company of Boy Long. "The pioneer mind only sees forward," D writes to Gwladys. "If it didn't it would never do what it does. But it seldom consolidated for the same reason." Taking responsibility for the mess, he admits, "I must make a real effort to straighten things out, and the only possible way to do so is to try and sell land at a low price. Things might improve and probably will in a year or two, but in the meantime one is in danger of being caught completely owing to my carelessness of my own business, and changes of management, in the year or two before I married you... if I could get rid of most of the ranching land we should be better off a good deal."

He tried to remain upbeat as his Loresho coffee lost more money: "One has to have these slumps to bring people back to reasonable costs. High prices always make people careless." His letter of 27th March reveals they are forced to live off Gwladys's alimony, telling her he's written to her father about her overdraft, urging her not to let such matters come between them, even apologising. "I thought it best to tell him that we should never have thought of bothering about Charles's allowance if I had not been infernally hard up. But as we are I do think Charles ought to pay, don't you?"

"We mustn't spoil our life by too much work," he writes at the end of April. "I shall never again be like I was when we first married about work." Although he was still active in politics, officialdom increasingly rankled with him, and he felt too old to fight any more. "I wish I was Governor of Kenya."

1930 was an extremely wet year, worsening D's lumbago, interrupting golf, ruining Kenyan harvests, destroying half Uganda's cotton, derailing the Kisumu train. "The rain is simply rotting the railway away," he writes shakily from the train on Rift Valley Sports Club-headed paper. He was devoting time to the Native Lands Trust bill, saving the maize (using driers) - and so the stresses and strains went on, in between stories of getting stuck in the mud on the escarpment road, jacking the car onto branches. Soon the road became so bad he was obliged to put Gwladys's car on the train, so he had a car each end. The children were under nets at night, serenaded by frogs, the mosquitoes breeding in a new lake behind the house. The Iringa hotel, which had made a profit up to the end of January, was struggling to get food and whisky. At the end of March, heavy rains closed the road to Dodoma and the factory ran out of supplies just when it was "within an ace of paying its way... It really does seem as if providence was against us," he writes. "But tout passe and...I am making great efforts to straighten out our affairs."

In spite of feeling unwell, D visited Manera to see his lucerne, resting on the veranda in the afternoon, his Somali retainer at hand to supply matches for his cigars. Watson had decided to leave to go to university and this time no amount of persuasion could change his mind. He noted that D ate no breakfast, listening to him ranting at Homewood for over an hour about calf deaths.

The Prince of Wales returned, meeting D in Laikipia to plant a European oak on Seagar Bastard's Sweetwaters ranch, neighbouring Ol Pejeta. D, Gwladys and Tom went on one of the royal safaris, notes Errol Trzebinski, along with Prince Edward's lover, Thelma Furness. Gwladys apparently tried hard to get the prince's attention, eventually sitting beside him on a chop box, where she was told she wasn't welcome.

The Labour Government's East Africa policy worsened government-settler relations, with fear for their future widespread among settlers. Even the East African Women's League sent a cable to the Secretary of State. D was sent as leader of a mission to London, sailing that August with Women's League delegate, Eleanor Cole. Feeling unwell, he was unable to attend all planned functions, but made it clear they weren't prepared to abandon Kenya's future to outsiders who simply didn't understand or care. 'An area of over a million square miles is awaiting development and British trade,' he emphasised. 'The only part of it which has been developed with railways and ports since Rhodes died and the railways of Rhodesia were carried into the Congo and the Katanga is Kenya - because it has a vigorous white population to push forward its development.'

After his final and hesitant speech at the House of Lords he confided to Cranworth: 'I do not expect to live much longer.'

CHAPTER 11

End of an Era

Seeing Uganda's exports fall by 50%, D was against its single-crop policy, favouring Kenya's mixed farming, which had actually seen her exports increase. But Kenya was now suffering from the global depression and, although his heart was in poor condition, D was more concerned about the economic crisis, spending hours poring over figures and details, advocating an agricultural credit system, neglecting his farms. "Curse all this work," he wrote to Gwladys, away again. "It is only because they put rabbits to govern who bolt into their burrows directly there is a chance of having to take responsibility." The Blixens had been forced to sell their coffee farm. D went to the station to see a heartbroken Karen off; after losing her beloved Denys in a plane crash, she was now leaving Kenya. Karen noted that D was now "a little older, a little whiter, and with his hair cut shorter than when I had tea with him in the Masai Reserve, but as exceedingly and concernedly courteous and polite now as then."

The new Governor, Joseph Byrne, turned out to be a mere spokesman for an unhelpful, distant government. Enraged, D pointed out that Kenya's loan commitments were now 17 million pounds. And what was the government doing about it? He wasn't well enough to lead the colonists' deputation to London for the final decision on closer union. Lord Sir Francis George Montagu Douglas Scott, uncle to D's daughter-in-law, Phyllis, went on his behalf and it was shelved. Kenya's Board of Agriculture, a non-racial entity representative of each major industry set up in May 1930, was abolished - to D's fury. Constantly worried for his country's future, unable to afford time for a holiday, he took Gwladys's advice and tried to play a regular game of golf.

Gwladys's eldest son, Charles Markham, was now at Pembroke

House Preparatory School above Gilgil. In the holidays the children stayed in the prefab house, often joined by Kathini, the daughter of D's golfing friend Charles Taylor who'd planted his coffee and also been a pillar of Muthaiga Club and the Jockey Club. She later recalled a "secret garden" beside the Mereroni River, a room in the house with trunk-loads of designer dresses, hats and tail coats, and a bright yellow sports car without wheels in a garage. Sometimes they went to Elmenteita, where the Indian shopkeeper, Mr Moolraj, gave them Indian sweetmeats.

***

Hugh remembered Moolraj: 'a thin-legged man who wore white... My grandfather was running out of money, and knew one way to get credit was from an Indian. So he got Moolraj, then the station master from Njoro, to come and open a duka, initially lending him £100.' Over time D had accrued huge debts with Moolraj. 'He died owing Moolraj £30,000.'

***

In August 1931, with Gwladys away again, D was busy with the budget, while also improving her Loresho bedroom. "All I want now is someone to talk to me about ordinary things or to read a rubbishy novel or two to stop me thinking even of business," he wrote. He managed to make a speech in the Legislative Council, catching the government out over an error. In early November he had a series of angina attacks, and Gwladys returned to nurse him. On Friday 13th he died in bed. He was still only 61.('He died of a broken heart,' was Hugh's verdict. 'He had asked the Kenya Farmer's Association - which he founded - for credit, and they turned him down.')

Tributes poured in, hailing D as the leader whose allegiance to the colony had never wavered. Despite differences of opinion, wrote the Chief Secretary of the Legislative Council at Entebbe, they held "whole admiration for the energy, the enthusiasm, the alert ability and the unerring consistency with which he championed causes and principals." Sir Donald Cameron, who'd once offered Delamere a seat on Tanganyika's Legislative Council, wrote, "He was the most satisfactory public man to do business with that I have ever met." There were messages from the Secretary of State in London, South African Prime Minister General Hertzog, former Prime Minister General Smuts, and the local native council at Embu.

"Lord Delamere was the only man of my acquaintance who was one hundred per cent for Kenya," his old friend Cranworth later wrote. Although he wasn't "generally loved," he added, "He never sought to inspire such a feeling...he was admired, trusted and respected to a degree miraculous in its time and place. That he was a great man I do not doubt, and Kenya will indeed be lucky if she sees his like again."

In spite of D's antipathy, Genesta paid her own tribute to the man who'd given her away at her wedding. "A grand fighter and a fine diplomat, he made Kenya and kept it going through every difficulty. We shall miss him in every way."

Elspeth Huxley's interviews reveal more contradictory postmortems. Truculent, evil-tempered, arrogant and overbearing were among words used, even amid acknowledgments of his leadership powers, quick mind, and astonishing ability to read several books in one night. Julian Harper, a farmer from Ruiru, found him rude: when they'd met up in England D 'picked up the paper and went on reading it, refusing to answer.' Then, as Harper was leaving, he 'suddenly put it down and started talking.'

'He thought in jerks,' said Powys Cobb. 'His thoughts flew from mountain top to mountain top, neglecting the intervening valleys.'

He was never law-abiding or diplomatic, said another friend, Jack Riddell, but 'he terrified the government people and hence his success.'

Robert Chamberlain called D a 'sixteenth-century feudalist come back to life,' while admitting he'd been 'one of the most loveable men possible to meet.'

Ormsby-Gore recalled him as an excellent man to deal with, one who saw the bigger picture, but also 'became infected with the Kenya complex of imagining that everyone at home was trying to do down the settlers…His ruling passion was a love for the country. He became emotional about it and when people become emotional about a country they are on dangerous ground.'

Ewart Grogan claimed that D had suffered small-man syndrome, combining 'pettiness and greatness of vision' with 'no philosophy and no consistency.' But from the outset, Grogan admits, D's mission was for Kenya. 'He lived for this and believed he should sacrifice himself and his family for this…he believed in a fair deal for the blacks, but always with the whites predominant.'

He was a man who kept his ego in check, said Thomas O'Shea. 'He never used the word I at all - always we.'

Women found him charming, alluding to his gift of winning people over. A female friend or acquaintance, Lady Kathleen Villiers, pointed out that had no small talk, that his bad temper was because he'd never learn self-discipline.

Eleanor Cole disagreed: 'His temper was quick and ungovernable, but not so out of control as he made out.'

Hugh Dempster heard the news that night. He'd just arrived at Ol Pejeta, but turned around and drove through the night back to Soysambu. At daybreak he supervised the digging of D's grave on a rocky ridge overlooking Lake Elmenteita. That same day, D returned to the earth in a brief and simple ceremony. Many people from all walks of life had driven hundreds of miles to be there; scruffy settler farmers, officials, employees, all supressing smiles as D's pall bearers were bitten by ants, as if D's final fit of rage was manifesting. Abraham Block, Lord and Lady Erroll, and Clutterbuck attended, but not Beryl; after Denys's burial on the Ngong Hills that May, she'd vowed never to go to another.

Tom, unable to get there so quickly, was in England digesting the fact that the farms owed £226,000 (£15.2 million today). But whatever Tom's thoughts on losing his father, few people could deny D's extraordinary contribution to a growing country, not only financial, but also economic and political. His devoted services to improving methods of rearing livestock, introducing innovative agriculture, and reducing diseases to both, would have lasting effects. In just over three decades D had seen the transformation of many parts of Kenya, not least of Soysambu itself. In spite of the fundamental wrongs of colonialism, the 3rd Baron's achievements would still be acknowledged in Kenya's government school history books well over a century after his arrival at Njoro on a stretcher.

One of Lotte Hughes' interviewees, a former employee of Gilbert Colvile's, told her that before he'd died, D asked Colvile to take care of the Maasai people and their interests. They certainly hadn't forgotten D. "A great many of them came to his funeral," wrote Genesta, "carrying spears and shining from head to toe with red mud."

On hearing the news from over three hundred miles away, one of D's old herdsmen caught the train to come and stand beside his grave. Wearing his traditional shuka, the Maasai elder would have witnessed the sun gilding the glassy surface of the water below, tinting the soda crust peach-pink as the flamingos took flight, a waft of darker pink against the darkening Sugonoi escarpment.

No gravestone was laid. "Delamere's grave is as he wished it to be," writes Huxley, "a part of Africa and out of the sight of men."

BOOK 2

1931-1979

Golden Years Beside the Pink Lake

"Soysambu did not lay itself out to attract man, or seem to care whether he came, or to take much notice of him when he did. It had a vivid beauty of its own, a beauty which slowly saturated and possessed the spirit..."

Elspeth Huxley, *White Man's Country, Vol. 1*

CHAPTER 12

A Woman of Importance

After D's death, a peak on Mt Kenya was named after him. A statue of him, paid for by the Settlers' Association, was erected outside the Stanley Hotel on Nairobi's 6th Avenue and a pencil portrait would be hung in the Reading Room at Muthaiga Club. But Soysambu would now see a decade and a half in receivership. One of the trustees was Wilfred Hunter, an accountant amongst other qualifications. Now he faced the depressing business of D's accounts.

***

'Grandfather was a great talker,' mused Hugh. 'Very persuasive. Always lent money by banks. And when the Bank Manager sent valuers to Soysambu, Manera, Ol Pejeta and the house at Loresho, they were valued at £60,000.' Not enough to settle the debts, Hugh said, which were double what Huxley had written. 'All Father inherited was a heap of debts and a house he couldn't afford to live in, with two acres of roof, off which the lead had been stolen in the first world war because my grandfather wasn't there and didn't care!' He told the story of how Hugh Dempster carried on managing the Kenyan farms 'without a shilling of capital expenditure,' employing Gerald Romer, who'd arrived in the colony around 1932, at £5 a month. When Romer found the long-drop at Manera collapsed into the rising lake, he duly moved it and asked Dempster to reimburse him the five shillings he had spent. 'I thought you'd understood there'd be no capital development!' said Dempster.

***

Gwladys now devoted much of her time to welfare work. The continuing difficulties of the depression were affecting both farmers and businessmen; impoverished British citizens, for whom there was no form of social security, required assistance in their return to Britain. At an African clinic, Gwladys washed and weighed babies, teaching young mothers about a nutritious diet. She was vying for a seat on Nairobi's Municipal Council, anxious to improve - amongst other things - life and housing for Africans. In 1934 she would be elected councillor, and after four years become Nairobi Mayor - a position to which she was twice re-elected.

Some said that Gwladys had never recovered from her great success with the Prince of Wales, but she shrugged off gossip and got on with life, continuing the tradition of D's generous hospitality. On New Year's Eve of 1932, she hosted a party at Muthaiga Club, where the notorious Lady Idina raised eyebrows by dancing intimately with current Governor, Sir Joseph Byrne.

Elspeth Huxley returned from England in 1934 to write D's biography, which would become the two volumes of *White Man's Country*. Her parents, Jos and Nellie Grant, were now farming 1,000 acres of D's former Equator Ranch which they'd bought in 1923. The commissioning of this promising young writer was an index of D's fame, and although the widely-travelled Huxley had been Assistant Press Officer to the Empire Marketing Board, this would be her first book. She would later become best known for her autobiography, *The Flame Trees of Thika*, published in 1959 and serialised on television in 1981 starring Hayley Mills, amongst other prominent names. I now found myself indebted to Huxley, as there was barely any archive material on Soysambu. ('Father burned all grandfather's papers as he didn't get on with him,' Hugh said, adding that Tom had pointedly refused to assist Huxley.)

In Out in the Midday Sun Huxley describes her voyage through the Red Sea - although Imperial Airways now offered flights from England, taking less than a week. She was pleasantly surprised by improvements in the train service from Mombasa, paying an "expensive" 60 shillings for her second class ticket: there was now a small washroom in each carriage, and a dining car serving five-course meals. Nairobi, its streets lined with trees and humming with box-body cars, was, Huxley wrote, "a frontier town no longer, but not yet to be taken seriously as a capital city."

Gwladys, "good at putting people of all sorts at their ease," writes Huxley, met her. "She had a striking appearance - chalk-white skin, jet-black wiry hair, dark-brown eyes - and gave out a sense of vitality, and of tenseness like a coiled spring." She quotes Gwladys's daughter, Rose, who described how she 'lit up a room as she walked in, smelling exotically of Chanel No. 5, usually with a gardenia pinned to her dress and often smoking a Turkish cigarette.' Gwladys took Huxley to the hairdresser to remove the dust, then to the new Torr's hotel, a popular meeting place for mid-morning drinks and after-dinner dancing.

The house at Loresho, surrounded by flowering coffee, was "a comfortable, creeper-covered stone bungalow with the usual deep veranda," Huxley noted, "built around a central quadrangle with a fig tree, sacred to the Kikuyu, in the middle." Gwladys lived in one cottage, her children in another. There were always visitors, and Gwladys "had the art of mixing together different kinds of people and keeping conversation on the boil. In argument she could be aggressive, but then she would disarm her guests with a deep throaty chuckle and a sudden unexpected turn of phrase." Somali servants ran the house as Gwladys was always busy. "Every minute of the day was filled with some activity. She seemed to be running away from something - perhaps her own company."

Huxley stayed at Soysambu with Dempster, rising with him and the managers at dawn, going around the ranch, returning for late breakfast on the veranda overlooking the lake. She also visited Nderit, noting Boy's seductive looks and garb: a "broad-brimmed Stetson hat and a bright Somali shawl (tomato red or electric blue) thrown across his shoulders...Women adored him. He was said to be one of the best stockmen in the country; he would not have been employed by Delamere for fifteen years had it been otherwise."

***

Curious to find out more about the enigmatic Gwladys, I visited her grandson, Sir David Markham, in Suffolk. Son of Charles, he'd never actually met his grandmother and his father hadn't told him much. He showed me Gwladys's beautiful portrait, hanging in his dining room, painted by Philip De Laszlo in 1925, commissioned by her father-in-law in 1912, for which he paid £1,200. But the war had intervened, and afterwards Gwladys had for a time maintained she was too old (at 27) to sit for a painting. I admired this painting, eventually completed, her black-hair contrasting with a sleeveless cream evening dress with green straps, a floating cream chiffon stole emphasising the paleness of her skin. She holds a small bunch of blue irises.

David also had the leather-bound visitors' book, used on Soysambu and Loresho from 1928, its many signatures including those of Eileen and Francis Scott, Genesta Long, Gilbert Colvile, as well as some less salubrious ones: Raymund de Trafford, Jack Soames, Lord Erroll and his second wife Mary (for whom he'd left Idina, although he wouldn't remain faithful to her either) - and royalty: *Edward P*, as he'd signed himself on Soysambu from 7th to the 12th October, 1928. Gwladys had recorded D's death in barely legible writing, continuing to note when she and the children went "home" to England, referring to herself as *Lady*. Visitors continued to stream into Loresho, good times illustrated in Hans Liechtenstein's carousing cartoon: respectable guests (Huxley, the Dempsters) rubbing shoulders with the likes of Idina (her latest married name Haldeman), Alice de Trafford (formerly de Janze), Derek and Patricia Fisher, and Fabian Wallace, all of whom hailed from Happy Valley's heady heights. The more I read on, the more the visits from Happy Valley-ites. One of the most frequent guests was Alistair Gibb, who lived on the fringes of Happy Valley in an imposing house backed up against the Aberdares.

David showed me his father's letters from Gwladys, dating back to school days, sent on Soysambu-headed paper, then *Elementeita* (sic); later headed *Mayor's Parlour, Town Hall, Nairobi, Kenya Colony*. I could discern their beginnings (*My darling Charles*) in her spiky right-leaning scrawl, but little else. The beautiful Gwladys had become even more mysterious. How did this devoted mother and strong advocate for better social justice for the less fortunate fit in with the wild party-goer? Here was a woman who would change considerably in the next decade, into someone with whom D might have struggled to live - although there's always room to understand that these changes could have been forged by loneliness and grief.

***

On 18th January 1934 Tom Delamere's wife Phyllis produced a son and heir.

'The year after Hitler came to power,' said Hugh. 'I was born, premature, in London - 23 Queensgate Terrace. It belonged to the Duke of Buccleugh.'

Tom was working for an advertising agency, and in 1938 became a partner, 'with a fellow called Everet Jones, who was Welsh and very clever,' explained Hugh. 'It made a complete change in the way advertising was done in England. It now became purely pictorial. I remember the Guinness ad: there were huge posters all over London, 40 by 20 feet, with two toucans sitting on a branch. The wording was, *It's amazing what two can do*. And right at the bottom in the left hand corner was a tiny bottle of Guinness.' It remained unusual for the aristocracy to *work*, Hugh added.

An American tenant, Rimmer, had leased Vale Royal after Robert Dempster died, but he left the year after Hugh was born, so the family moved in. 'My father was left with this house and park, and there wasn't even any good timber in the park,' sighed Hugh. 'Usually there's a few thousand oak trees, but all that sort of thing had been sold.' Jackson was still Estate Agent. 'Major Jackson from the Boer War. He always wore a coat and top hat to the office.'

Young Hugh disliked the clock tower ('Some idiot Victorian went and stuck that on. It made the most ghastly noise all night'), preferring the dovecot - 'raided at night by the monks who wrung their necks to eat for Lent. My mother fed the pigeons on yellow maize. When I was three I ate some thinking it was barley sugar.' A keen gardener, Phyllis planted King Alfred daffodils and Narcissus, but the extensive gardens that had once stretched down to the River Weaver now vanished beneath undergrowth. She taught Hugh to read when he was four and he always excitedly anticipated their regular visits to the local library.

The nursery wing was on the ground floor of the Elizabethan wing, on the eastern side, but Hugh set up his trains in the library, a nanny watching over him as he played. 'A huge great empty room, nothing in it except a few rows of bound copies of sermons by old bishops or something or other. I had one locomotive, one coach, one guard's van and one goods truck. All I had was an oval track, and I longed for somebody to give me a pair of points. Eventually an uncle gave me a pair, but that really wasn't enough to make a railway layout of any kind.'

There was a pause as we listened to the buzzing of the bees, encouraged out of their hives by yesterday's rain. It was a sunny May morning in 2015.

Hugh rescued a bee from his yoghurt. 'I had a wind-up Hornby. It was meant to be the Flying Scotsman, but it only had two driving wheels. However, I enjoyed winding it up. It would run for a long way - something like 60 feet - before you had to wind it up again.' His boyhood enthusiasm for trains undiminished, Hugh had built a train room in the garden at Main House, but his Parkinson's Disease increasingly prevented his fiddling with tiny wires. I'd seen the train room many times, been shown the volcano that erupted as the train went past, and the pornographic carriage where naked figures sprawled in compromising positions. 'I've been going at it for many years...still just a complete mess,' he'd said distractedly when he'd first showed me, an introduction that had taken up most of the morning, pointing out with a tinge of sadness that his son Tom never had the patience, nor were his grandsons interested.

When I visited Vale Royal in 2016 someone found an old photograph taken in the formal gardens: a tall and elegant Phyllis, a black Labrador, two little girls in woollen dresses, a greyhound, and three-year-old Hugh holding his mother's hand, with the same expression and smile he wore 80 years later. Vale Royal crouched behind, vast, dark and sinister-looking. 'A fashion magazine at the time had wanted to run a series,' Hugh observed when I produced it. 'We climbed fences and stood about with cows. There were acres of greenhouses in those days, with grapes, orchids, cyclamen. The greyhound was called Sally.' He sighed as he looked at the photograph: 'Mother was terribly shy. Before she went to a party she drank a tumbler full of gin just to steady her nerves!'

***

By the mid-1930s Beryl had made her name in the colony as a successful racehorse trainer, also discovering a passion for flying, a skill she learned in Kenya before rocketing on to international farm in 1936 with her solo flight across the Atlantic. The Happy Valley set were still enjoying their parties, but on a more muted scale, as deteriorating health and depression were beginning to afflict some of its main players. Alice de Janze, who'd by now married her lover Raymund de Trafford, had been deported from the colony, but was now allowed to return as a married woman. De Trafford had married her even after she'd shot him in Paris because he'd tried to leave her, before shooting herself. After they'd both recovered from their wounds, she was charged for murder and acquitted. Back in Kenya, she then did her best to avoid her new husband, a drunken philanderer, until he was deported in 1939. Meanwhile Idina had left her fourth husband, living with various lovers until she married a fifth time, a marriage which wouldn't last either. Erroll continued his political and extra-marital affairs, leaving his second wife at her Naivasha home, The Djinn Palace. He joined the British Union of Fascists in 1934, and was later elected to represent Kiambu constituency back in Kenya.

Meanwhile settler farmers were struggling through the depression and Dempster was doing his best to keep Delamere Estates going. When war broke out again in 1939 Tom was obliged to vacate Vale Royal. The government wanted to convert it into a sanatorium for injured soldiers. Tom rejoined the Welsh Guards, serving at the GHQ of Auxiliary Units near Highworth, initially as Motor Transport Officer. Phyllis and the children went to live with her father in Roxboroughshire.

***

'Mother had no money at all because father hadn't any to give her,'

Hugh pointed out. 'Her father, when he got married in about 1890, was given the magnificent sum of a thousand pounds a year, which enabled him to keep a carriage, four horses, two or three grooms and half a dozen hunters - and a motor car. A new-fangled idea but it seemed to work; he had an Austin 12 and it lasted for ever. My Scottish grandfather was our only grandparent, a charming old man, and of course in the war all his daughters (he had three) and their children descended on him because their husbands had gone off to fight. There wasn't even enough money to run a household - the princely sum of one thousand pounds a year wasn't much in 1939.' Hugh gave a faint smile, well aware that he'd be delighted to have that kind of money, worth £66,000 today, to keep Soysambu going.

The war was the beginning of the end of Hugh's parents' marriage. 'Father was away and mother felt lonely. There were quite a few Americans in Edinburgh, but practically half the Polish army was there. I suppose my mother was...what's the word I'm looking for?'

'Lonely?' I ventured.

'Lonely, yes, but unfortunately mother was rather over-sexed; she was very good-looking, and she felt it was her duty to entertain as many Polish officers as possible.'

***

On 24th January 1941 Lord Erroll was murdered on a lonely roadside a mile away from a house in Karen, on the outskirts of Nairobi, an event that plummeted Kenya into the headlines. He'd just dropped off Sir Jock Delves-Broughton's wife, Diana, with whom he'd been having a very indiscreet affair since their arrival in the colony the previous November. As he drove away from the Broughton house in the small hours, somebody shot him. His body was found in his hired Buick, which had veered off the road.

Diana's biographer Leda Farrant is not complimentary about her subject. Born in Sussex in 1913, Diana Caldwell had lived up to the adulterous role model set by her young mother, who aged 28 had reluctantly married Diana's 45-year-old father. As she grew up

Diana enjoyed no shortage of lovers before she became pregnant by a married one, then hastily married an unmarried one, Vernon Motion, before she miscarried.

Her liaison with Jock, considerably older and already married, who regaled her with family jewels and a flat in London, was conducted while she allegedly slept with her long-term admirer, Hugh Dickinson, who would follow her to Kenya when she arrived there with Jock, late in 1940, having just married Jock in Durban. It was a curious and apparently loveless marriage that involved an agreement stating that Diana would be financially taken care of should she fall in love with a man closer to her own age. Jock had visited Kenya in 1921 to buy a coffee farm, returning later and staying with D and Gwladys at Soysambu, and now, returning with his glamorous young bride, he'd stayed with Gwladys before renting a house in Karen. At Muthaiga Club, they were welcomed by Lord Erroll himself. And thus it had all begun.

More intimately known as Joss, Erroll left a trail of wronged husbands and jealous lovers, all of whom might have fired the fatal bullet, causing much tutting about the dissolute Happy Valley clique. Even Gwladys came under the spotlight. "She has been depicted as a bossy, bitchy and emotionally unbalanced woman, endlessly carousing at Muthaiga Club with Happy Valley-ites," wrote Elspeth Huxley, "and so possessively in love with Lord Erroll that she was even suspected of having shot him."

Erroll's biographer Errol Trzebinski shares Huxley's scepticism, writing that he and Gwladys were close friends due to "their joint concerns about the running of the colony...but they were never lovers." Gwladys was "the driving force behind productions at the Theatre Royal," Trzebinski writes, "shows Joss always attended. The last first night he'd have gone to would have been Agatha Christie's *A Murder Has Been Arranged*."

Sir David Markham felt that James Fox had been 'unkind' about his grandmother in *White Mischief*, published in 1982. 'My Aunt Rose was incensed and tried to take Fox to court,' he told me.

"By 1940, Gwladys had become somewhat more unbalanced," writes James Fox, "partly, it was thought, from the effect of a serious bout of typhoid, and from unhappiness in love." She had lost her looks, and "become exhibitionistic, touchy and unpredictable: loyal at one moment, she would cut you dead the next." Fox also accused her of being racist, sharp-tongued, intolerant of younger, prettier women, and strongly suggests that Gwladys was the author of some vicious anonymous letters sent to Broughton just before the murder.

Huxley writes that Gwladys had indeed suffered an unhappy love affair. As a woman unable to live alone, she'd fallen in love, but he "eluded her. This was her tragedy." This wasn't actually Erroll, I was informed by Gwladys's granddaughter Lucy Shilstone, who wrote in a letter that her grandmother "very likely had had an affair with Erroll, but at the time of the murder she was very much in love with Alistair Gibb, who she had a long love affair with." She even left all of her furniture to him in her will, which would upset her children. Gibb, another redhead, was separated from his wife. "My mother wrote many, many letters to James Fox before the publication of *White Mischief*," Lucy Shilstone continued, "as she felt very strongly that there were absolutely no grounds for pointing the finger of guilt at her mother for Erroll's murder."

But *White Mischief* would remain the popular text on the Lord Erroll murder, creating sufficient waves for the film of the same title to be released in 1987. The part of Diana was acted by Greta Scacchi, while Charles Dance played Erroll and Susan Fleetwood took the role of Gwladys. Charles Markham, by then 63, was most offended at remarks made about his mother. Lord Francis Scott's daughter, Lady Pamela, also complained at the many inaccuracies in both book and film, especially when it came to Gwladys.

At the time of the murder, Gwladys had been extremely busy, as Mayor of Nairobi, with non-stop good works, including serving food all night to soldiers and airmen who'd flocked to Nairobi, the Allied base for the Ethiopian campaign. She'd been one of the first to give up her house, which became a convalescent home for officers, Huxley points out. "She was tireless, her life became frenetic, and if at times she seemed unbalanced, this was because she needed to fill every minute and did not dare to stop." It was her "antidote to despair," Huxley believed, for Gibb had left Kenya, and would marry another.

The murder trial of Sir Jock Delves-Broughton commenced in Nairobi that May. According to the prosecution, Jock had behaved suspiciously before the murder, not least in insisting his wife was home at a certain hour that particular night. Joss's Buick had reeked of Chanel No. 5 - a perfume popular with Gwladys, Alice de Trafford, and Diana. But Gwladys was at Soysambu at the time, Alice had an alibi who'd been in bed with her, and Diana was sidelined.

Gwladys, called as a crown court witness, was said to have been a confidante for Joss, who'd allegedly confessed to her that he loved Diana, twelve years his junior, and that he'd never been so happy, asking her advice. She'd advised him to be honest with Jock. She'd then advised Diana to pursue her own happiness - after all, there was a war on, and her husband was past his prime.

Jock was acquitted, Alice de Trafford committed suicide a few months later, and Jock took his own life the following year.

Less than a year after all that, Gwladys, burnt out by stress, died of a stroke in the early morning of February 22nd 1943, at the age of 45. She'd been in a nursing home "after a brief illness" according to her obituary in *The Standard*. Her daughter Mary was in England serving with the FANYs, Charles was in the army, but Rose, still at school in South Africa, returned in time. The article mentioned Gwladys's medals during the previous war for her hospital work in France, and praised her for being the Colony's only female mayor for three consecutive years (and one of very few in the Empire), as well as President of the East African Women's League. It also noted her work with so many other charitable organisations and welfare services, including the British Legion, League of Mercy, Lady Grigg Home, the Pumwani, European and Indian Maternity Hospitals, the Lady Northey Nursing Home and the McMillan Library. Latterly, during the war, she'd inaugurated the Municipal Hostel and spent two evenings weekly at the Hardinge Street Canteen, where her work had included many menial tasks, "from preparing vegetables, to cooking and serving meals for hundreds of men," with whom Gwladys, never too busy to work at weekends, was most popular. Her funeral was at the Cathedral of the Highlands the afternoon after she died, followed by a procession in her honour along Delamere Avenue, Government Road and Swamp Road, to Forest Cemetery corner, and back. She was buried at Soysambu beside D, an occasion restricted to family and intimate friends. (Over half a century later, a simple engraved stone spelled her name *Gladys Helen,* stating that she was *wife of 3rd Baron Delamere,* plus her date of birth and death. D's and Gwladys's graves were the only two out of four that had gravestones. Neither Hugh nor Ann nor David Markham had any idea who might have placed them.)

After Gwladys's death the Loresho house was sold. ('One of my grandfather's trustees sold it to himself rather cheaply,' Hugh said. 'It later became a hotel.')

***

As a final tribute to Erroll, his suggestion that 6th Avenue be renamed Delamere Avenue was carried out.

CHAPTER 13

After the Murder -
Marriages and Moves

Conjecture and rumour continued to rage around Lord Erroll's murder, with many theories published over the next decades. In *White Mischief* James Fox was convinced of Sir Jock Delves-Broughton's guilt. In *Diana, Lady Delamere and the Lord Erroll Murder* Leda Farrant claims it was Diana, who'd been Lady Broughton at the time. Idina, one of the few Happy Valley-ites who wasn't a suspect, would always blame Diana for his death, according to Frances Osborne's *The Bolter*. Juanita Carbery, in *Child of Happy Valley*, states that Jock Broughton actually confessed his guilt to her teenage self. Paul Spicer, in *The Temptress*, firmly believes Alice de Trafford, formerly de Janze, pulled the trigger.

Errol Trzebinski puts forward a more revolutionary murder theory in *The Life and Death of Lord Erroll*. She believed that Joss's former allegiance with the British Union of Fascists and his political activities in the colony warranted his assassination by MI6, with Gwladys "a useful source of information" for the appointed secret agent. Trzebinski also pays tribute to D's influence on Joss, both as a farmer and politician; The two men were "utterly different types who stood for quite different things," writes Trzebinski, "but they were united in their love of Kenya and a willingness to use all possible means for their cause."

The political motive is expanded upon in *The Umzindusi Letter*, where Tim Topps (real name Alan Broad), briefly outlines his belief that Erroll's hired assassin was his own father, Daniel Broad and that Erroll's elimination was arranged by Lord Baden Powell - founder of the Boy Scouts movement - following orders from Winston Churchill. Alan Broad believes that his father's gratuity came in the form of a scholarship for his son, Alan himself. He further alleges that Broughton, Dickinson and Diana were all agents. Diana, he states, albeit without providing any references, was already known to MI5 and MI6, appointed to have some sort of affair with the Vice Chancellor of Austria shortly before Hitler's invasion. The Governor of Kenya, Sir Henry Monck-Mason Moore, the police, and Gwladys, Mayor of Nairobi, were also involved, according to Broad, making the trial a mere pantomime. He also links up his male protagonists through their association with the cavalry regiments.

Indeed, Leda Farrant points out, no finger prints were taken at Erroll's car, and that Diana was never questioned because she was "hysterical." Nor did she attend the burial. During the longest recorded trial in Kenya's history - all 27 days of it - an extravagantly-dressed Diana impassively watched the farcical questioning of her husband (who knew the truth, according to Farrant, but was covering for her) and listened to Hugh Dickinson lie in court - twice - about his whereabouts that night. After the trial she held a celebratory dinner at Muthaiga Club before Jock took her away to India, then on safari with Dickinson, where the suspicious trio could put their false stories to bed once and for all. As her final 'proof,' Farrant draws attention to an incident 25 years later when Diana encountered the Managing Director of the *Daily Nation* at Muthaiga Club. He attempted to apologise for the brief appearance of an incriminating article in an early-morning edition, later removed.

'Oh, everybody knows I did it!' Diana is alleged to have said.

Such admissions could of course have been offered with a hefty dose of sarcasm. It's also possible that Diana was playing to her audience. However, Farrant wasn't the only one to point her finger at Diana. In 2015 I received an e-mail from a woman who'd read my book *The Ghosts of Happy Valley.* Her mother's friend, a theatre sister at Nairobi Hospital, claimed to have witnessed Diana admitting to the murder on the operating table. Things had turned sour, in the writer's opinion, and Diana wasn't going to "get stuck with an impoverished womaniser." And the reason she had been prepared to go down to South Africa to find the best legal help was because Jock had helped her, by tidying up the murder scene. Diana needed to play along in case he was found guilty and came out with the real story on appeal.

***

I asked Hugh's opinion - after all, Diana later, remarkably, became his stepmother.

'Of course Diana shot him,' he replied without hesitation. 'She was always taking pot-shots at boyfriends who annoyed her. And she told Father and I that dinner at Muthaiga Club.'

***

'People were perfectly bloody to me after the trial,' Diana told James Fox in 1981. 'It was more fashionable to be sorry for Jock. The fact that I pulled myself together and went to the trial every day looking as tidy as I could infuriated some people. I remember the faces...I don't want to think about it.'

Farrant relates how Jock rented the Djinn Palace, beside Lake Naivasha, from Erroll's estate, but if he was trying to regain Diana's affection with this extravagant move, he failed. That August he wrote to the Nairobi lawyer, Humphrey Slade, citing her affairs: an Italian while engaged to him, an officer on the boat to Cape Town, another on honeymoon, followed by Joss, and now she was at it again. Jock wanted retribution, suggesting that she should be prosecuted for staging a fake robbery of the pearls he'd bought her. She never was and was widowed soon afterwards when Broughton killed himself.

Gwladys had apparently been one of many who refused to speak to Diana, but one man took pity on her and wrote to her. This was D's old friend, the reclusive Gilbert Colvile, who lived in bachelor squalor on part of his 155,000 acres bordering the estate of the Djinn Palace. They became friendly neighbours and, on 22nd January 1943, to everyone's astonishment, Diana married him.

***

Hugh, now nine, was sent to Ludgrove Preparatory School. 'It was an enormous house built by some Victorian manufacturer or somebody, and nobody could keep it up - it would have taken 20 servants, and so this chap A. T. Barbour bought it quite cheaply as a school.' He liked Barbour, although life was about hardships: frozen washbowls and limited food. 'The only thing I drew the line at was whale meat. I didn't mind horse - it was only once. I didn't see much of my parents, what with the war and things. My mother turned up about two or three times a term, but Father was away being a soldier.'

Soon enough Hugh had discovered his parents were getting divorced. 'We were staying in a hotel in Edinburgh, and I can remember being very miserable about it. My mother gave me a book to console me; it was called *101 Things for a Boy to Make*.' The divorce was finalised in 1944, and in June that year Tom, wearing army uniform, married the Hon. Ruth Mary Clarisse Ashley, whose father had been a Tory Cabinet minister. She was already twice divorced in England - firstly from Captain Alec Stratford Cunningham-Reid, with whom she'd had two sons, then Major Ernest Laurie Gardner. 'She was red-headed, Jewish and fearfully rich,' Hugh told me, 'a very pleasant stepmother but as mad as a cuckoo.' He acquired two older step-brothers, whom he didn't take to, he told me, and started at Eton, enjoying the social scene and winning a competition for blowing a hunting horn at the Perth Hunt Ball. He divided his school holidays between his parents. 'I remember whenever I went home to mother there was a different Polish officer. I can only remember one of them - he gave me a pair of German binoculars. He was rather a tiresome Pole - used to pinch my sister's bottom when we were climbing some rather narrow stairs in the house.'

Tom moved to live at his wife's family home, Six-Mile Bottom, near Cambridge. Hugh vividly remembers that a forest of trees had been felled on their family land, leaving great stumps. One had fallen naturally, but had been caught by another tree. Lying close to the ground it was the perfect place for a little boy to play. 'I had an imaginary friend,' Hugh said. 'I used to dig holes beneath the trees. I made a hole with steps going down, covered with corrugated iron.'

Life with Gilbert was a prelude to Diana's re-entry into society. He came from an old and noble family. More recently, in 1893, Sir Henry Colvile had been despatched by the foreign office to Uganda. His second wife, Gilbert's mother, Zelie Isabelle de Preville, was descended from French aristocracy. After Sir Henry died, she'd brought her son to East Africa in 1910, opening the Gilgil Hotel to cater for an increasing number of pioneers arriving after the war. Gilbert bought his Naivasha farm, calling it *Ndabibi* after the Maasai word - *en-dapipi* - for the clover-like plant that grew prolifically. Like D, he'd learned from the Maasai, preferring their company; they called him *Nyasore* because he was so thin.

For all his austerity, Gilbert was generous to Diana, happy for her to spend his money on clothes and jewellery, buying her a house in Muthaiga, a beach house in Kilifi (of special significance to her because Erroll had rented it), and even the Djinn Palace and its surrounding 5,000-acre farm, Oserian. According to Charles Hayes in *Oserian: Place of Peace*, Erroll's second wife Mary's first husband, Cyril Ramsay-Hill, had bought Oserian for £3,100 in 1925 from Leslie Tarlton, and had the Spanish-style Djinn Palace built, modelled on his grandmother's house in Seville, including quirks like a sunken bath, Spanish tiles, mosaics and art frescoes. When his wife ran off with Joss, Ramsay-Hill departed, Mary and Joss (by then Lord Erroll) married, and moved into the Djinn Palace in 1930, where they entertained Evelyn Waugh amongst others.

Diana seemed relieved to step out of the spotlight, and this marriage lasted twelve years. "Gilbert taught Diana to ride about the plains, sustained by Maasai snuff, and muster cattle," writes Elspeth Huxley In *Out in the Midday Sun*, "while Diana weaned Gilbert from some of his Maasai ways and, when she could, from some of his more parsimonious habits." According to Huxley, they had a son who died a few days later.

A visit to the knoll at Ndabibi in 2016, where the Colvile graves were now concealed from the sweeping views by a wall, confirmed it was actually a girl. Sarah Colvile had died in September 1947; *So Little and so Short a Time*, read the inscription. My aunt, Susan Platt, remembered the sad occasion. She was training at the Maia Carberry Nursing home, Gilbert Colvile had been a family friend, and she'd heard all the talk about her patient. 'She was very beautiful and very sad,' Aunt Susan told me. 'She had just lost her baby, poor thing. Her eyes were so blue, and full of tears that welled up and coursed down her cheeks.'

After Diana miscarried serially, the Colviles were advised to adopt. Cross-cultural adoption wasn't the done thing, but white babies weren't difficult to find in the colonies. A girl born in Uganda on 12th March 1948 was brought to Kenya at 12 days old. Her paperwork was quickly completed in the Nairobi courts and Gilbert and Diana named her Deborah.

***

When I moved to Soysambu in 1999, Deborah Colvile, whom everyone called Snoo, was a regular visitor, bringing a breath of fresh coastal air and cool boxes crammed with seafood. She was dark-haired, her skin bronzed by the sun; an attractive, fit, no-nonsense type, with an infectious sense of humour. She was nothing like I'd imagine Diana's daughter to be. She now lived for part of the year at Villa Buzza, her late mother's Kilifi pad, and in 2017 I accepted her long-standing invitation to visit. The large plot swallowed up the modest, white-painted bungalow, with its long, arched veranda facing the ocean, a shady orchard of mango trees behind. The house was open to the sea breezes; no window bars, nor even a fence - remarkable in 2017 when surrounding houses were fortified with security fences, alarms and guards. We took her dogs, of motley breeds, for an evening walk, watching them chase ghost crabs along palm-fringed white sand, gulls wheeling overhead, the shadow of a palm nut vulture suddenly passing over.

Gilbert had bought this place in 1943, Snoo told me, a two-bedroomed beach shack with an outside long-drop - which she'd been too scared to use when they visited. She had been christened at Oserian. The vicar had eyed the birdbath in which he was expected to baptise the baby and said, 'We need some holy water.' Snoo laughed. 'So Mummy said, "Bless it, then."' Until the age of eight she'd lived a happy, if lonely, childhood on Ndabibi, which stretched through the high country on the northern side of Naivasha that included a pea-green crater lake surrounded by sinister hills, and what Snoo referred to as 'a spooky and exciting place called the Caves of God; you could walk through a hill.' Schooling came in envelopes; the Rift Valley Correspondence Course supervised by her Scottish nanny, Mary Gregory. Snoo never met her paternal grandparents, 'although the Colvile family history goes back to the Norman Conquest.' Back at the house, over a glass of chilled wine Snoo told me she'd been very fond of Gilbert. 'He tried to teach me to call cattle...I regret not seeing more of him.'

CHAPTER 14

Money, Madness and War

'Do you know why we've still got this farm?'

It was August 2015, and Hugh, Ann and I were having lunch at Simon Thomsett's centre for rehabilitating birds, mainly raptors, concealed in one of Soysambu's southern pockets of forest and built out of local materials and a jumble of unlikely bits and bobs. We tucked into chicken, roasted in a highly efficient clay oven crafted by Simon's own hands, observed by a Tawny Eagle on a nearby perch. She was 'an imprint,' Simon explained, so she'd never be able to be released, although she enjoyed a good life, Simon flying her daily, like other people walk their dogs. She would be used for captive breeding to boost a rapidly declining raptor population. Simon was world-renowned for his knowledge, and Soysambu was fortunate to have him there, offering sanctuary to birds injured by ignorant people or by ill-thought-out and poorly situated wind farms and power lines. He was also involved in important research; I'd watched him catch, measure, ring and release eagles, and between September and April, when migrant species joined Soysambu's residents, he'd showed me a rare Greater Spotted Eagle perched on a thorn tree beside the lake and a Russian Peregrine atop an electricity pylon.

Before his sudden question Hugh had been lamenting the lack of funding for projects such as Simon's. Now, having failed to elicit an answer, he explained. The Second World War had generated a worldwide scarcity of beef, not to mention a substantial demand for tinned beef for Allied troops in Kenya. Even the Maasai were ordered to supply a quota of 2,000 cows a month, which didn't go down well, as Rupert Watson explains in *Culture Clash*; in 1946 Hugh Grant, District Commissioner at

Narok, a posting in the heart of Maasailand, ended up speared to death by a *moran*.

'We'd never have got out of debt if it hadn't been for the war,' Hugh concluded. Steers, he pointed out, had sold for 30 shillings each, but the war increased this to £30. In 1951, the year Hugh was heading to Cambridge, Tom had received 'the most extraordinary telegram any bank ever sent. Banks are, of course, organised robbers and thieves and bloodsuckers.' Hugh then quoted the telegram: '*You have repaid all the capital and in view of your father's services to the country we have pleasure in letting you off the interest.*'

After the war had ended, Tom had returned to Kenya in 1946 to have a look at his farms, said Hugh, 'to see if it was worth trying to get going again.' According to Hugh he flew into Kenya on a de Havilland DH.89 Dragon Rapide, a short-haul biplane airliner dating back to the 1930s. 'It had two Gypsy Moth engines and looked like a dragonfly. It could take eight passengers and could go 100 miles before it had to be refilled, so it hopped down the Nile, stopping everywhere you could buy fuel. It lost an engine in Malta, and buggered the other in a sandstorm in Wadi Halfa.' Deciding that Soysambu might be worth saving, Tom, moved to Kenya, where he fulfilled his obligations as Lord Delamere, joining Muthaiga Club and becoming a Jockey Club steward. Tom's advertising agency, said Hugh, 'was eventually sold very profitably to Bensons, who sold it on, and on it went until eventually it became Saatchi and Saatchi, which now has 114 offices in 76 countries.'

The following year Hugh flew out with his sister Elizabeth, 'in a train-spotter's version of a Lancaster bomber, with tin sides, wooden floors and basket chairs bolted on to the floor.' He was 13 when he gazed at Soysambu for the first time. 'My father warned me: "Don't fall in love with the place. It will ruin you." But like a lot of idiots, I'd fallen in love with it at first sight!' He went on to tell how his stepmother Mary 'insisted on bringing her Jersey cows.' Tom preferred horses, although according to Hugh he 'started cows properly. He brought cows from the Northern Frontier District to the 64,000 acres of Ol Pejeta he'd inherited, and to add to the scruffy mix here. Grandfather, with his 30,000 merinos, had nearly turned Soysambu into a desert!' In spite of Elspeth Huxley's claims to the contrary, Hugh maintained that Boran cattle hadn't been brought to Soysambu until after the Second World War; Ol Pejeta's manager, Brian Curry, had seen them while fighting in Abyssinia. 'Grandfather's cattle were an appalling mix. The Boran cattle have been bred up by Father since 1947, by selecting those with the biggest and best barrel. Wider-jawed bulls were chosen for breeding. Height isn't important.'

The railway line had recently been moved, no longer passing through Elmenteita, instead running below the Sugonoi escarpment, to the east of the lake. Boy Long, now retired and living alone, had returned to the stone house he'd built. 'Father hadn't the heart to try and turn him out,' Hugh said. Thus, with no other houses available on Soysambu, Tom rented one on the neighbouring farm, Oldobiye. '*Ol-dupai* is Maasai for sansevieria,' Hugh explained. 'We hired it from a Belgian... Now it's Gideon Moi's.' His father gave him a rifle - to his delight - and said, 'Shoot the two zebra,' (there were only two, according to Hugh). 'And that,' he concluded delightedly, 'was the end of them.' It wasn't, as by 2016, 5,000-plus resident zebra were daily chased away from the hay and water reserved for drought-stricken Soysambu's cattle. 'In a few years there'll be 10,000,' Hugh sighed. The CEO, Kat Combes, was doing her best to negotiate with the Kenya Wildlife Service about the surplus, but new laws of managing wildlife on your land were yet to be implemented. Meanwhile a lone zebra they'd called *Rafiki* (Kiswahili for friend) had moved into Hugh and Ann's garden and was now enjoying the dahlias. I detected a sneaking fondness for Rafiki, even on Hugh's part.

Tom sold the house at Vale Royal to Imperial Chemical Industries (ICI) and it would remain the Salt Division's headquarters until 1960. 'The bottom ends of the rafters had all started to rot,' muttered Hugh. 'Father got practically nothing for it.' Two years later the roof had fallen in - fortunately ICI's problem. 'They re-roofed it beautifully and it looked very nice, with a couple of Rolls Royces parked in front of it - just like father would have wished it to if he'd lived there.' Hugh sighed. 'Oh, well, delusions of ancient grandeur get you nowhere, I can promise you!'

Hugh often told a long story of two Jewish chemists who'd fled Prussia back in D's day, eventually persuading him to lease them some land at £40 an acre. They'd had a mysterious partner, Hugh said, benefitting over the years from ICI's profits. This turned out to be Dr Arthur Atkinson, who'd put up £1,600, making money until his death in the 1960s. 'The salt deposits were very deep,' Hugh added. 'They were the remains of a dried-up sea.' Atkinson, further living up to his reputation in East Africa for dubious dealings, had certainly proved a better businessman than D.

After ICI vacated their offices, Vale Royal lay empty before becoming, at various times, a conference centre, special education centre, country club, hotel - and eventually a golf club. By 2016 all that was left in England under the Delamere name, Hugh pointed out, was a fishing pond. 'It fetches 600 pounds a year in rent.'

Soysambu was finally entering its golden era. In 1948, a wet year, Tom was able to employ eight European managers, one of whom, William Fitzmaurice, built a new stone house below Sugonoi escarpment on the eastern boundary, close to the main entrance to the farm along the main road to Nakuru. ('Hugh's father was pretty mean about the whole thing,' Ann told me. 'He just galloped on his horse to the end of the water pipe and said, "*Jenga hapa* (build it here)!" Nothing about a nice view or anything.')

Michael Cunningham-Reid, one of Hugh's stepbrothers, arrived. Michael was a lot older than Hugh. ('He would tell me what to do,' recalled Hugh of their time at Six-Mile Bottom, 'and then pontificate, and was usually one hundred per cent wrong - it's difficult to be *more* than one hundred per cent wrong.' Noel, the other brother, 'was a bit older, and rather nasty. I didn't like him. I never kept in touch.')

Errol Trzebinski defended Michael Cunningham-Reid. He was "hugely generous - to a fault," she wrote to me, and "straightforward, whether expressing approval or disapproval." She sent me part of his unpublished memoir, titled, *What Was, Was,* in which Michael candidly describes his "spoilt, indulged, headstrong" mother, with her "bouts of manic depression." According to Michael she'd become obsessed with her father's employee, Captain Alec Stratford

Cunningham-Reid, a good-looking, charming, penniless war hero, at a shooting weekend at Broadlands - her older sister, Edwina, was married to Lord Louis Mountbatten - and although Mary's parents tried everything to prevent their marriage, she ran away to find him. After a nervous breakdown, then being sent abroad for a year, she got her way.

Michael was raised by a nanny, his mother getting out of bed at lunchtime and rarely visiting the nursery. Her close friend, Barbara Mcorkindale (later Cartland), would act as hostess at Six-Mile Bottom, when Mary's "swinging moods got the better of her and she was incapacitated." During the war when she remarried, Michael was palmed off on relatives in America. He got on much better with his second stepfather, Tom; they shared a love of horse-racing. "Tom was an irrepressible gambler and hard drinker," he wrote, "And I was the young apprentice." (Hugh objected to this characterisation. 'Father gambled, but he didn't drink much at all...' while Ann described Michael Cunningham-Reid as 'most unreliable.')

After the war Michael had left the Welsh Guards, then done remarkably little. After reprimanding his stepson as idle, and totally unqualified to do anything in England, Tom suggested he come to Kenya. Mary thus arranged a lavish safari to introduce her sons to a lifestyle to which she expected them to become accustomed. Afterwards Michael's brother Noel returned to Cambridge, Mary to Soysambu, and Michael was given a Morris Minor van to drive down the Rift Valley escarpment to Manera for his first job as farm-hand, with a salary of £10 a month. Gerald Romer met him and outlined his tasks. But instead of checking milk bales, Michael shot a leopard, then headed to the Lake Hotel for a drink, where he bumped into Romer. Fired the next morning, Michael sheepishly arrived on Soysambu. Tom, who rarely swore, did so now, losing his temper and dispatching his stepson to Ol Pejeta to join farmhands Robin Long (son of Boy) and Robert Shaw under the manager, Gerald Southey. Michael bedded down nervously, listening to the continuous roar of lions and trumpeting elephants. After a brief period there, he moved to Soysambu, along with Robin Long, where they joined Fitzmaurice and De Trafford (related to the infamous Raymund) in Sugonoi House.

By 1949 Beryl was in England, having left behind another failed marriage in America. Unwell and penniless, she wanted to join her father in South Africa. Tom, who hadn't forgotten the favour she'd once done for him all those years ago in D's hayloft, provided the money for her fare. The following year Boy Long died in the front bedroom of the stone house. Tom and Mary were finally able to move in, after Mary had made some improvements. In keeping with its enlarged grandeur, it was renamed Main House.

***

'Mary built on this wing, although we kept altering it!' Hugh indicated the veranda-lined wing to his left, containing their sitting room, bathrooms, dressing rooms and bedrooms: 'Originally this part' (pointing right) 'was the manager's house. Very small and three bedrooms, but only one bathroom. I'm told a gentleman's residence has two loos, a nobleman's mansion more than two. Well, I've got seven!' Main House certainly was no mansion - in fact it was badly in need of some repairs. I'd just visited one of the bathrooms, opened a tap in the basin which produced nothing, then tried a tap in the bath which had spat some lumps of mud. I didn't have the heart to wake the elderly retainer, Muiruri, dozing on a low stool in the corridor, the cow-tail fly whisk in his hand dropping to the floor as I tiptoed past.

***

Prone to sudden, sweeping decisions, Mary decided Michael needed his own farm, instructing her trustees to buy the 800-acre Spring Farm on the escarpment behind Sugonoi House. There were two springs above Soysambu, and the one on Michael's new farm fed the Mereroni. ('The name means devil thorn,' Hugh told me, although, he hastened to add, it was the incorrect version of the Maasai word *mere-ruanyei*. 'It grows in overgrazed areas on bare ground. It grows out like a star,' he said, 'sending tendrils in all directions. There are four spikes per thorn, so whichever way it lands is up!') The farm being on a slope meant its land wasn't able to be ploughed, and Hugh only recalled some Jersey cattle there, not enough to profit from. He thought it had later been bought by Fitzmaurice.

Michael didn't get on with the manager of his new farm, so opted to stay on Soysambu. His memoir suggests he was close to his stepfather; when he contracted cerebral malaria, Tom visited him in hospital. Mary didn't. "Waiting for Mother," he quips, "had become a theme in my life." His stepfather increasingly influenced his opinions, treating him with "a quiet and affectionate respect." Michael would even talk to Tom as the latter took his bath; sucking on a sponge he would reflect on life "that the most one could aspire to be was reasonably content and, if very lucky, gain a few moments of blinding happiness." He became acquainted with "Tom's demons… Today he might be labelled borderline schizophrenic. One of his personalities was dictatorial, conceited and foul-tempered; the other was of a deeply caring, tolerant, loyal, trustworthy, intelligent, witty and compassionate soul." Michael surmised that Tom had been intimidated by his father's towering presence, and unfairly compared to him ever since. Tom carried his anger with *his* father, Michael further noted, into his dealings with Hugh.

***

Hugh, who also often chatted to his father during Tom's pre-dinner bath, didn't believe Tom was as fond of Michael as Michael thought. 'Father put up with him,' he sniffed. He was also able to view his stepmother's mental condition with more understanding. 'She'd been badly treated by several husbands,' he pointed out, 'including my father.'

***

Tom and Mary were going through one of many turbulent phases in their marriage. Her mental health was deteriorating, something Michael found overwhelming and incomprehensible. "A depressive cloud hung over all our lives," he writes. As she hurled abuse at Tom, Michael would watch his typically English response: "stiff upper lip and talk about everything else but that which needed to be addressed." Michael, who confesses that he grew up restless, becoming a thrice-married compulsive gambler and drinker, writes with candour, "The abiding symbol of the shadow of fear that has dogged my life was my mother, Mary. She was the gauge by which I measured how I was getting on in life, and mostly, I found myself failing."

Besides suffering from depression, Mary had cause to be unhappy. The racing scene invited interaction with a glamorous competitor. "Mrs Gilbert Colvile wore a lovely tailored frock in powder blue with the new V-neckline," noted the writer of *Kenya Weekly News,* "set off by a round-brimmed cinnamon straw hat, adorned with cock feathers." By the 1952-1953 racing season, Diana and Tom were joint racehorse owners, their horses leading the field the following year.

Back in 1948 the Duke of Gloucester had arrived to give Nairobi city status, prompting a Kikuyu oath-taking ceremony at Kiambaa. Discontent with British rule had simmered for longer. A young Kikuyu, Johnston Kamau (later, and more famously, Jomo Kenyatta), Secretary General of the Kikuyu Central Association, had gone to London in 1931 with a land petition and stayed 15 years, losing touch with the Association to some extent, which had been proscribed unlawful in 1940. In 1944 the British allowed the election of a token Kikuyu to the Legislative Council, but little improved, and in 1947 an underground movement known as Mau Mau became active. In 1950 it too was banned. Oath-taking continued in secret, often in Kikuyu Independent Schools, created out of a reaction against mission ones and separate from government ones.

Perhaps Tom had a premonition that the situation could become serious, or he simply wanted his mother's grave to be more accessible. Thanks to further research by Monty Brown for his *Guide Book to the Nairobi South Cemetery* I discovered that Florence Delamere's grave, No. 227, in the first extension to the Christian cemetery, was exhumed on 21st March 1950, "her body being moved to join her late husband at Elmenteita."

Genesta Long, who'd moved to what she referred to as "cold, uncomfortable England," now returned with her new husband, Lord Claud Hamilton. "The country is more densely populated than when I went away," she wrote, referring to its white population, "from Thomson's Falls to Gilgil I saw farmhouses every five miles... As we drove through Kekopey and Soysambu it seemed so strange, forgotten yet familiar. The huge plain, the big, blue hills and the lakes were wonderfully welcoming." (Tom, like *his* father, didn't like Genesta, Ann told me. Hugh then made it clear that he hadn't liked her either, accusing her of many inaccuracies in her writings.)

By February 1952, the Duke and Duchess of Edinburgh arrived. Processions took place in Nairobi and there was a garden party at Government House. Governor Philip Mitchell's regime "surpassed itself," complains Genesta. "One card sent to Lady Mac (a widow) said *You and your wife will be presented*...and any amount of really important people - like Florrie Wilson, who started the airlines here - weren't asked at all." Fortunately, Genesta had been invited. After the pomp and ceremony, HRH went on to Nyeri - in spite of Mau Mau's activities there - where the Duke played polo, overnighting nearby in Treetops, a treehouse for watching game where the resident hunter, Jim Corbett, wrote his famous words in the register, referring to the death of King George VI which would lead to the coronation of his eldest daughter, noting that for the first time in world history a Princess had ascended a tree - and descended a Queen, "God bless her."

***

Hugh came out from Cambridge for his summer holidays. 'I did agriculture, because Father told me to do agriculture,' he told me. 'Father said, "You had better do something useful."' Tom kept Hugh busy planting pyrethrum on the Sugonoi escarpment. Hugh was more interested in gardening, in his spare time building a boundary wall around the garden, aiming to keep out the wind, building a terrace. 'You couldn't grow anything - you see, there was no soil,' he complained. 'Grandfather built on rock. Just below the old railway line, they dug up some red soil and carted it here. I brought in lorry loads of it. Moolraj at Elmenteita had a seven-ton lorry, and was willing to hire it out for 100 shillings.'

Tom, who'd had little further education himself, found it infuriating to bow to his son's superior knowledge. He was clever, 'a brilliant bridge player,' Hugh told me, yet lacking in so many skills. 'He couldn't even fix a car!' Hugh was more like his mother, tall and gangly, towering above his father, which further irritated Tom, as according to Hugh he didn't like anyone taller than him. Hugh had inherited the family red hair, but otherwise didn't look like Tom.

***

Mau Mau was hotting up, and in the dead of night freedom fighters came to the graveyard, keen to dig up D's bones to use in witchcraft. The old bull buffalo who used to lie around, guarding D's grave, had died, but there was a story, told afterwards by generations of Maasai herdsmen, that when these Kikuyu militia arrived in the dead of night they were met by a hail of stones - thrown by the ghosts. And thus the grave robbers fled empty-handed.

That August a curfew was imposed in certain areas around Nairobi. Mitchell had retired in June and the new Governor, Evelyn Baring, didn't arrive until late September. According to Charles Douglas-Home in *Evelyn Baring: The Last Protocol*, two weeks before his arrival a letter warned him of a "difficult political situation." So far he'd only been warned by Mitchell about how to behave around divorcees. "It is of somewhat unusual complexity, especially as we have the amateur champion out here, who has, I think, been divorced by five if not six husbands," wrote Mitchell, presumably referring to Idina. "The Delamere household is another not very simple one, particularly on the occasion of royal visits." Mitchell was likely referring to Tom's being twice married and Mary thrice, not to mention Tom's cosy friendship with Diana Colvile, which dragged the whole Erroll shenanigans into the equation. The British Government continued to ignore an inflammatory situation, Mitchell even informing Baring that

Africans were "largely apolitical." But soon after his arrival, Baring was on a tour of areas where the Kikuyu people were confined, when Chief Waruhiu was murdered for speaking out against Mau Mau. "I hope you will not think I have been carried away by panic on the part of excitable Europeans here," Baring wrote to London. "I have reached my conclusions very unwillingly and fully realize that the strong action I recommend will cause you much political trouble." The British Government announced its intention to send out troops, and on 21st October a State of Emergency was declared. A report by the War Council, amongst the Elspeth Huxley papers in Oxford, outlines colonial government plans; "intensive military operations, including bombing of terrorists in the forest" and "expansion and improvement of the police force."

Baring believed the trouble would only last weeks but, Douglas-Home points out, "atrocious intelligence" and lack of understanding of the Kikuyu created a very different reality. The situation was even underestimated by Dr Louis Leakey, the renowned paleoanthropologist and archaeologist who'd been born in Kenya in 1903 and spoke Kikuyu, as well as having taken initiation rites with them.

Accounts of Kenya's struggle for independence vary, depending on which book you read. Some called the perpetrators freedom fighters, others called them terrorists. Caroline Elkins' *Imperial Reckoning* (published in 2005) attracted criticism from former settlers for its one-sided view and sensational accusation of the British for committing war crimes on a far larger scale than had ever been imagined. 'We may argue indefinitely as to the method used to put down the Mau Mau rebellion - the number killed, and the justification of the policy of "villagisation," claimed R A Massie-Blomfield in a letter to the *Sunday Nation*, 'but what is beyond dispute is that the colonial forces, together with loyalist Kikuyus, were engaged in a struggle with Mau Mau rebels - not to deny Kenyans their independence but to ensure that they achieved it." J Smith, writing from Mombasa, disagreed: "If Britain had no shame or guilt, why are so many documents regarding this conflict missing?"

Undoubtedly the Africans had put up with enough. Fed up with segregation and lack of representation, amongst other indignities, they were demanding their land back. White settlers, who'd made their homes on the land they'd bought and developed, felt uneasy. "Kenya's present is darkened by a resurgence of primitive savagery," wrote Dr C. J. Wilson in the postscript to *Before the White Man in Kenya*, published in 1952 and on sale for five shillings.

In spite of Baring's hopes, Mau Mau would prove to be a long and complicated guerrilla war. Back in Britain there was little support for Kenya's white settlers, and taxpayers objected to the costs. The full-scale counter-insurgency was mainly centred in Nairobi and two adjoining provinces - Central, and Rift Valley (where the Delamere farms lay). Farms bordering the dense forests of the Aberdares or Mt Kenya were the most vulnerable, Happy Valley's amongst them, but the Emergency impacted all farmers. Many people lived in fear of attack, mistrusting their loyal workers. Most young white men in the colony had been called up to serve in the Kenya Regiment, a locally recruited battalion, leaving their wives to run the farms and sleep with pistols beneath their pillows. Older men, including Tom and Gilbert, were left to keep farms productive, although Tom, who was anti-war, remained very much in favour of Kenya's independence, which put him at odds with some settlers. He was also defensive of his workers.

***

'Lord Delamere was Chairman of the Employer's Association in the 1950s,' Soysambu's elderly manager, Stephen Koigi, told me. 'He protected his staff during The Emergency. He didn't let them go into detention.'

Interestingly, there were said to be a few Europeans who supported Mau Mau. While interviewing some elderly Mau Mau fighters in former Happy Valley in 2012, I'd been surprised to learn that they'd known some whites who'd assisted freedom fighters with food supplies and somewhere to hide, and that one such place had been Sugonoi House, where oath-taking had also been carried out. It's possible that with its young bachelor managers away fighting, and Tom's policy of protecting his workers, there were indeed Mau Mau activities being planned from there. Close to the forested heights of the escarpment, it would have been an ideal location, well protected by Delamere Estates, and as such, avoiding much attention. But even if some Europeans were supportive, or simply turned a blind eye for reasons of self-preservation, it's unlikely that Tom was aware of any such goings on at Sugonoi.

**

There were a few more houses on Soysambu by now: Flamingo House, on an east-facing bluff overlooking the lake, was Romer's residence, shared with his cousin, David Haselden, who'd arrived from Spain to be employed as another manager. Not far away another stone house, Lanet House, commanded fabulous views over the lake, the eastern walls of the Rift Valley and the brooding indigo hulk of Eburru. A new dairy manager, Jimmy Combes, moved in. His eldest son, Simon, aged 12, could now enjoy the idyllic boyhood neither Tom nor Hugh had. Although most people on Soysambu, Manera and Ol Pejeta beefed up their security arrangements, for Simon life went on as usual. With his African friend Soi, a rifle, and a couple of dogs, he spent school holidays roaming the bush, making himself an "eyrie," eloquently described in *An African Experience: Wildlife Art and Adventures in Kenya*. "A deep crack about a yard wide split the cliff from top to bottom," he wrote. "The upper end of this fissure was blocked by the tangled roots of a huge wild fig tree which clung to the rock like a giant octopus. Some three yards below the tree was a large ledge, accessible only by wriggling into the crack and clinging to the tree roots."

From here Simon could observe the lake, the valley, the Sugonoi escarpment with the railway and road below, and the distant peaks of the Aberdares. His adventures included being temporarily blinded by the venom of a 7-foot spitting cobra and meeting a leopard defending its kill. Back home, where he returned for sleep and sustenance, he raised an orphaned hyrax, a monkey, three young augur buzzards, crowned cranes and various gazelles. Beside the hot and inhospitable lakeshore with its expanse of hard-packed soda, Simon discovered the remains of a boathouse, a 12-foot aluminium dinghy hidden in the reeds. With his younger brother Rob he unearthed various sailing accessories in Flamingo House, learning to sail on an impossibly shallow lake in howling winds, pushing the dinghy through the mud, burning themselves raw in the alkaline water. He was even more thrilled to discover it was possible to borrow a .303 rifle from the old railway station, which had morphed into Elmenteita Police Station. The zebra always needed to be culled, but he preferred shooting buffalo - "the meanest of animals," as he describes them.

***

In 2017 I had to file a police report at Elmenteita Police Station, after I'd been hijacked at gunpoint along the Kekopey road, alarmingly close to Soysambu's Jolai gate; a rash of opportunistic crime had also included a huge increase in poaching and it seems I'd been driving in the wrong place at the wrong time. Inside this thoroughly rickety wooden structure on stilts, the policeman on duty didn't have a pen, so I waited while a runner went off at a slow walk to find one.

'We've just put in a new floor for them,' Ann told me later, 'after we caught some thieves and sent them to the police cells and they escaped through the floor.'

'It had rotted because they all had to pee in the corner,' added Hugh.

The new floor hadn't contained the runaways, who'd merely dislodged the back wooden corner wall, where it stuck out like a ballet skirt.

***

But in Simon's day the police station was still spruce and clean, its wall and floor intact. The borrowed gun had to be returned on time, especially as those were frightening times and guns could be stolen by Mau Mau freedom fighters.

Beryl returned in 1952, still totally broke, visiting Soysambu in the hope she could work for Tom, but he had enough problems with Mary, and nor was she prepared to have Beryl there, who, in spite of having been through menopause and a hysterectomy, hadn't lost her looks. Friends in Naro Moru offered Beryl their guesthouse, where she re-established herself as a racehorse trainer.

That October Genesta returned from England to find spotter planes patrolling by day, the army at night. A month later she would complain to her diary. "Now we, on the farms, are in the ridiculous situation of not being able to get rid of the dangerous Kikuyu when we want to, but having to spend a lot of precious time comforting and protecting them." All settlers were doing their bit, she added: "Claud, Gethin and Nicoll do their turns of all-night duty with the police at Elementeita (sic)."

Eleanor Cole, who'd adapted to wearing a pistol, never turning her back to the door, wrote about the complications of cattle management, with the risk of their being hamstrung by terrorists: "Security necessitated bringing all herds into guarded bomas at night - in the case of Kikopey twelve to fifteen herds of between a hundred and two hundred head each - which not only made much more work for the herdsmen, but seriously restricted the grazing hours for the beasts. Daytime-only grazing also made it almost impossible to carry out proper rotational grazing."

Mau Mau were crafty opponents, concealing themselves completely in the mountains, emerging at night to attack farms, vanishing without trace into the dense Aberdare and Kipipiri forests as night paled into dawn, their women secretly delivering food and conveying messages. 1953 brought a series of gruesome murders of white farmers, their wives and children. Settlers united to accuse the Governor of weakness, demonstrating in the grounds of Government House with shouts of 'Baring must go!' Two respected settler leaders, Michael Blundell and Humphrey Slade, were called in to pacify the mob while Baring remained indoors reading a book. Genesta recorded in her diary that by February, 15 white settlers and "hundreds" of Kikuyu women and children had been "slaughtered" by Mau Mau, criticising the authorities for not removing all Kikuyu from their villages at the outset, both for their own protection and to stop nocturnal food deliveries. Farmers were twitchy; many took on Maasai guards. The Hamiltons hired ten when Baring came to stay.

On 24th March a large gang of Mau Mau raided Naivasha Police Station, stole firearms and ammunition and released around 200 prisoners. The following day almost 100 Kikuyu men and women who'd resisted the movement were murdered along with their children at Lari, in the highlands between Naivasha and Nairobi. Jomo Kenyatta, who'd been among those arrested earlier that year, was sentenced to prison on 8th April. Emergency regulations were put in place, removing people from villages to transit camps in Nakuru and Gilgil, where, Elkins reports, they were kept in "squalid and overcrowded conditions."

Colonial life marched on. That June 4,000 people were invited to the Coronation garden party. Churchill-appointed General Sir George Erskine arrived as Commander in Chief, calling for reinforcements three months later. *Operation Blitz* ran through the Aberdares in late 1953, followed by the King's African Rifles *Operation Hammer*, with a shoot-on-sight policy. Genesta's diary reveals her increasing bitterness with "the poor deluded British Government." Gray Leakey, cousin of Dr Louis Leakey, had been buried alive. "The Europeans have made this country; they also make most of the trouble," wrote Baring to a colleague in Britain. The rift between settlers and administration deepened.

Life changed somewhat at Oserian. One night the police raided the house and took all their staff, only allowing those who were Muslim to return. (Snoo told me that Diana's driver, Simeon, had said to her many years later: 'I'm so glad we were locked up. We didn't have to kill you.') Diana hosted a neighbour and her children for five months, a generosity somewhat undermined by Charles Hayes' and Leda Farrant's claims that Diana had numerous lovers during the Emergency - including this friend's husband.

A young Kenya Regiment recruit, Sam Weller, later told Farrant about an occasion when dining at the Traveller's Club. His commanding officer, Guy Campbell, threw a bread roll from a nearby table, which Weller caught and threw back. It knocked an ice-cream onto Campbell's lover's expensively clad lap. This happened to be Diana. Furious, she wouldn't accept Weller's apologies, ordering Campbell to punch him - an instruction he ignored. 'I remember her face to this day,' Weller told Farrant, 'those eyes like ice.'

CHAPTER 15

Upgrades and Disposals

In 1954 Hugh returned to Soysambu, fresh out of Cambridge. His agricultural degree being deemed important enough to warrant his working to boost the economy, he wasn't called up to serve in the Kenya Regiment. Meanwhile Tom, who'd never reconciled himself to having such an academic son, sidelined him, taking on Arthur Newton as manager to sort out Manera's ailing dairy herd. So Gilbert Colville employed Hugh for six months.

'He couldn't stand me,' Hugh said. 'The only useful thing I did as far as he was concerned was shoot a lot of warthog. Between Oserian and Ndabibi there were seven gates, so every time I got out to open one, I shot two warthogs.' Hugh was given a house to live in and paid five pounds a month, enough to employ a cook. Gilbert was busy hunting down terrorists using dogs: 'Labradors and Dobermans,' Hugh told me.

In early 1955 Hugh moved to Solio to work for David Cole, Galbraith's son who farmed wheat, thousands of sheep and a few cattle. 'Half-breed foreign cattle, which was rather the state father inherited Soysambu in,' shrugged Hugh. 'In those days all the farms already had managers, so it was difficult to get a job.' The other side of the Aberdare mountains from Soysambu, this was rolling country freckled with whistling thorn that stretched from Mweiga to Naro Moru, the Aberdares and Mt Kenya rising on two horizons.

'David Cole had rather a difficult wife,' said my mother, who was staying.

'Difficult?' Hugh retorted. 'In a civilized century she'd have been burned as a witch. She was second- or third-hand - she'd been a mistress of the American Consul in Japan who moved to Kenya. I could never understand why he married her; perhaps she did very subtle things at night that he wasn't used to. She wasn't good-looking, her hair stuck out in all directions - so she was nicknamed "the Lavatory Brush!" When I arrived, Nancy had got through 17 managers in two years.' He recalled the manager, nicknamed 'Mbuzi' (goat), looking on in astonishment as Nancy insisted the carcass of a cow that had died of East Coast Fever was burned *immediately.* 'It was pouring with rain. Mbuzi said, "I resign," and handed the matches to her.' Hugh gave a faint smile.

Being Tom's cousin, David Cole decided to give young Hugh the opportunity to put all he'd learned at Cambridge into practice on a real African farm. 'Put up some fencing and get some cattle,' Cole told Hugh before leaving for America. Hugh bought fence posts, sold the sheep to a neighbour, Finn Ross, then built two more dips, having observed only one, 'afloat in a sea of arsenical mud.' On neighbouring Ol Pejeta, Tom was also trying to cut down on sheep, building cattle dips on a ridge to avoid the black-cotton, pumping water from the Ewaso Nyiro river up a hill, from where it gravitated across the farm - 'enough to support ten thousand head of cattle,' said Hugh.

Hugh saved up to buy his first car, a Ford Anglia that coped admirably with the narrow black-cotton roads, he explained, unless it was raining, in which case, when you had to get off for oncoming traffic you became stuck in the ditch. He visited his father once a fortnight, for dinner, occasionally on Ol Pejeta, which would only take a couple of hours if it wasn't wet, or on Soysambu, a day's drive away - after which he'd drive all the way back. 'He used to say, "Shut up, you stupid boy - you don't know what you're talking about."' Hugh frowned. 'I remember Father bought a stallion called Prince Yaki, terribly well bred, and one day he said, "Now, Hughey, you're fresh from school." (I wasn't, I'd finished Cambridge.) "Come and look at this stallion. It's got a very swollen neck." 'Yes, I know what's wrong with that. It's got hypertrophy of the thyroid gland,' was Hugh's verdict. 'What causes this is a deficiency in iodine. So what you ought to do is get a solution of iodine in potassium and give it about six drops a day in its evening hot mash.'

'I went away,' Hugh continued, 'and the world's best vet,

whose name I forget, came out from Newmarket to stay, so father took him to see the horse. The next time I saw Father, the vet had been and gone. "You're quite wrong about that horse, Hughey," said Father. "It hadn't got that long-winded thing, whatever you said it was. It had goitre, and the vet wrote a little prescription for it and it was right as rain in a week."' Hugh laughed. 'What do you think goitre is? It's hypertrophy of the thyroid gland! No point discussing matters veterinary with Father; we just agreed to differ. Agriculture at Cambridge had included veterinary medicine, draining, building cowsheds...Oh well, Father paid to have me educated, and I thought he might as well make some use of it.' He paused and looked out from my veranda towards the blue bulk of the Aberdares, on the other side of which lay Ol Pejeta. 'We discovered, interestingly enough, that when we brought up a few bales of star-grass hay from Soysambu to Ol Pejeta during the drought, in the places where the cattle had eaten them the bare earth popped up in the next rains as star-grass, which rapidly spread.'

Boy Long's diaries had told how a young Tom had enjoyed hunting in Laikipia, accompanied by Mesubeio. Now it was Hugh's turn. 'Father bought me a rifle,' he said, 'because giraffe kept walking through the new telephone line. Father paid for a new telephone line every time they broke it - about twice a day - so father said, "Shoot the bloody giraffe." I did – went and shot seven of them, and after that never wanted to shoot another.'

There was a pause - Hugh and Ann were especially fond of Soysambu's endangered Rothschild's giraffe - before Hugh added that he'd been fired many times by Nancy - 'although I ignored her, and left when I was ready!'

To raise some capital Tom sold a share in Ol Pejeta to his friend Marcus Wickham-Boynton, and eventually Tom would sell all his Ol Pejeta shares to him.

'Marcus Wickham-Boynton was an expert on pictures,' said Hugh. 'At Vale Royal we had a couple of nice Leylies, about eight feet high, slightly bigger than life size. King Charles II's brother gave them to the Duke of York, and when father had to sell up, Marcus Wickham-Boynton was kind enough to pay him something for these pictures - I don't think an awful lot.'

'A thousand pounds each, wasn't it?' asked Ann.

'Now they'd get about a quarter of a million each...or perhaps a little more.'

Tom invested some of the money in Manera, but he spent most of it on Soysambu - on 420 miles of fencing. D had only satisfied the fencing ordinance, Hugh said, by putting a boundary fence. 'A terrible waste of time - look at it now. The zebra have got the lot.' He sighed: 'In those days it cost 100 pounds a mile to build. A coil of 100 yards of wire was 1,000 shillings. I remember it was 11 by 13 oval gauge, high-tensile steel, galvanised, made in Belgium. Cedar posts were cut in the badlands. There isn't any cedar to be had now.'

***

In 1970 Ol Pejeta was sold on to an American called Parfet (who also owned Solio). Almost fifty years later, it had gone the same way as many large ranches, including Soysambu, partly for the sake of their own survival, and become a wildlife conservancy. Ol Pejeta Conservancy, all 90,000 acres of it, was now owned by Fauna and Flora International, having passed through various hands on the way, including Adnan Khashoggi, the billionaire Turkish-Saudi Arabian arms-dealer and businessman. Lonrho Africa had also owned it, creating Sweetwaters Game Reserve in 1988 to protect its wildlife, including black rhino, descendants of the one that had killed Kolb over a century earlier, now securely fenced in to keep out the growing population outside its boundaries with their dwindling plots of land, desperately trying to survive.

***

Mary, meanwhile, had filed for divorce, citing Tom's affair with Diana Colvile. She'd always referred to Diana as "the murderess," while Diana had warned Mary she'd take her husband one day. 'I will never allow that woman to cross my threshold,' Tom had said, according to Farrant. Nevertheless, in November 1954, at the Nakuru races, he announced his engagement.

'Well done, Tom!' said a friend, thumping him on the back. 'That makes you the third.'

He was actually the fourth. The news galloped gleefully around the colony. "The latest Kenya romance is that Tom Delamere is going to marry Diana Colville (sic)," Nellie Grant wrote to Elspeth Huxley on 21 November. "Did you ever? Apparently Tom took a great liking to the Colville (sic) house, formerly the Erroll mansion, and moved in. It is said that Gilbert Colville (sic) moved out with joy to his old shepherd's hut; Lady D is quickly divorcing Tom, and Gilbert, ditto Diana; and there we all are."

**

When Hugh was first introduced to Diana, he thought, 'Well, that woman smells nice!'

'You'd better get to like her, because she's your stepmother,' Tom said shortly.

On 26 March 1955, Marcus Wickham-Boynton witnessed the marriage of Diana, in her early 40s, glamorous as ever, and 55-year old Tom, shy and taciturn. She married him for his title, Hugh insisted. By 2016 he couldn't remember whether he'd been at the wedding. 'Perhaps it was in London?' He shrugged. 'It's funny, isn't it - my second stepmother had been married to a Broughton when Joss Erroll was shot, and after the war my sister went and married his son. Evelyn, he was called. They had a flat in London, Ebury St. She was desperately longing to marry him, and about a week after she married him she said, "This is absolutely hopeless - he never makes love to me." You'd think she'd have taken the trouble to find out first.'

Mary returned to England, where Edwina Mountbatten decided to have her certified insane. Michael and Tom protested, eventually reaching a compromise: she could continue to live at Six-Mile Bottom, while having regular treatment at Midhurst mental institution.

Diana's divorce and marriage within such a short space of time didn't seem to change things much, apart from her living arrangements and title. She, Tom and Gilbert had been a happy trio of friends before the move, and thus they continued. According to some of those who knew him, Gilbert remained very fond of Diana, but seemed happy to live apart, while maintaining their friendship. Hugh suggested that Gilbert and Diana's relationship had been largely platonic anyway. Charles Hayes writes that Diana took both husband and ex-husband to England on honeymoon, after which Gilbert returned to the simple life, never staying in the special wing Diana reserved for him at Soysambu, but sending Maasai guards to ensure her safety throughout Mau Mau. Diana remained fond of 'the little man', as she called Gilbert, and he continued to be seen with her and Tom at the races.

'I loved him dearly,' said Ann over pre-lunch drinks at Main House. 'He amused me. The first time I was taken to Oserian by Hugh to meet Gilbert, he came out on their great big marble veranda, which was covered in a huge lion skin. I, of course, managed to get my foot in the torn bit.' She'd apologised, embarrassed and he'd replied, "Oh, that's all right. That's where I speared it."'

I asked how she thought he'd ended up marrying Diana.

'Well, I think *she* married *him*,' said Ann. 'He was the richest man in Kenya. She used to whizz off to here and there and everywhere. Obviously she whizzed off for the hunting in England and this and that and the next thing. Gilbert rather liked travelling too; he took her to Mexico and South America and all sorts of places.'

Having been promised by Gilbert she'd still inherit his estates, Diana set about transforming Main House, improving Mary's upgrades, brightening up the barren surrounds. She had a penchant for pink bougainvillaea.

'Knicker-pink!' retorted Hugh.

'I think it's called *puce* now,' said Ann.

'When Diana lived here, the house hadn't got any verandas. She always felt cold, so liked it to be as hot as possible. She built this patio, without any roof, just trellis and *knicker-pink* bougainvillaea.'

Old photographs show there'd only been a covered walkway before Diana added a black and white tiled floor, furnishing this back patio with a set of white wrought-iron chairs, formerly Erroll's, adding yellow cushions and painting the window frames yellow. She had D's old bull box converted into a two-roomed

Diana also upgraded Villa Buzza - although the name on the gate was misspelt. It should be Buzzer, Diana's pet name for Tom (He called her Buzzy) and the name she gave her fishing boat. Gilbert, who continued to visit the Kilifi house, was called Pooh Bear or Pooey. When I visited, the interiors were much as Diana left them: cane furniture, tiled tables, painted chests of drawers, black and beige floor tiles, Spanish tiles set into walls. Diana's passion for big-game fishing, passed on to Snoo, remained embodied in chipped china fish on the shelves, plaster-cast heads of marlin on the walls, framed photographs boasting of grand catches.

Tom hadn't been a fisherman, and neither had Gilbert, although Gilbert had been a keen sailor, keeping his boat at Oserian, Snoo told me as we walked to the swimming pool over sun-scorched grass shaded by a medley of indigenous trees and planted exotics, the orange-flowered flamboyants brightening the scene. Kilifi had suffered water shortages, a combination of drought and incompetent governance, so the pool was half full, awaiting a bowser that also needed to fill the house tanks. She'd been fond of Tom, she said as we joined a host of white butterflies beside the pool. 'It's every little girl's dream to have two daddies!' Some noisy Hadada Ibis alighted, the red on their beaks clashing with the bright pink of the bougainvillaea, their harsh cries (*Ha DA da!*) transporting me to Soysambu, where a loud and messy flock inhabited the fig tree above the pool at Main House. Diana's marriage to Tom was a very happy phase of her life, Snoo added. 'Mummy always said she'd made several mistakes in her life and finally got it right.' This feeling was reciprocated by Tom, who often said to Snoo, 'There are only between five and ten people in the world whom one can truly love and live happily ever after with.'

Sarah Seth-Smith had been a childhood friend of Snoo's, accompanying her to Kilifi, visiting her on Soysambu to ride horses across the plains. In 2016 she was living on part of Colvile's former estate. Diana, she said, 'was very clever at making sure both her husband and her former husband were friends - all very civilised.'

All of them, she added, had treated her kindly. 'Gilbert taught me to play Piquet...Diana had an engaging way with children, holding them spellbound with her bright blue eyes; she was never in the least condescending.' We were having lunch on the Seth-Smiths' upstairs veranda, overlooking Lake Naivasha. It was a dry February, and I was constantly jumping up and walking away to talk to my house-help back on Soysambu, who was trying to dissuade a hot, thirsty, six-foot cobra from taking refuge in my living room.

'I don't remember so much about Tom,' Sarah continued, 'but I do remember Diana riding out at Soysambu dressed in jodhpurs, a flat black Spanish sombrero and immaculately laundered, tailored, white matador-type shirt. She had a stunning figure.' The budding writer Nicholas Best would later note in *Happy Valley* that he sometimes spotted Diana in the only street of Gilgil, "horribly overdressed."Nuptial bliss apparently hadn't stopped Diana's roving eye. Leda Farrant mentions Peter Leth as a lover of Diana's, relating how they took Hugh's visiting older sister, Elizabeth, on early-morning rides around Soysambu. When Elizabeth was visibly charmed, Diana took Leth aside. 'I want you to know one thing, Peter,' she said. 'Never, ever, am I going to be your step-mother-in-law. I want you to understand that.' Tom even sent Diana, with Leth as companion, to England and France for a few months to get away from the Mau Mau. On their return to Oserian, Leth expressed his desire to leave Kenya, and Farrant relates their alleged conversation.

'I think you know too much about me, Peter!' Diana brandished the gun she kept at hand.

'Don't talk rubbish,' Peter replied. 'And put the gun down!'

'Yes, Peter, you do know too much about me...'

After she shot him, growing concerned by the amount of blood, she made him promise not to tell the truth, calling Dr Bunny, who lived further around the lake. When the doctor insisted Leth be taken immediately to hospital, Diana replied, 'Not in my new Mercedes.'

'A car was ordered to take him to hospital,' Sarah Seth-Smith's husband, Tony, told me, 'and dinner went on as if everything was normal.'

Leth complied with Diana, and was paid handsomely with Gilbert's money. Years later, he still referred to her as 'that bloody woman.'

And he wasn't the only near-miss, claims Farrant. On catching Ron Watts with another woman on Soysambu, she fired at them both. She also shot at the Muthaiga Club ceiling when annoyed with another lover, Peter Kennedy.

As we finished after-lunch coffee on the Seth-Smith veranda, watching the sun shift over shimmering water, the Djinn Palace somewhere behind the spit of land called Hippo Point, the talk inevitably moved to the Erroll murder.

'*Diana* did it!' Tony said.

A Fish Eagle atop a nearby yellow-barked acacia threw back its head and let out a haunting cry.

CHAPTER 16

The End of Mau Mau

In April 1954, in *Operation Anvil*, around 65,000 Kikuyu, Embu and Meru were rounded up in Nairobi and detained. In retaliation, the following month Treetops and Nyeri Polo Club were burned down. "It is virtually their war, they dictate the terms," former Police Officer Peter Hewitt wrote of the elusive Mau Mau in *Kenya Cowboy*. On 3rd May he'd visited his inspector. "Like many others," Hewitt recorded in his diary, he was "at loggerheads with the local settlers, they like to dictate."

By early 1955, Genesta, tidying up scattered pamphlets ("polluting the lovely forest trail," she writes) that urged terrorists to surrender, wrote about *Operation First Flute*, a sweep through the forest to catch Mau Mau. This failed, she says, "because of leaky intelligence (what else can you expect when officers have mission-trained 'former' Mau Mau Kikuyu, able to speak, write and read English letters and dispatches, for servants?)" Meanwhile, she reports, the Lancashire Fusiliers were having snowball fights with Samburu soldiers up Mt Kenya.

Caroline Elkins sets out a more modern perspective, writing of a "civilian war, one that was far more complex than anything that had taken place in the forests," and "far more significant in scope and impact than the military campaign against the guerrillas." General George Erskine, she points out, had defeated only two per cent of Mau Mau; Baring had broken the allegiance of over one million through the "Pipeline Project." which aimed to rehabilitate and "cleanse" Kikuyu people in detention camps, places where Elkins recounts many atrocities committed by the British.

Half a century earlier, in a government-issued booklet, *The Mau*

Mau in Kenya, Kenya's Public Relations Officer Granville Roberts calls Mau Mau, "this menace to the future of the country," its "foul atrocities" illustrated in graphic photographs. Press office handouts provided further "background" to be broadcast by Voice of Kenya: "The greatest cry of the agitator is that Europeans turned Africans off land belonging to them," one begins, going on to claim this as untrue. *The Guarded Village*, a report dated 5th September 1955, remarkably outspoken and plain-speaking for its time, admits that the introduction of the village system had brought to the Kikuyu people "upheaval and disruption, and the compulsory abandoning of their age-old customs for a life of considerable restriction...it might be asked whether these villages are not approaching perilously near to the Nazi concentration camps of dreaded memory." But October's notes for the press hailed the success of the village programme, recording the increasing success of the security forces, claiming that of the 1,660 civilian deaths since the start of the Emergency, 1,604 were Africans murdered by Mau Mau. One handout referred to its "bestial savagery." The Kikuyu, it continued, lived in the best, healthiest areas, had an "astonishing" rate of fertility, and had experienced the closest contact with Europeans and education, adding patronisingly, "with all the disasters that half-baked learning can produce." It conceded perceived errors by the administration, including the creation of chiefs, disregard of heredity, inability to foresee erosion and population pressure, and a "lack of good manners" towards the Africans displayed by some Europeans, not to mention the "colour bar" in many places - including hotels.

By the end of the year Mau Mau was winding down, but the State of Emergency would not be lifted for several more years. "I frankly loathe this place and the job," Erskine wrote to his wife. "A sunny place for shady people." Nor had he found any common ground with the settlers. "I hate the guts of them all, they are all middle-class sluts." When Erskine left, some Mau Mau leaders still eluded the British, including Field Marshall Dedan Kimathi, who would continue to evade capture until late in 1956. Meanwhile Lt General Sir Gerald Lathbury arrived for the next phase, sending pseudo-gangs into the forests, while the RAF continued their bombing.

Evelyn Baring, exhausted and depressed, left for six weeks' sick leave before returning to see out his seven years as Governor.

In November 1956 the military campaign was almost over, although security remained tight. The boys' boarding school in Gilgil, called Pembroke House, was still surrounded by barbed wire, part of it electrified, recalls Nicholas Best, who was a pupil at the time. "Boys who ran away had to be recaptured quickly, before Mau Mau caught up with them. One pair got 17 miles, pursued by tracker dogs, Kikuyu spearmen from the Home Guard, and a spotter plane from the Kenya Police Airwing."

The popular Moral Re-Armament movement was seen by some as a way to rehabilitate Mau Mau fighters back into Kenyan society in preparation for independence. Eleanor Cole became involved, visiting South Africa and speaking to a group of women advocating this envisaged new world for black and white people. As Tom was also in favour of an amicable solution to Kenyan independence, he accepted Eleanor's invitation to a Moral Re-Armament meeting at Kekopey, taking Hugh along.

***

'Somebody got up and said he'd slept with so-and-so,' Hugh recalled, adding that the woman, who was present, vehemently denied it. The man then replied, 'In my dreams.' Hugh continued with a cynical smile: 'Then Wilfred Hopcraft told how he used to sell his lucerne full of thistles before he got morally rearmed, but now he'd stopped.'

As it happened, that morning at Soysambu they'd received a lorry of baled lucerne full of thistles. 'Come on, Hughey,' Tom had said in disgust, and they'd left, briefly united in their disagreement.

In 2015 I chanced a visit to Fairseat, a care home near Muthaiga, to speak to Eleanor's daughter-in-law Tobina Cole. Now elderly, she didn't do telephones, but I found her sitting before a crackling log fire, a puppy on her lap.

Tobina, who'd married Eleanor's son Arthur, didn't think much of Moral Re-Armament either. She was one of the few people who still remembered Tom. He'd been a good friend, she said, with whom she'd had much in common. 'He wasn't interested in the things Arthur was interested in,' she explained. 'He didn't shoot, and so quite often he and I talked. We were interested in growing things. He was interested in politics too. He was friends with African politicians and the local DC. He was always very much in touch with what was going on. He believed Kenya should be independent.'

Tobina had also liked Gilbert Colvile - 'always a friend, a great help when Arthur and I started farming' - and Diana. 'She lived a very good life and had no nonsense at all.' She paused. 'Diana was a very good wife when she *was* your wife. It may not have been forever, but she was very good at bolstering the self-confidence of her husbands. When I got cross with the children they'd go over to Diana.' Tobina firmly called Snoo Deborah - 'I hate nicknames. We saw quite a lot of her,' she went on, 'because her governess was a friend of my children's nanny.' As an elderly neighbour arrived, Tobina turned to me dismissively: 'Fondest to Hugh and Ann.' She paused and gave me a searching look. 'I hope they're alright. They're very vulnerable, those two. I've always worried about them.'

***

Tobina had died by 2017 when I visited Genesta's daughter-in-law, Liza Long, who'd married Robin Long, after which they'd moved to Nderit. Liza, now 89 and a widow, lived on the southern side of Kilifi creek, which had acquired a bridge in the late 1980s, rendering redundant the unreliable old ferry where a radiantly happy Diana had once been pictured with Joss. Liza hadn't been well and was only half awake, reclining on a bed that looked over the midday glare of the ocean.

'Tom was a terrific...a terrific...' Liza said, between bouts of coughing, 'I think the word would be raconteur. He always had a story up his sleeve, and he was the greatest of fun.' They'd shared an interest in horses. He wasn't handsome, she added, 'short and dumpy. Like his father!' He'd introduced her to Robin over dinner at Muthaiga Club.

When I asked about Diana, she hesitated. 'Well, I don't know that I *knew* her all that well; she very much preferred men to women...' Fishing had been their common ground. 'She was a mad keen fisherman - and a lucky one. I was a mad keen fisherman and not a lucky one!'

Was she beautiful, I asked?

'She was rather glamorous. I wouldn't say she was beautiful, but she was attractive and she hit you with a kind of a bang.'

Had there been a kind side to Diana?

'I think if I really thought about it, I'd have to say *no*. It was Diana first. She always had a string of - I don't know what you call them — hangers-on!'

I slipped away as she fell asleep; she hadn't heard - or possibly didn't remember - that Tobina had died. Later that year I heard Liza had died too.

***

In between the annual splendid Christmas lunches Diana hosted for her managers, beginning with imported salmon and caviar and washed down with expensive wines, there were regular lunch parties, every last Saturday of the month: sometimes roast Soysambu guinea fowl, always plenty of puddings - all eagerly anticipated by a lonely little girl called Jennifer Mason, whose father, Dick, was a manager on Soysambu, living in a house he called The Old Chateau. Jennifer's mother, Ruth, had left her father during the war and remarried the future Lord Portsmouth. Now Jennifer Falkiner, she wrote to me about her happy childhood on Soysambu; riding with her father each morning, checking on herdsmen and stock, sometimes driving a buggy pulled by a horse called Tinga Tinga (Kiswahili for tractor). She especially loved visiting the stables, where the horses were obliged to share accommodation with Mary's Jersey bulls. Lunches were a sit-down affair, she wrote, recalling "the big long table, plenty of pink gins, and the booming laughter, with lots of stories and jokes." Tom and Diana were always kind to her. Tom called her "Dark as a Dog's Mouth" because of a dog-shaped torch with a bulb in its mouth she'd bought at Moolraj's *duka*. According to Hugh, his father lost patience with Mason after giving him £5,000 pounds to clear the thick bush and build a house on the south-western end of Soysambu known as Ol Jolai. ('He built a house that was far too big,' Hugh explained. 'He hadn't budgeted for a roof, but as he had to finish it another £1,000 was produced and the house downscaled.') Mason was fired, although Tom and Diana had been sorry to say goodbye to Daphne, his second wife, of whom they were very fond. The Masons would still be neighbours, moving up the western escarpment to Mau Narok. Meanwhile Sam Weller, another assistant manager, whose wife Judy would later marry Mason, moved into Lanet House.

By 1957 Baring, a keen bird watcher, was drafting a new constitution for Kenya in between weekends on Soysambu, observing flamingos from his raft. Their nocturnal flight patterns had been impacted by large pylons, built by the East Africa Power and Lighting Company Limited in 1954, to bring power to Kenya from Uganda's Owen Falls Dam. These marched through Soysambu, close to the southern and western shores of lake, inevitably snaring flamingos. The government compensation for this assault on the birds was pitiful. ('Father was paid two shillings and fifty cents a pylon,' Hugh told me.) The still mysterious flamingo migrations between lakes were being studied by the biologist Leslie Brown, who would discover their breeding site on Lake Natron. "Personally I hope no one ever will fully rationalise flamingos,' he wrote in his book *The Mystery of the Flamingos,* 'and that they will remain the supremely beautiful, elusive, opportunistic, unpredictable beings that I like to think they are."

Hugh left Laikipia and returned to Soysambu. His relationship with his father was not helped by their sharing the typically fiery temperament associated with red hair. Hugh was an enthusiastic botanist, determined to plant trees. Tom didn't believe in trees. ('They didn't show up on the balance sheet,' Hugh said. 'He used to say, "If God had meant there to be trees here, there would be." If he had planted gums we would now be harvesting them for telegraph poles.') Leda Farrant claims that Hugh's allowance from his father was extremely mean, especially when Tom was spending more on a girlfriend at Thomson's Falls, adding that Diana also continued to enjoy her lovers, although James Fox quotes an unnamed friend of Diana's who said Diana was always faithful to Tom - "a difficult man" - and that she was very patient and kind during his long bouts of bad health. Tom, on the other hand, "was rather strict. He didn't want her running around."

***

In 2013, I was in Stow-on-the-Wold during my book tour, when an elderly woman introduced herself as Anne Fitzmaurice. She had married one of Soysambu's managers, William Fitzmaurice, whom she called 'Fitz,' living with him in Sugonoi House, where she'd brought up their two sons. Aged 93, she looked back on those Soysambu years as 'the happiest' of her life. She'd grown fond of young Hugh, who'd often dropped by, chatting to her while she washed nappies. 'I remember his visits so well and looked forward to him coming.'

***

Although it was plain Hugh's brain and skills were being under-utilised, Tom stubbornly continued to deny him more responsibility. In 1958, impressed by Arthur Newton's work at Manera, Tom promoted Newton to assistant manager at Soysambu, where he lived in Jolai House. The Fitzmaurices had left and Hugh was given Sugonoi House to live in, and 60 acres below it which Tom instructed him *to do something with.*

'I planted oranges,' Hugh told me, 'in the days that the river used to run, before they pumped the Mereroni River dry upstream. I planted potatoes and beans in between, but there was a big male bush pig who was rather fond of them. Every weekend we went out shooting buffalo; I got six one day – I was rather pleased. The others went back to Eburru forest.' He sighed. 'Unfortunately now we've got far too many buffalo on this farm, and they can't go back to Eburru because they've cut down all the forest.'

Hugh then further irritated his father when he tried to sell him a bag of oranges - well-watered by D's furrow - to make a point about his father's meanness.

***

Joseph Mwangi Wakaba had arrived in 1958 to work as Newton's gardener, before moving to Melia, the north-western end of the farm, to build fences. Sixty years later Wakaba, as he was always called by his fellow workers, was retired near Elmenteita, a small town referred to as "centre" by those who lived there, that had sprung up around the old railway station and Moolraj's former *duka*. He lived with his youngest wife, who tilled his few acres of land while he tended to his 19 beehives. When I invited him to tea, he arrived punctually – for Kenya - despite having set off from home that morning on his motorbike, which had broken down. He'd hitched a ride on the back of a friend's, bumping across Soysambu dressed in his glossy suit and tie. Locally revered for his 47 children, he was now a *mzee* (an old man), with white-filmed eyes, gap-toothed and hard of hearing, but his memory was crystal clear. He'd been born the same year as Hugh, he said, and now, in 2018, he knew the exact ages of Hugh's grandsons, remembering every manager on the farm.

'Newton was very *kali*,' he laughed, using the Kiswahili word for which there is no literal translation, as it can describe a hot curry, a sharp knife, or a fearsome dog or person. 'So was I, so we got along fine!' He'd been an excellent manager, Wakaba confirmed, adding that there'd never been one to match him since. Romer was also 'very *kali*...those were the days we Africans were just like animals to them.' He laughed. He'd heard that D was different, deeply respected by the Maasai, not least for his attitude to cattle theft: 'If they stole five, they must return ten!' Elders, he added, still talked of D's blood-brotherhood rites with their grandfathers. Wakaba had liked Tom - he wasn't a racist and 'he knew how to work!' There were 13,000 cows back then, and Lendani, then a young herdsman, had a 'big *manyatta*' by the lone blue gum tree on the road to the hayfields not far from Jolai gate. 'It was called *Lemeluk,*' Wakaba continued. 'Lendani still comes to stay with me and visits Lord Delamere.' They both greatly preferred Ann to Diana. 'She did not look after her employees,' Wakaba explained, adding disapprovingly, 'She had too many husbands!' He recalled

Nyasore, as well as Snoo, who became 'too friendly with Newton.... She went riding into the bush with him.' Wakaba warned them against such foolishness, adding with a knowing smile: 'Newton *listened* to *me!'*

My house (which Hugh told me had been built by Haselden 'after the war,') was there when Wakaba arrived, lived in since then by various African assistant managers and herdsmen, and eventually Wakaba. 'You are the first *mzungu* [white person] to live there,' he announced. Nearby, at what was now Jolai One *campi* (a cluster of basic mud huts accommodating herdsmen and their families), there had been a 'very smart wooden house,' he continued, 'but one day in 1962, *Mzee* Kafango was smoking out bees from its walls and he burned the whole house down. Do you know his son? He is still a tractor driver on Soysambu. The stone kitchen is still there.' This explained why, when Dick Mason's daughter Jen had returned as an adult, she couldn't find The Old Chateau, which she described to me as having a separate stone kitchen and "a stone part, which adjoined a wooden structure on stilts."

As Wakaba's *boda boda* (motorbike taxi) arrived to collect him, he cast a final glance around my home, pointing at the small living room. 'This used to be my office. I had a phone in there. And my children slept in there.' He pointed at my son's bedroom. 'Are there still bees in the roof?' He lingered at the corner, noting that I'd removed the bougainvillaea, commenting on the trees I'd planted. 'There used to be many snakes,' he said as he departed. 'Big black snakes!'

I smiled. 'There still are!'

CHAPTER 17

All Change at Midnight

Jomo Kenyatta was released from prison in April 1959, initially remaining under house arrest in Maralal, safely out of the spotlight in this small market town in northern Kenya. Baring left later that year. In 1960 the State of Emergency was lifted by the new Governor, Patrick Muir Renison, and the British Government invited Kenyan leaders to conferences at Lancaster House. Kenyatta attended the second, demanding a date for independence. Harold Macmillan, Britain's Prime Minister, had been thinking of granting Tanganyika independence around 1970, and Kenya five years later, but with some prominent settlers, including Humphrey Slade and Michael Blundell, promoting the New Kenya Party, envisaging a mixed-race government, the 1962 Lancaster House agreement set the date for Kenya's independence the following year, the World Bank leading a willing-buyer-willing-seller scheme to redistribute white-owned farms to Africans.

Finally Kenya could leave behind the racism and segregation that had become ingrained in so many of its institutions. Political correctness became the new norm, 'rapid social change' was the phrase on everyone's lips, while 'indigenization' meant city jobs formerly reserved for Europeans now being taken by Africans. The *Kenya Farmer's Weekly*, November 1962 edition, amongst its farming advertisements, articles, notification of Royal Agricultural Society shows and women's section (limited to clothes, afternoon bridge, gardening and cooking), printed a speech by Tom, then President of the Kenya Farmers' Union. "Surely the last thing that anyone would wish to see would be the creation of white highlands of the past," he said at the opening of the 15th annual conference. Referring to suggestions in respect of the new Settlement Scheme, he called for adequate Land Bank Finance and extolled the importance of setting up an Agricultural Credit Organisation. D would have agreed with Tom's argument that, without capital to finance its development, land was "a liability and not an asset to its owner." In spite of the disagreement of some white farmers, Tom was insistent on the importance of the Union's offering a graduated subscription, so that *all* people could take advantage of it.

A list of East African milk records in the *Farmer's Weekly*'s last pages prominently features cows from Manera: Arthur Newton, who'd been transferred there as Senior Manager the previous - and very wet - year, had produced results.

Tom was now a prominent figure in the colony, sitting on numerous committees and boards of public agricultural companies. In early 1962 Patrick Renison and his wife accepted an invitation to Soysambu, asking if they could bring their daughter Ann.

***

'I'd left my first husband and run home,' Ann told me, 'and they couldn't very well leave a 22-year-old daughter in Government House with its 32 bedrooms, all by herself with the male Private Secretary. Diana was unamused! This dining room table only seats eight, and it ruined her numbers, so she had to rout around for another man. So it was family-elbows-in; Hugh was told to brush up his dinner jacket and get here.'

Ann Willoughby Renison had been born in Ceylon on 8th October 1938. The second name was her paternal grandmother's, she told me - 'Try writing that in a hurry!' She had arrived two weeks late: 'They took me for a ride in an ox-cart and out I popped the next morning, which is why I'm used to bad roads.' At the time her father was Private Secretary to the Governor of Ceylon, while her mother, Eleanor Hope Gibb, painfully shy, was finding the social expectations of a civil servant's wife a challenge. This was the Gibb family that had settled on the fringes of Happy Valley, and Alistair Gibb, who'd broken Gwladys's heart, was Ann's cousin.

Ann vehemently denies that she was ever pretty, although plenty of people said she was, and in 2018 she still had a beautiful complexion. Her mother hadn't helped. 'Darling, such a pity you'll never be beautiful,' she would say, 'but at least you're *bonny*,' while visitors touched Ann's small upturned nose and said, 'Press the button!'

In 1942 Eleanor and Ann were evacuated to a wealthy paternal aunt in Cheshire. 'Mummy loathed it,' Ann said, explaining further: Eleanor felt inferior as her daughter had nothing, while the cousins had beautiful prams and tricycles. As soon as she was able, Eleanor rented a house near Mayfield until after the war, when they joined Renison in India. 'I remember Simla because it was lovely there and I had a pony called Snow White,' Ann said. 'But I don't remember the rest much.' Finally, after 10 years, her father was given six months leave, which they spent in Ceylon, after which he became Colonial Secretary of Trinidad and Tobago, then Governor of British Honduras (now Belize) four years later, and three years after that he was sent to British Guyana. 'I went to school wherever we happened to be, if there *was* a school,' Ann told me. At the age of eleven she was sent to Queen Anne's in Caversham, where her mother had made her mark in ladies' lacrosse; 'They were one of the first British teams to travel - to America and Canada. My mother was frightfully athletic - she played ladies' cricket as well—'

'Did she wear a tin bra like Boadicea?' Hugh interrupted.

Ann ignored him. '—and they expected me to be. I wasn't, but I could swim. Then I fell down the shiny polished wooden stairs; I was in the attic bedroom and I was late. The school said "Growing pains" and did nothing about it for six months - and I've had trouble ever since.' She was finally sent for an x-ray, then put in plaster 'from the armpits - for three months.' There followed four years of steel braces and physiotherapy, leaving one leg shorter than the other. 'I didn't care for school much,' commented Ann with characteristic understatement, adding: 'the Colonial Service allowed one eight weeks a year with one's parents.' Holidays were usually spent with her Gibb cousins and after school she went to the House of Citizenship. 'A bit like a finishing school,' she explained: 'You could do a year of secretarial skills or public speaking, or the whole lot - which I did.'

Having perfected her new skills, now aged 20, she'd joined her parents in British Guyana. Back then in 1960, she said, 'there was one road to the airport and one road along the coast and that was it.' Newspaper headlines were typically: "Two donkey-carts collide on sea Wall," while a tiny little paragraph on the back was titled: "America Invades Cuba"...' Georgetown, although hot and humid, boasted some lovely old houses and a wooden cathedral. Government House, also built of wood and raised on stilts above the damp, was 'patched together with packing cases from the 1850s.' There wasn't much else to do, so Ann married a sugar farmer called Michael Tinne, moving into his house, double-storey - 'to see over the sugarcane' - where her only happy moments would be spent with his dog. 'I wept bitter tears over leaving the Alsatian,' she concluded.

Soon after her arrival in Kenya, Ann found a job as PA for a Greek herpetologist called Constantine J P Ionides, her work taking her all over Kenya to catch poisonous snakes.

'Ionides sent snakes to the Miami Serpentarium,' Hugh told me. 'They could be posted in special cloth bags - customs wouldn't look in a bag labelled: *One live poisonous snake*. It would have been an ideal way to smuggle heroin or cocaine, although I was never into any of that.'

'Iodine was such fun!' Ann added, using her boss's nickname.

Her snakes in their cloth bags in the back of a Land Rover, she'd once phoned her mother from Nanyuki: 'I should be back for dinner,' she'd said, 'and I've got 105 poisonous snakes with me.'

To which her mother had replied, 'Well, don't let them anywhere near the dogs!'

'She wasn't worried about her *daughter*!' commented Hugh.

'They were Russell's carpet vipers,' Ann explained, 'and there was no known antidote for their poison at the time, so Iodine sent them to Miami to develop a serum using live horses - an expensive process.' She paged through my old book, *Snakes of the World*. '"Mexican Dwarf python,"' she read out. 'Never met one. I've seen pythons on Soysambu of over 18 feet. There are less around now... If the gardeners find a snake they don't tell me.' Like most Kenyans, the gardener instantly killed snakes, however small and harmless.

The young Ann who came for dinner at Main House that night was petite and pretty, with very long, thick, rich-brown hair. Her endearing smile spread over her entire face, half-closing her lovely brown eyes when she laughed. She was very taken by the very tall, thin, ginger-haired Hugh, with his kindly demeanour, faultless manners and dry sense of humour. 'He was absolutely divine - if he was allowed to get a word in edgewise.' She smiled at the memory. 'Diana was very much in command. She liked the sound of her own voice, so other people didn't get much chance.'

Snoo told me that Tom and Diana had been determined to match-make: Ann was well-travelled and well-bred - she'd do very well for Hugh, who'd been seeing an unsuitable young woman in Nakuru ('the bus driver's daughter,' Diana deprecatingly called her), who'd fallen pregnant and been hastily dispatched back to England. Thus Hugh was actually summoned at tea time, after which they had the obligatory family walk to look at the brood mares. On reaching the end of the drive, Diana said pointedly: 'Why don't you two go off and walk that way?'

After her step-brother had obligingly diverted with the Governor's daughter, a teenage Snoo, home from school in England, hissed at her mother, 'Don't *ever* do that to me!'

Hugh gave me his version. 'The Governor and his wife had a rather nice-looking daughter who was still married to a rather tiresome fellow called Tinne, a Dutch name. He was an odious fellow - an old Etonian. She swore she'd never marry another.' He'd quickly been smitten by Ann's poise and sophistication. 'I was rather disappointed to discover she was married - I fancied her strongly. That weekend I squired her round the Nakuru races. I thought, "This is actually rather a nice-looking woman. I wonder if she's actually nice." You can't tell by looking at 'em: you have to talk to them. So we did a bit of that - and it turned out she *was* nice. They stayed a few days so I drove her up the Mau on the Powys Cobb road and we sat in the car and discussed things. I said, "I think I'd rather like to marry you." And she replied, "Delighted, but I'll have to get rid of my husband."' Hugh glanced over at Ann. 'I'm still rather fond of her. Having got her properly trained I see no need to get another wife... haven't broken a walking stick over her for 51 years.'

In spite of Diana's efforts, Ann believed Tom wasn't in favour of the match: for a settler family, especially one of such standing, marrying into the dreaded Colonial Service simply wasn't the done thing. Tom, like most settlers, would have seen officials as the 'bastard herd,' she told me. Ann's mother was equally put out. 'Don't marry aristocracy,' she'd advised her daughter – 'and don't marry in Kenya!' Now she was obliged to invite her daughter's suitor, who fell into both categories, to Government House.

"The cool, twilit spaciousness of Government House was like a dream," Vivienne De Watteville had written three decades earlier: "…against the torrid sky and the smell of dust, the tall white pillars with shadows of pure cobalt had a freshness that was almost alpine; in a country where the grass is nearly always brown, the soft deeply green turf of the courtyard had something of the dreamy delight of Omar Khayyam."

She further praised "the mediaeval thrill of having luncheon (or even breakfast) with Their Majesties looking graciously down from their long gilt frames at either end of the room; and beyond the cool shades of the awning you had a glimpse of the red cannas flaming in the glare of noonday," and how, after dinner, "everyone stood up for the solemn toast: *The King.*"

By Renison's day it was *The Queen.* Otherwise it hadn't changed, said Ann. 'The original little house, before Hugh's grandfather instigated its expansion, was still there. It was used to house senior staff.' But Hugh was far more intrigued by his fiancée, who had a habit of working at her desk with one of her pet snakes around her neck.

'They felt the cold,' Ann explained, 'so it warmed them up!' When some formidable *memsahibs* were bustling around Government House in preparation for a Red Cross Ball, she related: 'one of these double-breasted battle-axes paused to say, "That's a pretty necklace, my dear." At which point the snake put up its head and regarded her coolly, and the ladies fled. My mother was delighted - she'd been trying to get rid of them all morning.'

Ann's parents left that November, buying a 13th-century retirement house near the village of Mayfield in East Sussex. A few months later the BBC quoted Sir Patrick Renison referring to Jomo Kenyatta as "the African leader to darkness and death." His remark has often been quoted since, usually out of context. People who knew him say he certainly wasn't a racist.

***

On 4 January 1963 Malcolm MacDonald arrived, to govern up until Kenya's rapidly approaching independence date. That April the East African Women's League published *They Made it Their Home*, dedicated to Kenya's pioneers: "For they are the people whose faith and brave endurance have built a fine country." The book contains a collection of photographs of embroidery panels made by dedicated members, depicting life in different farming communities, the Gilgil one showing Lake Elmenteita, behind it Eburru and the clefted hill known as Delamere's Nose. Although she hadn't been correctly acknowledged in the book, Eleanor Cole had stitched the centre part. She was one of a minority of settlers who would remain, happy to be part of a changing Kenya. Others were emigrating to countries they hoped wouldn't be too different from Kenya - South Africa or Australia.

Tom and Diana weren't leaving, although they hastily moved their investments to the Channel Islands, anticipating exchange controls. They were also about to increase the size of Soysambu, by a stroke of luck. In 1954 a New Zealander, Sandy Pilmer, had bought the neighbouring farm, originally called Congreve Farm. Named after its former owner Major Congreve, it was a 6,000-acre parcel of land bordering Soysambu to the west and Nderit to the north. Pilmer had bought it for £17,000, renaming it Kiwi Plains. It generally enjoyed better rainfall than Soysambu, but the Pilmers had struggled, obliged to replace old fences and buildings, adding three boreholes, which had better water than Soysambu, being farther from the lake. The land had proved good for fattening Boran cattle and Pilmer had planned to plant 1,200 acres with trees, 640 with lucerne. But he didn't expect Kenya to become independent so soon. In an angry letter to his nephew, 30 years later, he raged at visiting politicians, who'd been reassuring settlers in the late 1950s, while "London was quietly negotiating with a few missionary-trained malcontents there about an immediate hand-over." The debacle had cost "the poor tax-ridden Pommies billions," he continued, with the Africans "the biggest loser." He quotes his elderly African labourers, pleading with him before his departure in 1962, 'Don't go, *bwana*, who is going to look after us?' (Hugh was disparaging about Pilmer, explaining that Tom had bought the farm cheaply to offset tax owed: 'Pilmer had only paid half; Father paid the other half.')

This new corner of Soysambu took back its former name, Congreve, and the house Pilmer had built was now called Congreve House. It was a pleasantly rambling bungalow, which by the twenty-first century had housed a series of Soysambu managers, tenants, a giraffe researcher and various groups of students.

Nairobi itself was now a "fantastic mushroom city" with "gay, glittering new air-conditioned skyscrapers," wrote Huxley in 'Kenya's Clouded Future: Can the European Survive?', published in the *Daily Telegraph*. Since the start of 1961, 5,586 more Europeans had left than arrived, while half a dozen schools built for Europeans had been forced to close, she pointed out, paying tribute to those European farmers who'd "built from scratch, in half a century" the productive farms that provided "Kenya's economic sinews." Now, over a million acres of the seven and a half million farmed by white settlers were being bought, costing the British Treasury £12 million. At the time she was writing, around 230 farmers had been bought out, with another 250 in process. "The confidence-exuding president of the KNFU Lord Delamere points out that last year more than 150,000 acres were sold or leased privately, as against 180,000 acres bought by the government," Huxley continued. "Applications to borrow money from the Land Bank for development are running three times the level maintained in 1960. The snag is that the Land Bank has run out of cash and can advance only about one-fifth of what is asked for." Tom, backed by Michael Blundell, believed that only 40% of Kenya's white farmers would depart, but opinions varied daily. Huxley had been reliably informed that 90% of farmers from the Uasin Gishu planned to depart within four years. In her view it was less about politics than demographics. "Kenya's population is now increasing at the fantastic rate of 4% a year, one of the highest in the world...it is hard to see how white mixed farmers can survive in an all-black, land-hungry ocean."

Alongside two political parties (KANU and KADU, the latter more moderate in Huxley's opinion), plenty of "foreign cooks" were trying to spoil Kenya's broth, "pouring money into KANU's coffers for the election campaign." Kenya's lack of "constructive African leadership able to transcend the deep-seated factionalism based on race and tribe" also concerned Huxley. "The balance between those forces making for an eventual *modus vivendi* between the races and tribes, and those working towards collapse and perhaps chaos, is delicate and even," she concludes. "Never has there been a cloudier crystal ball. Sadly, those who are departing feel sure of only one thing: wherever they go, they will never find another Kenya. There isn't one."

That June in the *Weekly News* Huxley wrote of an widening gulf between Kenya settlers, who saw British policy as "betrayal and disaster," and public opinion in England, to whom this was "a shedding of onerous, unwanted responsibilities, relief from a burden of guilt, and every prospect of better trade in future, all rolled into one - something almost too good to be true."

But settlers who planned to stay on were determined to make a go of it. The cover of the 1963 *Kenya Church Review* pictures two babies, white and black, side by side. White kids in the background look delighted, while adults of both races wear determined smiles. The editorial talks about the need for prayers for a peaceful and smooth transition. Raymond Harries, the new provost of Nairobi Cathedral, voices his approval at Nairobi's cosmopolitan nature.

Delamere Avenue was renamed Kenyatta Avenue in both Nairobi and Nakuru, and Nairobi's statue of Delamere was removed from its pedestal. ('The new government wanted to melt it down and remould it into a Mau Mau hero,' Hugh said. 'The settlers said, "No! It belongs to us!" So the whole statue was taken up, with its plinth, and sent up here on a lorry. Father didn't know where to put it, so stuck it where it is.')

The 73-year-old Jomo Kenyatta addressed the nation, calling for tribal and racial differences to be buried in favour of national unity. 'We are not to look to the past,' the BBC quoted him as saying on the 27th May – 'racial bitterness, the denial of fundamental rights, the suppression of our culture...Let there be forgiveness.' On 12th August Tom, already on excellent terms with Kenyatta, escorted him into the crowded Nakuru town hall to face an audience of over 350 white farmers. 'We are going to forgive the past and look forward to the future,' Kenyatta told them, adding that he hoped they would stay on and build the nation in a spirit of togetherness – *Harambee*. It became his token word. (My grandfather, who was also there, told me that Kenyatta received a standing ovation.)

Some white farmers took a dimmer view of change. Genesta complained of all-night drumming in the Ol Kalou forests two days before independence, "newspapers squirming before the former murderers, like dogs on their backs," and her "Luo boy sulky and swollen-headed." She wouldn't stay here, she wrote, "if it wasn't for Claud and the Masai...I am bored, slightly scared and utterly fed up when I think of my 41 completely wasted years here, when I might have been building up a lovely, safe and permanent home in some safe country." Scathing about the Government House garden party on the 12th December 1963, snobbish about clothes worn by Kenyan wives, she watched the final descent of the Union Jack, admitting that she now loathed Kenya, which she still had the audacity to refer to as "my beloved country."

That night at midnight was Kenya's *uhuru*: Kenya became independent, with Kenyatta, head of KANU, its first Prime Minister. He referred to Mau Mau as 'a disease which has been eradicated' and didn't appoint any former Mau Mau leaders to his cabinet. Government House was renamed State House, although Kenyatta apparently disliked sleeping there. Some said he imagined it still full of the colonial ghosts of those who'd passed through its high doors.

In the preface to the 1968 edition of *White Man's Country*, Huxley offers her thoughts on what D might have felt: "He always recognised that, in the long run, Africans would rule their own country," adding that had he lived to see Kenya becoming a black man's country "it is certain that he would have wished all Kenya's people well, for the love of his adopted country was the love of his life."

Europeans sealed their faith in the new Kenya by taking up citizenship. Tom was one of the first, renouncing his British nationality in 1964. Hugh followed suit. When I asked him about this he said emphatically: 'Kenya's a very lucky country because the people are so nice - and when you think what the British did to them!' He returned to his Kenyan newspaper, a sign the subject was concluded.

Diana kept relevant newspaper clippings, later pasting them into her photograph albums. 'I believe in the future of this country,' ran the shout line of one piece that featured Tom. Another clipping pictured Kenyatta meeting members of the European commercial community at State House at a leaving party given by the former Governor. Tom was alongside another pro-independence white, Bruce McKenzie. Never one to be upstaged, Diana's picture graced the opposite page, receiving a cup from Kenyatta, who'd been invited as guest of honour to a celebratory race meeting at which Diana's Sea Port won the aptly-named Uhuru Cup that had been brought from England for the occasion by Diana and Tom. She wore her pearls with their diamond clasp, the ones that some people speculated were the Erroll pearls.

That September, however, the *Sunday Express* ran a less positive piece: 'As Britons in Kenya today are losing hope.' A small headshot of Tom appeared beside one of Ian Henderson, an Intelligence officer in the Kenya Regiment who'd played an integral part in the pseudo-gangs aiming to track down those Mau Mau who'd still remained hidden in the forests. Henderson had now been deported, his book, *The Hunt for Kimathi*, banned. In spite of Kenyatta's campaign, the piece claimed, fewer than 200 Britons had become Kenyan. Of the 2,500 farms in the white highlands only 1,000 remained, and their farmers were fast being replaced by 30,000 Africans. "We don't want people in this country with one foot in Kenya and one in the House of Lords," senator John Kebuso had told Parliament, adding that the likes of Tom should renounce his title or get out within 24 hours. The common (albeit tongue-in-cheek) exchange between whites was: 'What, are you still here?' or 'See you on the next plane.' The Minister of Home Affairs, Oginga Odinga, was busy signing expulsion orders. But, the article pointed out, there was a great deal of British money invested in coffee, tea, sisal and pyrethrum, as well as other areas, and Britain had only three months earlier given £60 million in grants, long-term loans and military installations. In Kenyatta's new scheme to settle a million Africans on two million acres, Britain was now being asked to find another £30 million.

Feeling a need to stabilise the situation of his workers, Tom trimmed Soysambu down to 48,000 acres. Several of the descendants of these old retainers told me they were 'given' the land, although Hugh told me his father had sold it: 'Good agricultural land above Sugonoi House...for twenty shillings an acre. That was a pound an acre in those days. Unfortunately, he sold them the spring that fed the Mbaruk river!' When Hugh told me this in 2017, the Mbaruk was feeling the effects of climate change; alternatively flooding, spewing mud into Lake Elmenteita, and drying up completely.

CHAPTER 18

Black Man's Country

Divorcing Tinne complicated Hugh and Ann's marriage plans. 'He was born in Scotland,' Ann explained, 'so counted as Scottish - and in Scotland a woman couldn't divorce her husband unless there were two eyewitnesses to him committing adultery with somebody else *in* Scotland.' Tom paid for their flights and Ann's parents lent them a car. They stayed at the George Hotel in Edinburgh, where the lawyer and his secretary duly arrived at 7.30 the next morning for a cup of early morning tea, 'and there we were sitting up in bed!' concluded Ann triumphantly.

The wedding took place on 11th April 1964 on the veranda of Main House. Ann tied up her long hair and wore yellow, a colour she didn't suit; Diana's idea, expensively and virtuously resplendent in white herself, upstaging the bride.

'We couldn't get any vicar to marry us as Ann was divorced,' Hugh explained, 'so we were married by a PC who hadn't brought his glasses. He was called Mahihu, and he was Mama Ngina's brother' (referring to Kenyatta's latter wife). 'He had trouble with pronouncing *Willoughby* and *Cholmondeley*.'

'He warned us against *pigamy* and *puggery*,' Ann added.

'Not many people were there. Diana, of course, all covered in lace and frills, plus Peter Barclay, my best man, Meynell from Naivasha - he was also keen on model railways, but he spent all his money looking after his aunt - and Robert Howon, who plugged up the exhaust pipe with a potato. I ended up trying to remove it with a toasting fork but ended up pushing it further in. Diana who loved double *entendres*, cried, "Oh, look! He's put it in too far!"'

'Apart from the Barclays, it was very much Diana's friends,' said Ann. Snoo was away at school, and Ann's father wasn't allowed back into Kenya for five years as per Colonial Service regulations.

She pointed out the wedding guests in the photographs: 'Romer, Haselden, Aunt Nell (Eleanor Cole), Arthur and Tobina, Pam and Hugo Dent, and Patricia Fairweather - who fought with Pam at the wedding.' Two years earlier Diana had built a cottage in the garden for Patricia Fairweather, daughter of the Earl of Inchcape, and a childhood friend. She had a crush on Diana, Ann said: 'We were relieved when she left. She drank secretly at home - the house was full of empty bottles.'

The newlyweds honeymooned at Mnarani Club, where Hugh broke a toe water skiing. 'I hit the beach on one ski,' he said, 'and almost ran over Hayley Mills, who had the most objectionable Spanish boyfriend.'

Hugh now had a job as Settlement Officer, based on the Kinangop. Formerly known as "the white highlands," it was being divided up for African settlement. 'I worked for the *Sediment* Board,' he quipped. 'I applied and I appeared to be honest, so they employed me. Initially I worked in the Naivasha office.' His fellow European officers were 'all either drunks or thieves. The Africans were much better.' To Hugh's relief he didn't have to choose who benefitted from this settlement scheme. 'All the European houses were bought for £1,300, so those with mansions lost out. The Catholic Bishop of Nyeri bought a few. It was a World Bank scheme, but it was too complicated. It didn't work.' Hugh paused. 'Towards Ol Kalou people got more land, up to sixty acres, but on the Kinangop they only got two.'

These former settlers had left, many embittered by what they saw as all their hard work going to waste. 'Kenya is, if anything, a more unhappy country than when I knew it,' wrote Venn Fey in 1964 in *Cloud Over Kenya*: 'unemployment, hunger and disillusionment are some of the fruits of freedom. Law and order are precariously maintained...The Kinangop where I lived and farmed is today a shambles, stark testimony to ill-conceived planning and expediency."

After six months Hugh was promoted to Senior Settlement Officer, moving into a former settler's house. After a life spent travelling the world and roaming Kenya in search of snakes, Ann found it dull and lonely with their African neighbours giving them a wide berth.

Shivering through the coldest months, she observed gangs of youths who came to cut grass, aware that they were talking in Kikuyu about taking everything once these last white people had gone. 'Water was pumped into a small roof tank which always overflowed,' she told me. 'We nicknamed the house *Funga Maji!*' (meaning 'Turn off the water!') 'There was a bathroom upstairs; you couldn't let out both baths at the same time or water came through the ceiling of the dining room. The septic tank for the loo was under the front step and the sewer pipe under the lawn, but only by six inches. A lorry crushed the pipe the day the Settlement Officer came to lunch.'

I pointed out that Hugh's job was an interesting denouement of his grandfather's dream.

'*White Man's Country?*' Hugh said scornfully. 'Of course it isn't. It's *always* been an African country.'

***

In 1965, Hugh's work completed, they returned to the orange plantation and Hugh's bachelor pad at Sugonoi, which didn't offer a much better social life. There was nobody their age. David Haselden was managing Soysambu, Gerald Romer now General Manager of Delamere Estates. They had little in common with Genesta, who recorded in her diary her mounting hatred of the new Kenya: "the politics, the boredom, the inefficiency and the dust." Finally she left, returning to visit in 1979, when she would find fault with everything. By that time, their former farm had been incorporated into the 18-year old Nakuru National Park, while Nderit House was being reinvented as a tourist lodge.

Although they were also older, Hugh and Ann enjoyed the company of Arthur and Tobina Cole. 'He was very amusing,' Hugh told me, 'and they had a sheepskin pouffe in which lived a family of mongeese. Ratty and Mrs Ratty and assorted ratlets!' These weren't introduced to their greatest enemies, snakes - Ann's collection had also moved to Sugonoi. A couple of harmless ones, Hugh added, 'a mole snake, a house snake and various others, fed on white mice until these were liberated by some visiting children, after which we released the snakes.'

On 10 November that year Sir Patrick Renison died in London during hip surgery, at the age of 54. Hugh built a cottage at Sugonoi for Ann's mother. While Lady Renison would grow accustomed to her son-in-law's ways, she never took to Tom and Diana.

'She thought them mean,' said Ann.

Hugh shrugged: 'Father was always broke.'

'He was a dreadful little man. He was getting old and he was scratchy. We weren't particularly cosy with Diana either.' Fortunately, Ann added, they'd lived the other side of the lake.

Hugh was now one of the first commercial producers of oranges, acquiring a prestigious customer in the new Hilton Hotel. The river hadn't yet dried up, and life seemed good.

CHAPTER 19

Racing, Fishing and a Dog's Life

The name Delamere continued to be synonymous with horse racing. Hugh remembered 'over a hundred racehorses. There weren't all these zebra then,' he explained. 'Zebra carry horse-sickness - there are over 30 types of it, and only seven can be inoculated against - but they never suffer from it.'

Races Past (August 1954 - February 1956) listed Diana and Tom as leading owners, Diana second on the list of winning trainers, Delamere Estates second among leading breeders. Shel Arensen writes of one occasion when Sir Charles Markham was staying and Tom's Mercedes had two punctures on the way to the races. Markham changed both tyres, noting how worn they were, while Tom sat in the back of the car, angrily contemplating how late they'd be. Markham tactfully suggested he replace his tyres, to which Tom replied, 'Don't worry, I'll get my money back in the second race.' As predicted, his jockey Groombridge won by ten lengths, but after an objection over weight Tom lost the very large bet he'd placed, which didn't improve his temper.

With the departure of two-thirds of Kenya's European farmers, up-country racing dwindled, until the racing scene was centred on Nairobi. As a trustee of the Jockey Club, Tom had helped design Ngong racecourse, replacing the old one at Eastleigh. He and Diana had their own box in the grandstand, to which friends might be invited - at their peril; Tom once threw out the Chief Steward for questioning a result. He and Diana each had their own racing colours. "Delamere's colours were brown and cream and I still put money on a horse in those colours here in Australia!" Jennifer Falkiner, nee Mason, wrote to me. She couldn't recall Diana's so well, but was pretty sure they'd had pink in them. Confirming this, I found a photograph in a drawer at Main House of a jockey wearing pink and green, riding a beautiful grey mare. These horses were ridden by top jockeys, while their trainer, Diana Black, kept producing winners. Diana preserved newspaper cuttings about her horses, especially when there were pictures of her triumphantly leading a winner or receiving prizes wearing elaborate hats, highlighting sections with red biro.

With second homes in London, Kilifi and Muthaiga, Tom and Diana still found time to be involved in England's racing scene, where they hired well-known trainers, including Sam Hall and Bernard van Cutsem. Their horses' names harped back to Kenya: Baragoi and Ndabibi, the latter once pictured being ridden by Lester Piggott.

Fishing remained Diana's other passion and, although she initially suffered from seasickness, she persisted in going out to sea (bedecked in jewels, according to James Fox) until she got the better of it. Tom preferred staying on the veranda at Villa Buzza playing backgammon, often with the Duchess of Westminster (owner of the famous racehorse Arkle), until she and Diana fell out over some fishing rods. Patricia Fairweather usually accompanied Diana, along with David Partridge, assistant manager of Mnarani Club. He'd first arrived in Kenya in 1947 as a policeman, stayed on, and met Diana when he was ranching near Colvile's Laikipia property. Now he was her skipper, there when Diana's new boat *White Bear* arrived on a cargo liner at Kilindini harbour, in Mombasa, photographed by the press being unloaded by crane before her first spin around the Indian Ocean. Thirty-eight feet long, with a beam of 12 feet and a draught of two foot ten, *White Bear* had been custom-built, her hull of hard chine form, finished off with blue and white upholstery and a blue pile carpet, as well as all mod cons and facilities, but most impressive of all she had a flying bridge with full alternative controls - the first on Kenya's coast and the envy of the fishing fraternity.

Diana's albums contain endless photographs of fish they'd caught during many seasons, making trips north to Lamu or south to Shimoni, Diana wearing her captain's cap, her African crew dressed in navy-blue sailor suits. On one occasion her team won the Lady Delamere Fishing Cup on *White Bear*, their catch boosted by Patricia Fairweather's 215 lb black marlin, which David Partridge helped her land. Another time, Diana and Patricia caught six marlin during a six-day competition at Shimoni, using an expensive artificial lure called the Honolulu, only used by one other boat.

Partridge was soon promoted to Diana's full-time majordomo, in charge of everything from carrying her jewellery around in an old camera case, to putting together Diana's photograph albums, and even accompanying her to England. He and his wife Pam moved into Patricia Fairweather's cottage after Tom was finally able to persuade her to leave. (Ann told me she'd come for a week and stayed years.)

Diana loved dogs, her indulged pugs often accompanying her. *The Pug Car,* as Romer called it, was a Mercedes, its sole purpose being to drive the pugs to Muthaiga. Tom was less enamoured. Ann told me she'd once watched Tom 'bouncing up and down on the sofa repeatedly shouting *"Bastard!"'* - which turned out to be addressed to the pugs lying on the Persian rugs. Gilbert had always favoured working dogs, but Diana had introduced him to pugs, giving him one as a consolation prize when she married Tom. According to Farrant he became devoted to "Peggy." Diana, meanwhile, was the fashionista at Nairobi dog shows.

***

Hugh Cran was a Scottish vet who'd arrived in Nakuru in 1966 and was still treating Soysambu's pets in 2019. 'Oh, my goodness,' he said with a hollow laugh when I asked him about Diana's pugs. They'd been difficult dogs to treat, although less grumpy than Tom. 'Once when I went to look at the horses he was hollering at a syce,' he said. 'Diana calmed him down. She was easier to deal with. And charming.' Horses on Soysambu, he added, seldom did well due to a calcium deficiency. Cran's book *And Miles To Go Before I Sleep*, offers an amusing record of farming life at the time, including wrecking his car getting to Soysambu to treat a horse, the sprouting village of Elmenteita:

"an equatorial mock-up of the scene in *Shane* in which Alan Ladd guns down Jack Palance in a welter of mud in the one and only street. Elementaita (sic) didn't really have a street. The road just ran through it." He details the many livestock diseases, tick-borne ones carried by buffalo making farms like Soysambu and Nderit highly vulnerable: "No sooner had one problem been solved than others appeared to torment the latter-day pioneers." Then there was *Nakuruitis,* identified in D's day, making cattle listless, anaemic and susceptible to disease.

When Hugh and Ann first met Cran his yellow Volkswagen Beetle wouldn't start. Hugh gleefully rolled up his sleeves and prepared to rewire it. The end result was that when Cran was ready to chug off to his next appointment, he had to manoeuvre himself into the driver's seat, ducking between two wires which ran along each side of his head. These wires were tied to the steering wheel, and when you touched them together the car gurgled into action. Cran hadn't been in Kenya long, Hugh told me, so he'd been fairly impressed.

***

On 17th June 1966, Gilbert Colville, now 78 years old, had a stroke and died soon afterwards in Nairobi Hospital. He was buried at Ndabibi, on the same knoll as his tiny daughter: a suitably remote spot with its 360-degree view of his land. *SI MONUMENTUM REQUIRES CIRCUMSPICE* ran the inscription: if you want to see his monument look around you.

Hayes' and Farrant's books are contradictory on the subjects of coffins, pug names and burials, but it seems that there was a "smelly old pug" of Gilbert's as Farrant put it, who outlived his master and ended up being pushed around by Diana in a child's pushchair, tenderly covered in a blanket, a spectacle borne out in photos. Farrant further states that after this dog's demise, in Diana and Tom's absence one of the managers buried him in the family graveyard. On their return to Soysambu, Diana and Tom insisted, to the astonishment of the staff assigned to undertake the grim task, that it be dug up - an even smellier old pug by then - and transferred to Ndabibi. When I visited the Ndabibi graveyard, there was a gravestone, inscribed *OUR FRIEND AND CONSTANT COMPANION*, confirming that Gilbert's pug Peggy had died aged 12, five months after Gilbert, and was buried at his feet.

Along with the pug, Gilbert left his entire estate to Diana. According to Hayes this was in a two-line will, along with a three-page letter detailing how to deal with rinderpest in cattle. Diana, then in England, felt it might not be wise for a white woman in Kenya to own so much land. On her return, therefore, she sold Lariak, Gilbert's Laikipia farm north of Thomson's Falls, then prepared to sell Oserian. While sadly going through his things in the basement of the Djinn Palace, she was further upset by finding some of Erroll's, prompting her to send all the Djinn Palace's antique furniture to a Nairobi auction. Thus Diana closed another chapter of her life.

***

Snoo, meanwhile, had done a secretarial course in Nairobi, before being sent to Paris 'to be finished' as she put it. Diana was now ready to launch her 18-year-old daughter into high society, although the debutante season in England was definitely not Snoo's scene. Farrant writes that Snoo's "coming out" was a mean affair, involving cost-sharing with other parents of debutantes, and some "fussy dresses." With her hair in a fashionable bouffant, Snoo looks exceedingly glum in a photograph of the occasion, standing beside Tom and an exceedingly dressed-up Diana. ('I got awfully sick of the chinless wonders,' was Snoo's only comment.)

James Fox had been trying to meet Diana for a while, for the book that would become *White Mischief*, and finally set eyes on her that year at the races. "She was smallish, like English royalty, and she dressed and seemed to behave like royalty too..." Her appearance he defined as "*discreetly* rich," although she wasn't a "classic beauty."

Hugh disagreed: there was nothing subtle about her expensive dressing. 'Diana wasn't beautiful in the same way that Beryl was,' he said. Beryl Markham, who'd never had that kind of money, had what it took to look beautiful without the need to be pampered or preened. She simply 'carried herself well.'

***

Soysambu's new assistant manager, Ken Doig, moved to Lanet House, extending the garden and planting plenty of indomitable bougainvillea, given to him by Diana, to add colour during the long dry season. He had plenty of good snake stories, like the large black cobra which had headed into the garden where his two-year old son was playing on the rocks, vanishing, then turning up again a week later beneath the sofa in their living room. Ken called Dick Behr, the farm mechanic who lived by the workshop. Armed with shotgun and long stick, both wearing sunglasses in case it spat, they persuaded the snake out, where it made its way up the back of the sofa and, before it could escape through a window, he relates, 'it got two barrels of SSG from my 12 bore.'

Then there was the cobra they ran over by mistake that became pulverised in the engine; and the python curled up by the artillery gun when the army were on exercise near Sugonoi. This had a happier ending: Ken and Dick enlisted a couple of soldiers to help, Dick grabbed it behind its head and Ken, with four others carrying the rest - all fifteen feet of it - released it into the Mereroni River.

Ken and his wife Janice enjoyed regular prolonged Sunday lunches at Flamingo House with Romer and Haselden. At one of these, after plenty of home-brewed beer, they decided to run a competition to see who could put the phone down before their boss. A taciturn man, Tom would bark orders over the phone, addressing his managers by their surnames ('Doig - meet me in half an hour. I want to see the cattle!') ending by abruptly hanging up. 'I beat him!' they'd boast at subsequent lunches.

Janice had been taken on at Main House as Diana's PA, where she was frequently summoned into Diana's bedroom to take letters in shorthand. She was in awe of Diana's clothes, designed for Ascot by Hardy Amies, who sent drawings of outfits and snippets of material for her approval. Janice secretly copied these, shared them with other managers' wives, and thus the Nakuru tailors did an excellent trade in Hardy Amies outfits for a fraction of the cost. 'Let me show you some of my new outfits,' Diana announced on one occasion, beginning to undress. As Janice would later tell Ken, she didn't know where to look, but didn't dare disobey. Then came the sound of Tom's car. Diana hissed at Janice, 'Get in the wardrobe quickly!' Concealed in the closed cupboard Janice waited nervously until Tom left and she heard Diana's cool voice. 'Shall we continue where we left off?' As Diana had plenty of her own money, Tom probably would have been less upset by the expense of Diana's latest outfits, than the presence of a secretary in his bedroom.

Hugh and Ann enjoyed the company of these younger managers and their wives, and were delighted when the Behrs moved into D's old prefab. This had been fortified against Mau Mau by enclosing the veranda and creating a corridor to access rooms without going outside, and thus it remained until Marcus and Annie Dunn moved in some decades later and opened it up again.

Hugh and Ken enjoyed hunting buffalo together, and Ann was particularly pleased that Ken shared her interest in motorsport. He encouraged Hugh to take up rallying in his Peugeot 504, volunteering to be navigator, but discovered how loudly Hugh snored when they shared a hotel room having downed a few drinks before bed. 'After four hours of trying to sleep through the snoring - this was The Rt Hon Hugh Cholmondeley - the snoring was more than any man could take,' Ken told me. Eventually, leaning over Hugh's bed, he thumped him over the head with a pillow. Hugh murmured, turned over, and started snoring again. 'Another couple of blows finally did the trick,' Ken continued. 'I had good sleep, Ken,' Hugh announced in the morning. 'How about you?"

In time Ken, whose daily work began at six in the morning, became concerned by Hugh's sleep requirements. 'He got out of bed near lunchtime,' he said, 'which irritated his father.' The relationship between Tom and Hugh wasn't improving. With his father continually undermining his ideas and work, Hugh perhaps didn't feel that there was much to get out of bed for.

Meanwhile Tom and Diana had their own health issues.

CHAPTER 20

Heartache and a Silver Spoon

Tom was losing weight and suffering chest pains. 'Indigestion!' he told Dr Gellert in 1967, who referred him to a Nairobi cardiologist. Dr Silverstein diagnosed a heart attack, ordering a month in hospital, followed by medication and a strict diet. Although the latter didn't include cigarettes, Tom continued to smoke. Diana secretly pricked every cigarette with a pin before replacing it in the packet, and at their next visit Silverstein asked if he'd given up smoking.

'I had to,' said Tom. 'I didn't enjoy it any more - I couldn't get a puff.'

The following year when Diana returned from Vienna, Hugh and Ann noticed that she seemed to be having difficulty walking.

'I've had flu,' she said dismissively.

'Run up and down to the beach,' Tom suggested. This didn't help, and Diana ended up in hospital, where it turned out she'd had a stroke.

Meanwhile, back on Soysambu, Ann, who'd struggled through two unsuccessful pregnancies, carried a baby to full term, then lost it.

'I can't remember a lot about it,' she told me. 'I do know that Hugh was out doing something on the farm, and my Mama didn't know what to do, so she sent for the enormous Maasai driver and they bunged me into a motor car and took me to the War Memorial Hospital.' Her voice was becoming drowned by the pre-lunch bird brigade; I had to lean forward to glean that Diana hadn't been particularly sympathetic. It was probably simply too painful for her to allow herself to get involved. Keeping her own chagrins at bay, she'd busied herself on the War Memorial Hospital committee that D had supported in its early years. Hospitals were no longer segregated, but there were still mostly European patients and nurses at the War Memorial. Ann described the latter as 'battle-axes in their late sixties,' who weren't sympathetic; neither was a drunken doctor. 'They wouldn't let Hugh come in and talk to me, only Diana and Pattie Fairweather - of *all people*.' She took a thoughtful sip of vodka. Then she told me that the baby had been a girl, named Eleanor after her mother. Still bedridden and extremely distressed, she hadn't attended the burial.

When she fell pregnant again, Ann was confined to bed for two months in Nairobi Hospital. Occasionally she was allowed out to lunch with another expectant mother, Jay Hewett, whose husband remembered Ann as a lonely teenager in England who spent most of her school holidays with her pony. Hugh gratefully sent the Hewetts bags of oranges, and Ann managed to get some exercise wheeling the library cart around the hospital.

Thomas Patrick Gilbert Cholmondeley was born on 19th June 1968, and automatically registered as a Kenyan citizen. Under the Kenya constitution there was no option to be dual-British, and it was decided he would take his father and grandfather's nationality. As two Toms in one family would be confusing, initially his parents called the new arrival Patrick.

Hugh became a hands-on father, taking over the midnight feed, patiently holding the bottle until two in the morning. Patrick was an exceptionally long, large baby, with hands and feet to match. From the outset it was evident he'd got Hugh's genes, inherited from Phyllis.

'He was a healthy poppet,' Ann smiled. 'I had no idea of how to look after him.'

'He wouldn't be hugged,' Hugh recalled.

'Yes, he recoiled and went all stiff. He wouldn't stay in his swaddling clothes. He thrashed about and got free!'

Tobina was asked to be godmother, and the christening took place at her mother-in-law's Church of Goodwill. Hugh and Ann's happiness spills out of the photograph as they proudly gaze at their baby outside the church. Patrick wore the hand-embroidered christening gown that had been worn by Hugh's grandmother. The family had been reluctant to lend this to their Kenyan relatives, and unfortunately the gown was later stolen from Sugonoi House.

Jay also had a son, and the Hewetts became regular visitors. Jay observed her friend's cool relationship with Diana and Tom, finding him unfriendly - 'and particularly bad with Hugh,' she told me. Her father knew Diana, so she'd met her before. 'A nice lady,' she told me, '*if* she liked you! She always looked beautiful, wore her clothes beautifully.'

But beneath the perfectly groomed exterior, Diana was suddenly struck again, as she watched the happy new mothers with their babies. Perhaps the pain of her own buried sadness was manifesting itself as she suffered a mild heart attack. Silverstein diagnosed angina. Living at sea level would have been better for her heart, but this would have meant leaving the good life on Soysambu. Under Arthur Newton's expert eye the Manera dairies were generating plenty of capital, and James Fox writes of peacocks on the lawn, servants dressed in khaki tunics, long trousers and green cummerbunds, topped by a fez, discreetly in the background, arranging everything to perfection. Guests took breakfast in their bedrooms, cards placed on the dinner table the evening before so they could complete their orders. Tom and Diana had servants to dress them for dinner and separate drivers. After Tom's elderly driver, Simeon, crashed the car, Diana sent him for eye tests. On his return Ann watched him peer through his new glasses at the pink-fringed lake. 'I have never seen all that water before!' he gasped. 'And those birds!'

By now Diana had overseen the building of a swimming pool, perfectly placed at the edge of her beautifully landscaped garden. An elegant gazebo housed changing rooms, a shower and washroom, with fashionable Spanish tiles set into its walls, its white arches a pleasing foreground to expansive views of golden plains and mauve hills. She then built a nautilus-shaped pool at Kilifi, planting frangipane trees around it, decorating its surrounding walls with more Spanish tiles.

'It cost about £11,000 to build,' Hugh said. 'A lot in 1970. Do you remember it had a little fountain like a tiered wedding cake?'

'Yes,' Ann replied. 'And all the birds shat in it.'

'Diana never swam. She just sat about in her bathing suit, displaying all her jewels.'

'Diamonds and what-not. Diana collected diamonds.'

'She had a monkey - a nasty, biting one - in a cage in a corner of this patio.'

Diana's albums had photos of the unfortunate monkey - which wasn't any Kenyan breed - being played with by various unnamed children. It bit people because it was miserable, Ann agreed, and in the end it died. 'My godmother went to school with Diana in Hove,' she told me. 'Daphne, Diana's sister, was one of the stupidest women that's ever been. She married a Marquis.'

'Diana wasn't clever either,' Hugh added, 'but she had a marvellous elocution teacher. Her father was a rather dishonest horse dealer.' According to him, Diana hadn't been particularly honest herself. He told a story of her arriving at Lake Naivasha on a Solent flying boat, pretending to stumble and drop her blue jewellery case into the water, claiming it contained £30,000 worth of diamonds. 'But BOAC sent a diver down and dredged it up - and all they found in it was a brick and a curtain ring.'

She might not have charmed her son-in-law, but Diana endeared herself to others, especially men. 'She was a beautiful lady,' insisted Ken Doig, praising her generosity in allowing them use of the pool. Diana was also growing very attached to her step-grandson, who was quietly endearing, albeit alarmingly wordless. When Christmas arrived, she flung open the drawing room door with a flourish and Patrick beheld the most amazing sight: the whole room was crammed with teddy bears, jostling for space on every surface, sofa and table. With her penchant for bears, Diana had persuaded a Nairobi toyshop owner to lend her his entire stock.

'Choose any one you want, darling,' she said.

Patrick chose a large white one, which he would keep for the rest of his life. It was seated on Hugh and Ann's sofa in 2015, looking somewhat battle-scarred. 'It came here for a nose job,' Ann said, 'after a dog chewed it off. At some stage it lost its ghastly green nylon shorts...'

Patrick still hadn't uttered a word, although his beaming smile exuded pure joy. 'We had awful panics,' Ann added. 'Perhaps if your father talks as much as Hugh, then you don't need to be in a hurry.' Eventually, aged two-and-a-half, he came out with a sentence, after somebody - Ann couldn't remember who - told Patrick a story about a cat and a mouse.

'Whose side are you on?' asked the storyteller.

'I'm on my side,' responded Patrick.

Patrick's childhood was far removed from that of the majority of his peers, even those white-Kenyan kids who had *ayahs* to watch their every move. Patrick had a nanny - from Seychelles - and a 48,000-acre garden, much to the amazement of his playmates, one of whom was Philip Coulson in Gilgil. Philip was two years older, although Patrick's height made him appear much older.

'Everybody always said, "Oh, you must tell him not to be nasty to people because he's bigger than they are,"' Ann recalled. 'But he wasn't aggressive.'

When he went to play with Patrick, Philip told me, he addressed Hugh and Ann as Mr and Mrs Cholmondeley, while Patrick was 'this rather pretty little boy - long socks, Clarke's sandals, and he had a *nanny...*' Patrick's nanny, Mrs Laurence, had a daughter called Rosa - 'a solid little poppet,' Ann said, an ideal playmate for Patrick. Mr Laurence, a mechanic in Nakuru, was even better with children: 'He could do anything with them. When he came for the weekend the children behaved like angels.'

***

Towards the end of his life Patrick, by then known as Tom, would write two unpublished memoirs, both of which contained details about his early life. With Rosa as companion, he writes, her mother in charge, and an expansive life on their doorstep, he only saw his parents for a few hours a day. They had no idea that his biggest treat was to go to the workers' houses and drink sweet stewed milky tea.

From a muddle of photos in a drawer at Main House it was evident Patrick wanted for nothing material and never lacked for attention. Rosa pushed him on his tricycle, Hugh took him for swims in Diana's pool, and there were regular excursions to Kilifi and England. In another drawer I found Diana's old albums, carefully labelled *Fishing, Trips, People* and *Soysambu* by Partridge. Here Patrick stands out as the only child at adult gatherings on Diana's veranda, sitting politely poised. There are endless photos of Diana, her friends, especially Patricia Fairweather, a few of Hugh and Ann, and almost none of Snoo - just one with her in the background as Diana and various others inspect the stables, her head bowed as she walks behind a glamorous group. But it was Snoo who'd first put Patrick on a pony, taking him riding around Soysambu, helping him to develop an early love for the unique landscape.

At 21, Snoo, who'd been temping in London in between visiting Kenya for holidays, got married.

'He was a sergeant or something in the army,' Ann told me. They hadn't attended the wedding, which was in England, but they'd heard that cups of tea were served after the event, as opposed to champagne. Snoo later told me that Tom and Diana hadn't attended either, not being delighted by her choice. It had been an act of rebellion, and she remained Mrs Moorland for only three years, before her serially unfaithful husband left her for his girlfriend who was threatening suicide.

'I reminded him to take his suitcase,' laughed Snoo.

***

Kenya was developing rapidly. Nairobi boasted the new Kenyatta Conference Centre, while a satellite station at Longonot was speeding up international phone calls. There were growing educational facilities; polytechnics, colleges, Nairobi University and the largest hospital in Africa, Kenyatta Hospital, as well as new housing, blocks of flats, and new buildings at the main airport. Wilson Airport, where Beryl had once learned to fly, was the busiest in Africa. In the 1972 Olympics Kenyan athletes won nine medals, and the East African Safari Rally was branded the world's toughest event. The tourism industry was taking off - a booklet produced by the Ministry of Finance and Planning (*Kenya 1963-1973*) claimed that in 1972 428,000 visitors came to enjoy Kenya's wildlife, bask on the beaches, and climb Mt Kenya, staying in new lodges and hotels.

Lake Nakuru's concentration of flamingos was the world's highest, but Elmenteita remained largely undiscovered, its colonies of Greater Flamingos breeding in peace. The President came to visit with his large entourage. Tom was 'very close friends' with him, Wakaba had told me: 'Kenyatta wanted to build a big hotel by the lake, not far from Head Office. Everyone on the farm came to see him and Delamere killed many cows.' The feast was enjoyed, the hotel never built, but Kenyatta had written a letter, Wakaba claimed, 'to say that nobody in the government could grab Delamere's land!' With the rising population there was increasing demand for land, although this tended not to be acquired by the poor. Wealthy Kenyans, notably those in politics or well-connected, were busy building up land empires, not always by fair means. According to Charles Hornsby in *Kenya: A History Since Independence*, Tom financially assisted the socialist politician, Josiah Mwangi Kariuki, as did Jack Block, the wealthy son of Abraham Block to whom D had once lent money. Kariuki was a wealthy Kenyan, formerly Kenyatta's Private Secretary, but now critical of his policies. Popularly known as "JM," he was assassinated in 1975.

In 1973 Gerald Romer retired, returning to Britain with David Haselden. Arthur Newton, now married, was appointed General Manager and invited to join the Board of Directors. His young son Robert and his half-sister Tania joined Patrick at nursery school in Gilgil run by a homely teacher called Barbara Terry, whose husband Ray ran the diatomite mines at nearby Kariandusi. The school was in Gilgil Country Club, which wasn't required by its hard-drinking members by day. Two young Terry daughters had boosted the numbers, as had Philip Coulson and his sister Mary-Jane. Patrick had initially attended twice a week, diplomatically cast as King by Barbara in the Christmas nativity. Quickly tiring of his royal role he'd knelt down and put his finger in a crack that snaked along the floor the floor. Pretending to be a train with the accompanying *choo choo* noises, he followed the crack with his finger, disappearing behind the audience, oblivious to what Mary, Joseph and the rest of the bunch were up to.

At five, Patrick started going to school every day. A driver would do the school run, taking Patrick, Rosa, the Newtons and the 'rather portly' Mrs Laurence, Ann told me. 'She had a bad habit of sitting on the eggs.'

'Patrick was very clever,' recalled Barbara, who in 2018 still lived in a cottage beside Gilgil Club. 'He picked things up *very* quickly.' She leafed through photographs of her pupils - sitting under a tree, doing sack-races, posing as a group with a blond, beaming Patrick standing tall in the centre, Rosa grinning broadly beside him. 'You had to keep Patrick interested,' Barbara continued. 'He loved learning new things, but didn't like practising what he'd learned. He became bored easily.'

Before he went over the road to Pembroke, Philip took the role of Gabriel in his last Nativity, sticking angelically to his script while Patrick was busy neglecting his duties as shepherd and dismantling an old fridge in the corner of the room. 'Every father watching was dying to help,' Philip recalled with amusement, 'while Hugh and Ann were hysterical with laughter.' Hugh was more of a thespian, he added. When he was at Pembroke House, Philip was one of a group taken to *Dracular Spectacular* at the Nakuru Players Theatre. Hugh was Count Dracula, a role he played with demonic delight. Pembroke boys were known for good behaviour, but on this occasion one ran onto the stage at the crucial moment just before the exciting denouement, grabbed a vital prop, a Gladstone bag, and ran offstage, pursued by Count Dracula, who eventually returned to the stage empty handed, apologising to his audience.

I would have expected Patrick to have had the kind of African childhood his father and grandfather had missed out on, enjoying a unique freedom that comes with growing up on a place like Soysambu, but, according to Newton's wife, Mandy, he was often confined to his nursery, expected to stay clean. On one occasion when she'd taken her children to Sugonoi, they'd escaped Mrs Laurence to play in the mud, making Hugh 'livid,' Mandy said. Barbara Terry also felt Patrick might need more adventurous stimulation; when driving to Nakuru she'd often observed him standing at the fence with Mrs Laurence, watching the cars and lorries. As she and Ray regularly ran rally checkpoints in remote places, making a family safari of it, she invited Patrick along. Back then they took wildlife for granted; there was plenty of it around, so living on Soysambu was no big deal for Patrick. Watching rally cars roar by in a cloud of dust, on the other hand, was far more exciting, and he decided that when he grew up *he* would be behind the wheel!

'It was great fun taking him on safari because he was very observant,' Barbara told me. 'You had to keep an eye on him because he wasn't very experienced at camping in the bush, but he learned fast.' They began taking him on more adventurous trips - to Taita Hills to watch the eclipse and Mugie Ranch in Laikipia.

'What are these?' Patrick asked once, pointing at the pink finger-like objects sizzling in the pan.

'He'd never seen a raw sausage!' Barbara smiled at the memory. 'Everyone helped on safari, so I gave him a tea towel, but he had to be shown what to do with it...'

***

The Newtons were living in Flamingo House, which Arthur Newton had calculated would cost more to improve than rebuild, so Tom had given him the go-ahead to knock it down. Hugh was critical of Newton's rebranding of a 'perfectly good house' as what he dismissed as 'an exact copy of a 1960s Nottingham council house.' Neither he nor Ann had liked Newton, partly because he had been notoriously tight with funds, but Philip Coulson told me he'd done wonders for Delamere Estates, working well with Tom to ensure excellent profits.

Mandy Newton liked Tom, and had great respect for his negotiations with the British Government to help organise the buy-out scheme at independence. 'He wanted to ensure the best for the settlers *and* the people of Kenya,' she told me. 'He was a dear old man, always very fair. He took no nonsense, but he was unassuming, always dressed in his tatty old shirt with a frayed collar and an old jacket, unless he was going to the races.' Diana, on the other hand, 'wasn't my kind of woman...and she wasn't very nice to Hugh.' Mandy had found Hugh interesting and amusing - 'He played his guitar so well and made up funny songs' - but it was obvious that he was too academic for his father. 'Ann was very beautiful,' said Mandy. 'She had the most gorgeous hair - her plait reached her bottom' - prompting the bottle-blonde Diana to be 'very bitchy; she told Ann that at her age it was *unbecoming*...so she cut it.'

'Absolutely not,' said Ann when I asked. 'It didn't go with babies!' Her hair was so thick, she explained - 'like wearing a horse blanket' - so she'd worn it in a plait, which Patrick had discovered was perfect to swing on. 'Hugh used to cut four inches off it a year with the kitchen scissors.'

Arthur and Mandy Newton's son, Robert, was full of praise for his late father. He'd been a farmer and engineer of note, he said, building a reputation that extended through Africa and beyond. In 1973 Newton was invited to judge cattle in Germany due to his success at Manera with Friesians. 'He personally selected every animal,' Robert said, expanding on how good his father was with horses: owners sent theirs to Soysambu for livery and high-altitude training from as far away as the Middle East. Farm vehicles, all less than three years old, mainly Mazdas, and 56 Ford tractors, were all replaced regularly and the farm workshops were run with precision and care, Tom and Diana each getting a new Mercedes every year, although Hugh and Ann evidently didn't receive the same treatment, Robert referring to 'Hugh's ageing Lamborghini' and their 'old Peugeot.''Lord Tom,' as Robert called him, had been generous in improving workers' housing and water supplies, offering free healthcare for all employees and their families and discounted food and milk, and investing in their children's education. 'Top performers went to university in Nairobi, even abroad,' Robert said - in 1996 he'd gone to a party in Brighton where he'd been pleasantly surprised to meet several young professionals, originally from Elmenteita, all of whom remembered his father.

'When my father was in control,' concluded Robert Newton, 'Delamere Estates Ltd was a multi-million pound business visited by agricultural professionals and universities from all over the world to study the farming techniques that my father adopted - for dairy, beef and arable. Everything made money back then.'

CHAPTER 21

Masters and Servants

In 1974 Kenya was gripped by a countrywide drought lasting two years. According to a study by Julius M Huho and Edward M Mugalavai (*The Effects of Droughts on Food Security in Kenya*), the Maasai lost up to 80% of their cattle. But life for the wealthy was barely affected: the 1974 racing season had been excellent and, between presenting and winning cups, Diana and Tom took Mediterranean cruises with their old friend Marcus Wickham-Boynton, attended the Royal London Yacht Club Ball, and went salmon fishing in Scotland.

At just seven Patrick started at Pembroke, strictly a full-boarding school. He felt bewildered by his new sponge bag, shoe-cleaning kit and geometry set (how would he ever remember which bit of equipment went in which bag?), let alone the task of settling into this 1950s-British institution, in which he shared an open-plan dormitory (the entire ground floor of an old house) with 50 other boys, mostly sons of white farmers. He snuggled beneath his blanket, brought from home, wondering how he would fit into this different world.

It was quickly discovered that this new boy, whose grandfather was both titled *and* Chairman of Muthaiga Club, wasn't good at sport. Patrick became increasingly solitary, finding better conversation with an old Kikuyu cook who told great stories about his time as a Mau Mau fighter. Aware Patrick was possibly being bullied, Philip tried to look out for him, but being two years above him meant their paths didn't often cross.

'He was bullied witless,' Ann told me. 'So badly that he became incontinent - and then of course the matron bullied him because he wet his bed.' As soon as she and Hugh became aware of the problem, they sorted it out and life at Pembroke improved for Patrick. By then he'd worked out that being too near the top or bottom of the class thrust you into an unwelcome spotlight, and therefore ensured that he coasted along somewhere in the middle. His school report dated December 1976 confirms that, although seven months below the average age, he'd come 4th in exams (1st in history and geography), startling his teachers, for whom he'd always performed poorly. He worked slowly and untidily, his English teacher complained, although his reading was "above average." He wasn't lacking in ability, said his maths teacher, but needed to "overcome his dislike of putting pencil to paper." His science teacher summed it up: "A good brain, used sporadically." However, he impressed the drama teacher. When the boy playing the main part in a forthcoming play fell sick at the eleventh hour, Patrick learned the lines in two days and acted the part faultlessly.

The jangling of bells, signalling military-style punctuality, irked Patrick. Hugh gave him a watch to help him keep time. He left it on muddy ground near the playing fields, where he'd been alone as usual, watching a tractor ploughing.

'Why did you do that?' Hugh asked.

'I don't wish to be bound by the tyranny of time!' was the reply, the sort of statement that continued to fail to impress his fellow-Pembrokians.

The holidays were better. Robert Newton, who'd always looked up to him, was delighted to join him in building Meccano gear boxes and clutches, enjoying Patrick's Asterix books (some of them in Latin) during the obligatory two-hour after-lunch siesta at Sugonoi. He especially remembered one of Patrick's birthday parties: building kites and flying them at the lake. Both boys longed to play with Hugh's forbidden trains, but even when Patrick was old enough to join his father in the train room he lacked the patience, preferring it when his father taught him to drive a tractor and to shoot a gun.

When Patrick grew out of Mrs Laurence, Rosa was replaced with a more adventurous companion. Patrick Waweru had also grown up on Soysambu, his father having been in charge of milk distribution. Although quite a bit older, he happily undertook the task of accompanying Patrick during school holidays, alternately amazed and amused by this young *mzungu* (white man) whose background was so different. Patrick, rapidly becoming fluent in Kiswahili, proved a kind and entertaining companion. 'He used to come here with his water pistol on his bicycle,' Waweru told me in 2007, indicating the school beside Sugonoi House, that had originally been built as sheds to accommodate Mary's cows, and then donated to a government primary school just before independence. In spite of their less affluent circumstances, the children at the school felt sorry for this lonely white boy, making him wire cars to play with, Waweru said, adding with amusement how Patrick had made poisoned arrows with which he shot all the headmaster's chickens.

'Tom [Patrick] used to sit quietly behind the sofa listening to Hugh rabbiting on,' Ann explained. 'His godfather, Roger, gave him a beautiful chemistry set, so he studied the set, listened to Hugh talking, and discovered how to make arrow poison from the trees in the garden.'

'*Acokanthera fresiorum,*' Hugh added. 'It's all poison - the berries, leaves, all of it. It has pink and white flowers.' Below Sugonoi House, huge flocks of great white pelicans began arriving, escaping the civil war in Ethiopia where they'd always bred on Lake Tana. They congregated on the hard-baked soda flats beside the lake before taking over Elmenteita's black lava-rock islands created by rising water levels. Still doing his research, Leslie Brown recorded up to 8,000 pairs beginning to breed, displacing the Greater Flamingos.

There's a photo of Patrick fishing in the lake with a sieve, catching fish for their aquarium. The tiny fish which survived in the alkaline waters of Elmenteita, providing food for the many pelicans amongst other birds, were *Tilapia Grahamii*, Hugh told me. 'After a Scotsman.' They'd been introduced to Lake Nakuru from Lake Magadi in 1962 'by those who mistakenly thought the lake fly were mosquitoes. They brought the fish in milk churns to eat the mosquito larva - which was a waste of time because lake fly breed in grass. The first lot died, but the second lot survived, and they were then transported to Lake Elmenteita in the beaks of pelicans.'

'We went fishing in boots,' Ann said, 'but Tom [Patrick] had no shoes and the water was too hot.'

'Yes we were near the hot springs at the southern end. We caught two females and a male. Bluebeard, we called him. He had blue lips. He was a cannibal.'

Kat Combes came bustling by to tell us that she'd seen one of the hippo - 'near the rocks.'

"Hippos were plentiful in the lake up to 1951 when the lake dried up," Eleanor Cole wrote in *Pioneers' Scrapbook*, also recording the disappearance of hyena and Grant's gazelle from the area. Now Soysambu protected thriving populations of hyena and Grant's gazelles, as well as four hippo, which had suddenly returned at the end of 2011 when the lake was higher than it had been since 1962. They'd left dinner-plate-sized footprints on dusty farm tracks miles from the lake. 'Two came from Lake Olbolossat,' said Hugh, 'and two from Nakuru National Park, from up the Nderit River! They come and go. Every seven or eight years the lake dries up to a little puddle at the south end.'

***

In England, Phyllis, Hugh's mother, was suffering from terminal cancer. Receiving news in 1978 that this was consuming her fast, Hugh begged his father for a fare to England. In spite of Diana making regular trips to London to re-stock her wardrobe, Tom declined, adding that Phyllis was in 'the most awful condition,' Hugh told me, 'and he didn't want me to remember her that way, which was probably a good thing. Father had been very fond of her, so he sent her a bottle of gin a day.' Perhaps because of his mother's heavy drinking, Hugh only drank in moderation, his one weak whisky outlasting my and Ann's equivalent of two doubles. As Hugh spoke about his mother's death, there were frequent power cuts, dark patches in our conversation when we couldn't see one another, let alone find our drinks. 'Pattie Fairweather was a real stirring-up bitch,' Hugh went on. 'She told Father that Ann had said to some people who lived up at Subukia that I hadn't got enough money to go to England that year, and Pattie Fairweather distorted it into, "Your daughter-in-law says you don't give him enough money."'

'Pattie used to set her sausage dog on Tom (Patrick),' Ann added.

'I hadn't said anything like that. Then Father came storming into our house and said, "I'm going to throw you out of the house. I'm giving you plenty of money." Tom [Patrick] got very upset. Father growled at Ann until she had hysterics.'

Tom (Patrick) later recalled this vividly; his "fierce and domineering" grandfather coming to tea, losing his temper, and shouting at his parents. Then he'd turn on Patrick: 'And that goes for you too!'

'I vow I shall never be like that to my own son,' Hugh had said after his father left.

'Are we going to be able to come back here?' Patrick had asked anxiously. 'Are we homeless?'

"My grandfather did not let my father be involved in any way with the farm management," Patrick would later write, "and took a cruel delight in marginalizing him and disrespecting his opinions."

Phyllis died soon afterwards. Patrick had known his step-grandmother better. He'd liked Diana, impressed by her impeccable appearance - she changed into fresh outfits five times a day. Besides, she amused him, even though his parents "were slightly uneasy and cordially polite" in her presence. At one of her lunches, he continued, "she displayed on the table some of the china she'd gathered from her travels along the south coast of Spain, including a mustard pot in the shape of a cat. Someone remarked brightly about *how pretty* it was. With the timing of a pause to perfection (a la Stephen Fry), Diana arched one perfectly pencilled eyebrow and remarked, 'I always keep mustard in my pussy.'"

As loud laughter rumbled through the gathering, Patrick tried to keep a straight face in case his parents realised that he 'got' the joke.

***

I often wonder what lies behind the see-all-say-nothing masks of

Kenyan staff, silent witnesses to everything that goes on in such households. One hot February morning in 2018, I watched the elderly retainer, Muiruri, pour Hugh and Ann's vodkas. After he'd hobbled off in slippered feet, Hugh told me Muiruri had started out as Diana's 'pantry boy.' She'd been simultaneously training up a young woman to be a lady's maid - until she received a letter in which the woman confessed that she was pregnant, by Muiruri. Diana's reaction was simply to fire her. Muiruri had lasted, however, now a senior member of the Main House establishment, although he wasn't majordomo, Hugh hastened to tell me; that was reserved for Peter Ndung'u, who'd been Arthur Newton's driver until he'd refused to work for him any longer, fleeing to Main House, where he'd remained, now too elderly to drive much. He'd recently been in hospital, one of the expensive private hospitals in Nairobi where Hugh paid his bills. Talking to him, he seemed as fond of Hugh and Ann, as they were of him.

Then Hugh related stories about their former employee, Josphat, who'd worked his way up from being *kitchen toto* (a child apprentice in the kitchen) to top man. He'd briefly worked for Idina in Happy Valley, Hugh added, where he never knew which rooms required early morning orange juice or tea, as guests were all sleeping with one another's husbands or wives, let alone where to return 'the see-through cami-knickers.'

'I remember his face as he told us that these turned up anywhere in the house,' Ann laughed. 'He referred to their cocaine as snuff!' added Hugh.

Stephen Koigi was another employee who, like Muiriri, had been at Soysambu for decades. Born in 1947 in Elmenteita, he'd started work in 1974 as a clerk on Manera. Things were expertly run by Newton, he said, while Lord Delamere was 'a very good businessman, he was *kali* and expected high standards.' But he was kind and generous too, giving out some of his land 'very cheaply' to his workers, keeping on friendly terms with the government before and after independence. Diana 'wasn't friendly to the staff,' Stephen smiled, 'not like Lord and Lady Delamere today.'

Now Stephen was Soysambu's manager, and feeling somewhat torn about the prospect of retirement - how could he leave his old friends, he asked? 'Lord Delamere treats all his employees very well, like family. He worries if money is short and wages are paid late.' He looked through the open doorway of the century-old office building where children from Kiboko primary school ran by, some of them barefooted. Stephen had gone to school there, all those years ago, but today the school was much larger, with an increasing number of children enjoying Kat's school lunch programme, which she'd set up after discovering they were fainting in class, having left home before dawn, walked to school for up to an hour, then done lessons until mid-afternoon, all this with nothing to eat or drink.

An elderly *shuka*-clad Maasai leaned against one of the veranda posts, waiting to see Stephen, so I returned to Main House and sought out Muiruri. Sitting stiffly on a worn chair in the pantry, in his uniform of navy-blue trousers and navy-blue apron over a white shirt, he leaned forwards to hear my questions. We conversed in Kiswahili as, like many of his generation, he didn't speak English. Like Koigi and Ndung'u, he praised his employers, emphatic that he had no intention of retiring. Sometimes it's difficult to dig deeper with long-term employees; they're either fiercely loyal or frightened to tell all - especially to a *mzungu* to whom the standard reply is '*Mzuri*' - good! Muiruri was only prepared to outline his career: born in Elmenteita the year D died; beginning work here in 1960; initially cleaning the office, then cutting grass. He remembered Romer and *Karaia* (meaning "thanks"), as they'd called Haselden, who'd dispatched him to work in Main House with the warning, 'It is your problem if you get sacked.' Hugh was still growing oranges and planting trees above Sugonoi - 'so many trees...there was very much water then' - but Tom and Diana treated him well, he insisted. Patrick, he said, was 'a very good boy.' After Tom died he'd once accompanied Diana to Kilifi - which he disliked: it was hot, sandy and useless for cultivation. When Hugh and Ann moved into Main House, Hugh had told him he could stay as long as he wanted. 'I am still here,' he concluded, his deeply lined face creasing into a broad smile.

CHAPTER 22

A Very Human Man

With no interest in fishing or racing, Hugh and Ann enjoyed their increasing involvement with motorsport, which forged their friendship with my parents, notably my father who competed in and organised many rallies, including the annual East African Safari Rally. Hugh and Ann were in charge of the Rally Headquarters at the Rift Valley Motor Sports Club in Solai.

'She did the work and I took the credit,' said Hugh. 'Solai Club was built by a man with a very pretty wife - and was originally a tennis club. We used to play bridge there.' Philip Coulson reminded me of the club's quiz nights where Hugh and 'another genius' Robin McLellan always knew all the answers. Hugh was also renowned there for his hearty carol-singing, usually tasked with a solo part - *Ten lords a-leaping* - for 'The Twelve Days of Christmas.' My parents and I sometimes stayed at Sugonoi House. Patrick, a polite schoolboy, wasn't particularly interested in talking to a teenage girl, and would slip away after polite pleasantries. On one occasion, leaving my mother to talk to Ann and Lady Renison on the veranda, Hugh took my father and me for a spin in his rally car. There was no time to look at flamingos or anything else as we skidded in circles around the soda flats.

'Flying with him is even more alarming,' my father told me afterwards.

It was Ann who'd persuaded Hugh to take up flying, perhaps in a bid to boost his self-esteem. He'd had lessons at Nakuru, building up his hours flying around Soysambu in the Cessna 182 he'd bought. 'It was painted dog-sick green,' Ann said. 'I used to get out matching it every time.'

'Three landings for the price of one,' Pat Neylan, son of a

neighbouring farmer, commented while watching Hugh bounce along the Nakuru airstrip.

Charles Njonjo, a good friend of Tom's, sat on the Delamere Estates Board; he'd become Kenya's Attorney General at independence, a position in which he would remain for sixteen years. 'Thank you,' he said tactfully to Hugh after he'd been given a lift, bouncy landing thrown in, 'but the Government require me to fly in twin-engine planes.'

By 1978 Soysambu had 12,500 beef cattle, an extended outdoor slaughtering area attached to Dairy House, next door to Flamingo House, and a new cold store. 'It was pretty well much an inherent part of the Delamere-Colvile hierarchy that it was deemed a privilege to work for them,' Desmond Bristow, whom Arthur Newton had brought in to manage beef and arable at Ndabibi, later told Lotte Hughes. 'They just paid you what they liked, within reason.' Such frugality came easily to Newton; he was tough by nature, but it made him widely disliked, and Mandy told me how she found it increasingly awkward to be part of up-country Kenya's small white community, her social life running her into people her husband had offended - or fired.

That year Soysambu lost its buffer zone, part of an important migratory route for wildlife, when Kekopey was sold to a co-operative. It was quickly stripped of all its assets as its upper reaches became densely settled. A year later the land was showing signs of becoming overgrazed, its topsoil swept by storms into the lake. Kenya's dramatic population growth and the inevitable neediness of these neighbouring smallholders concerned Tom, not least the worry of what would happen to Soysambu after he'd gone.

The Easter weekend of 1979 Hugh and Ann were at Solai in the middle of the Safari Rally when Hugh, trying to relay information to Nairobi over a crackling radio handset, was told there was an urgent phone call. For once the Rift Valley Motorsports Club's phone was working.

'You know your father's very ill...' the doctor at the other end began. Hugh listened as the doctor told him that he needed to come and say goodbye. Solai was some distance out of Nakuru, even further from Elmenteita.

'Anyway we couldn't get away,' Hugh now told me shortly. It was a cold July morning, and he'd developed the habit of retiring back to bed after breakfast until fifteen minutes before lunch, when he would hobble back to his usual chair, wrapping himself in a fleece blanket. I suddenly imagined him as a young man, weighed down with inertia, his feelings of worthlessness exacerbated by his father's relentless undermining. Perhaps this had darkened into a state of mind which wouldn't have been understood back then; his father (along with most other people) would simply have told him to pull himself together and take some exercise. A depressed state of mind might explain his apparent lack of grief at the time of his father's death. But now, as Hugh waited for lunch and relived an event that had happened over 35 years earlier, he seemed upset by this recollection of his refusal to hasten home to bid his father farewell as he lay on his deathbed.

Tom had died at home on Good Friday, four months before his 79th birthday, of congestive heart failure.

'...Anyway, we *couldn't* get away...' Hugh repeated, taking little interest in his vodka and tonic. In the silence that followed I could hear the clock ticking loudly, until a mobile phone suddenly jangled and we were jerked back into the present.

***

When his grandfather had died, Patrick was with the Terry family in some remote spot, so he didn't know about it until Easter weekend was over. They hadn't been especially close.

Arthur Newton arranged for the driver Mwangi to take the body to Nairobi. 'It was a very sad day,' Wakaba said, when he visited me. He paused, his milky-white eyes looking inwards. 'Before he died Lord Delamere asked me to look after his son because he was *mpole*,' he said softly. Amongst its other uses, including as a condolence, the Kiswahili word *pole* describes someone with humility, translating as "gentle, humble, polite and meek." Tom had never wanted Hugh to run the farm, Wakaba explained, 'but when Lord Delamere died I was able to help him. I told him when to check the cows. I told him everything he needed to do.' After a moment's silence as he looked into the distance, he repeated his late employer's words. 'Look after him when I die...' I followed his gaze to the large silhouette of a Verreaux's Eagle Owl, perched on a branch of one of the vast eucalyptus trees planted back in Tom's day. It was too far away to see whether it was watching us, or merely asleep.

Needing space to grieve, Diana went to Ndabibi, where Desmond Bristow found her sitting quietly beside Gilbert's grave. Farrant records that a week later she summoned Bristow to Soysambu, where she received him in her drawing room. Bristow had been planning on leaving Ndabibi, but Diana persuaded him to stay on. 'I don't trust Arthur Newton,' she said, before breaking down in tears.

'Lord Tom and my father were very close. They seemed to understand each other very well, as well as understanding the needs of the business,' Robert Newton told me, infuriated by Farrant's portrayal of his father. Both Newton and Robert had been devastated at the loss of Lord Tom, whom Robert viewed as his Kenyan grandfather. Tom had always given Robert special attention, he claimed, ensuring that he had a seat at the dinner table. Although still young, Robert had noticed Tom's treatment of Hugh. 'He was always being called *useless*!' While Arthur Newton had been something of 'a tyrant,' Robert added, this was because he was dedicated to ensuring that the farms, which they'd so successfully built up, continued to prosper. 'When Lord Tom died,' Robert explained, 'everyone wanted their bit. There was plenty of animosity.' But Newton's tight financial control, his determination to curtail excessive and unnecessary expenditure, would now be a great deal harder without Tom to back him, especially where Diana was concerned.

There was a coffin ready; Tom and Diana had undertaken the task of having decent coffins made well in advance. Ken Doig recalled Romer saying at one of their Sunday lunches, 'Ken, you won't believe what I had to do for Tom today,' then proceeding to relate how Tom had materialised in his office with a tape measure.

'Romer, just measure my height!'

'Of course, sir.' Romer performed the task, then ventured, 'Can I ask you why I need to measure your height?'

'It is to make sure I have the right size for my coffin, as I do not want to be uncomfortable.'

The funeral was held on Friday 27th April at Nairobi's All Saints' Cathedral. Hugh didn't have much to say about it apart from: 'People *would* keep photographing me.'

The choir sang an anthem before Humphrey Slade, the renowned lawyer who'd been a trustee of Delamere Estates when D died, delivered the eulogy, telling the many mourners who'd gathered between the sombre, grey-stone walls, that Tom's 34 years in Kenya 'were undoubtedly the fullest' of his life. He hailed Tom as an 'industrious and imaginative builder of the economy and society of Kenya.' Tom had always admired what his father did for Africa, Slade said, and he'd hoped to carry on the good work, although he was not as politically inclined. But he'd quietly made his own contribution with his involvement in businesses, sitting on many boards. He was 'a man of great practical ability,' who had 'a real zest for many facets of life, a great sense of humour, and a most infectious laugh: a friendly man of personal charm and kindness, especially to those younger than himself: in all respects, a very human man.' Slade also complimented Diana on being 'a wonderful wife to him.'

After they'd sung *The King of Love my Shepherd Is, Now Thank we All our God*, and Psalm 121, Reverend Wigram, Provost of the cathedral, gave the blessing before everyone spilled out into the afternoon sunshine, crystal clear after the rain.

Ann had kept Slade's handwritten letter to Diana, on Messrs Hamilton, Harrison & Matthews-headed paper. "It was a privilege and big responsibility," he wrote, 'to have been asked to contribute." He acknowledged her bravery in facing what was indeed "something of an ordeal" for her.

'He had to be buried on *her* farm over there...' Hugh said, referring to Ndabibi. 'Diana insisted.'

Snoo was in England and couldn't attend Tom's funeral, nor his burial near Gilbert and the pug, a space between her two husbands left for Diana when her time came. The inscription on Tom's grave included his full name, *Thomas Pitt Hamilton Cholmondeley, Fourth Baron Delamere,* his dates of birth and death, and simply: *So Great a Man*. I'd first visited the volcanic hill with my father in the late 1980s when we were looking for rally routes on the untravelled roads of Ndabibi. We'd climbed over the low square wall surrounding the little graveyard and read the engravings, puzzled that the three adult graves were together, the pug at their feet, while Gilbert and Diana's daughter lay alone in a corner.

When I re-visited in early 2016, the wall had been raised above clambering height, the metal gates padlocked. I peered through them at the neatly tended path leading up to the graves, now shaded by a leafy fig tree. Two peach-coloured bougainvillea spread their tendrils over clipped green grass. Behind the far wall rose the blue bulks of hills, denuded by their human population. The view behind had also changed considerably; far below, hundreds of school children scurried around, ant-like, their shouts punctuating the stillness up on the hillock. Hugh had told me the graves had been desecrated at some point - 'by Maasai who imagine rich white people are buried with their valuables.' Alongside the southern wall, in the late afternoon sun, a youth reclined with three desperately thin dogs. A dozen more youths were approaching, carrying large sticks. As we drove away, bumping over ruts, they shouted at us, waving their weapons. I felt sad for them - school drop-outs without a clear future.

And what future for places like this little colonial graveyard? I suddenly recalled Slade's hopeful words, as he wound up his eulogy. "The name Delamere is written long and deep in the history of Kenya. May it continue to be so written for many years to come."

BOOK 3

1979-2019

A Fragile Sanctuary

"It seems to me that we all look at nature too much, and live with her too little."

Oscar Wilde, *De Profundis*

CHAPTER 23

Rebellion, Degeneration and Death

After the death of his father, Hugh wasn't inheriting a fortune, nor even the land; Tom had placed the farms in trust soon after he'd moved to Kenya.

'I'm just a tenant for life,' he shrugged. 'I draw a small salary for my contribution to the farming.' He was now the Right Honourable Hugh George Cholmondeley, Fifth Baron Delamere. 'A bit of a mouthful,' he told me. 'I ought to have a trumpet fanfare for all that...' As a Kenyan who didn't even live in Britain, he added, he had no intention of sitting in the House of Lords: 'I felt it would be rather cheeky to tell the British what to do!'

A few months after Tom's death, Jomo Kenyatta passed away. There was brief panic, but when Vice President Daniel Arap Moi stepped into Kenyatta's place and all seemed calm, there was a national sigh of relief.

Patrick, now able to be called Tom, was coasting at Pembroke - until he momentarily forgot his tactic of staying unnoticed and came out 'blazingly top,' as Ann put it. Realising that he was 'loafing,' they dispatched him to Ashdown House back in England, not far from where Ann's mother now lived. Pembroke being such a more-English-than-English institution, Ashdown was no shock, but England felt alien, and Tom writes how he missed Kenya's "huge human energy and love of the outside." Although relieved to escape Pembroke's pressure to excel at sport, he did admit to missing its "air of excitement and adventure" - his English peers didn't even climb trees!

Diana arranged a hasty sale of Tom's London house in Mayfair; in those days of exchange control, it was illegal to have property overseas. She then rented an apartment behind the Ritz to use for three months each year. It was here James Fox finally met her in 1981, a triumph he recorded in *White Mischief* released the following year - a publication Diana would find offensive. She was, Fox noted, "one of the most striking women" he'd ever met. Although she maintained her excellent figure, she was becoming more cantankerous with age, making her elderly housekeeper Paterson's life increasingly stressful, and it took Fox several visits to muster courage to broach the subject of telling her story. She'd *rather die*, Diana told him. She didn't want the past revived, and would 'go for him' if he wrote about it. Being a journalist, Fox was determined to talk about the Erroll murder, and finally, after a dose of vodka, Diana told him she'd had a pact with Tom never to talk publicly about it, but now as both men were dead, she opened up.

'I didn't do it if that's what you think,' she allegedly told him - adding that there'd never been an argument. 'There are only two men I have ever loved. Tom Delamere and…Joss. I always felt that it was because of me that he was killed, although he probably would have been killed anyway. He was that sort of man.' She added that Jock never admitted to, nor denied the crime. Afterwards he'd had nightmares - and she remained sure it was him.

By now Newton was running Delamere Estates as an increasingly tight ship, infuriating Diana, who saw no reason why she should bow to his edicts. The racing stables were doing well, the past season producing 38 winners, her pictures gracing the papers. She had no intention of cutting expenditure on travel, fishing, or facelifts either. Mandy Newton told me Diana would happily go through £80,000 annually, 'and that was just pocket money.'

On medication since her stroke, Diana had been forced to accept for several years that she couldn't live at altitude for more than a month annually, although she'd ignored medical advice to give up fishing. She enjoyed a good life in Kilifi. Partridge drove her to Malindi to have her hair done every Wednesday, where she always dropped by the Fishing Club for a pre-lunch drink. She lavishly entertained friends, favoured employees and even her doctors at Villa Buzza. Ndabibi Manager Desmond Bristow was a regular guest. On one occasion, he told Diana's biographer Leda

Farrant, heeding Diana's summons to her bedroom before he left, he was a little taken aback when Diana received him "without a stitch on." Her plastic surgeon Robin Beard, and cardiologist David Silverstein, were also regulars. Newton, notably, wasn't invited; he'd annoyed Diana further by enlarging some of her stables for his prize-winning Holstein Friesian bulls, whose sperm even sold overseas for artificial insemination. But although Diana hardly ever used Main House, she couldn't bear to give it up.

'One year she spent as many as five days here,' Hugh told me. 'It cost up to £20,000 a year to keep this house up.'

Tom moved on to Eton, and covered every surface of his room with memorabilia from home; with the Safari Rally now sponsored by a cigarette company, he had no shortage of *Marlboro Safari Rally* stickers and posters, inevitably ripped down by older boys. Eventually he settled in, having learned not to talk of what he'd done during school holidays - his peers never believed perfectly true stories such as his leading a team of motorbikes on a failed attempt to herd zebra into Nakuru National Park!

Kenya now began a slide into corruption and dictatorship. Oginga Odinga, the former Vice-President and a Luo politician who'd supported Kenyatta's rise to power, was banned by the ruling party from running for parliament. During the 1982 English summer holidays, Kenya's winter, there was a brief and abortive military coup. The postmaster from Elmenteita rang to advise Hugh and Ann not to venture off Soysambu, although they weren't to worry; Europeans, who generally kept their noses out of political wrangles, were mostly tolerated as being harmless, while useful for their contribution to economic stability. Hugh switched on the radio to realise that VOK had been taken over by militants who constantly replayed the same song and announcement. The insurgency was quickly extinguished with brutal force, and was followed by over a month of curfews in Nairobi. Fair trials and freedom of speech became even remoter ideals, with many alleged dissidents detained and tortured.

Anthony Rowan was a new young manager employed to try arable farming on the slightly better watered south-western side of Soysambu known as Ol Jolai. Arthur Newton and Wakaba both had great respect for Rowan, and Robert Newton recalled the purchase of a massive baler, 'the biggest outside the USA.' Two male lions had also taken up residence on Ol Jolai, killing cattle indiscriminately, like cats thrown into a roomful of mice. Dick Behr's son, Peter, sat up for most of the night and shot them both. Ken Doig, who'd left in 1975, returned to visit eight years later, to discover that after a cobra had been seen vanishing into a hole in the Lanet House rockery, labourers had followed a manager's orders to dig deep, where they'd discovered a cobra lair, housing at least 40. With the aid of plenty of kerosene the unfortunate reptiles had been cremated. A portly hippo had turned up on the veranda of Flamingo House, determined to enter through the French windows. Hugh was called to shoot it, and sadly the hippo met its end before anybody knew it was a "pet" hippo from Lake Nakuru Lodge. There was no point in Tom repeating these stories at school either.

After falling behind in his work, however, Tom was expelled from Eton, his O level examinations behind him, but A levels still looming. Ann maintained it all stemmed from Tom's revenge on a fellow pupil who'd poured milk on his suit by peeing on his, but he was still out. He came back to Kenya to spend the summer concentrating on his motorcycling skills, Soysambu's remote and rocky roads being perfect for a teenager whose only ambition at that point was to compete in motocross. All too quickly September arrived, and he was sent to a 6th form college in Worcester.

1983 had seen a country-wide drought; water shortages and hordes of skeleton-thin cattle driven by their Maasai owners onto farms or cramming Nairobi's roadside verges, causing traffic jams. In 1984-1985 the Rift Valley had suffered further drought, bringing food shortages and long queues in supermarkets for imported maize meal. In 1985 Hugh decided to close the stud. He wasn't interested in horse racing like his father had been, objecting to dressing up in a suit to attend the Nairobi races. 'Couldn't afford it,' was his blunt reasoning. 'Horses eat.' There wasn't enough grazing, they didn't grow oats and there was always the threat of horse sickness from the zebra. Newton backed Hugh, the artificial insemination business being more profitable.

A public horse auction was held at Soysambu, where a welcome downpour didn't deter a large crowd of buyers. Thus departed many champion steeds, including the stallion, Longonot, who'd been there since 1974, siring many winners. After this, although they were occasionally obliged to attend the races to present the Delamere Cup, Hugh and Ann were relieved to bow out of the racing scene. But it was the end of an era for Diana, and perhaps accounted for her sudden decline in health. Charles Hayes and Leda Farrant both tell the story of when David Silverstein arrived at the coast, planning to avoid Villa Buzza, where he was usually obliged to stay. Upon hearing that Diana was in the Intensive Care Unit of Mombasa's Aga Khan Hospital with pneumonia, he gave up all hope of a quiet getaway from his busy Nairobi consulting rooms and hastened to her bedside, accompanying her on a Flying Doctor plane to Nairobi Hospital, where she spent the next month on a ventilator, during which time she suffered another stroke. David Partridge stayed by her side, and Snoo was summoned from England.

But Diana was tough, a week later regally demanding to be wheeled to the hospital salon for her manicure, eyebrow and eyelash tint - and to have her hair done - before receiving visitors. Few men could avoid dancing to Diana's tune; Nairobi's top restauranteur, Alan Bobbe, brought his haute cuisine to her bedside, and Silverstein resignedly – albeit reluctantly - agreed to Diana's command to spend the festive season at Villa Buzza. Delighted to be home, Diana, resplendent in her silk evening gown, cast aside her wheelchair and entertained her entourage as if she'd never been away. Silverstein was presented with his Christmas gift - a pair of gold and diamond cufflinks. Photos show Diana smiling - not too hard because of the facelifts - at the centre of a host of girlfriends, also dressed in silk evening gowns. But although Robin Beard had done his best, Diana was having to conceal her ageing complexion beneath increasing layers of makeup.

***

In 1986 Beryl Markham died. Four years earlier a restaurant owner in California had read about her memoir, *West with the Night*, in Ernest Hemingway's letters, in which he described it as "a bloody wonderful book." He'd persuaded a publisher to re-release it, although these much-needed new royalty payments would only see Beryl through her final three years. Much of her second round of fame would be posthumous, and would include books, an award-winning television documentary about her life and a series, *A Shadow on the Sun*, in which Beryl was played by Stefanie Powers. It seems astounding that this glamorous aviation pioneer, who'd had affairs with British royals and made a name as a top racehorse trainer, had ended up on the breadline, living gratuitously in a cottage beside the racecourse, drowning her financial woes with vodka when kindly friends supplied a bottle. Hugh and Ann regularly took her out to lunch at Muthaiga Club, including the much talked-about day, immortalised in a cartoon on the club's walls, when it had been the military coup; Beryl had driven furiously through a military roadblock, determinedly arriving punctually for her customary pre-lunch vodka, her elderly Mercedes laced with bullet holes.

'She wasn't remotely bothered,' Ann told me. It was good to know Beryl hadn't lost her sparky spirit, although sad that while she so fondly remembered D, Florence, and Tom, Soysambu, it seemed, had not remembered Beryl. 'Diana didn't want her near the place,' explained Ann.

***

Fed up with Soysambu's unreliable telephone lines and impossibly dry conditions, Newton moved to Manera, taking the Delamere Estates office with him. Soon afterwards a large gang of thugs attacked Manera farm workers, many of whom were injured, some admitted to hospital. Newton reported the incident to police, then visited the DC, who warned him that these attacks were intended to intimidate, but that he was powerless to stop it as orders came from 'very high up.' As rumours circulated that a high-ranking politician was after a slice of Manera, the alarming incidents escalated. An assistant manager, clearing acacia seedlings rampant in Manera's dairy cattle paddocks, was accused of flouting laws banning tree-cutting, and locked in police cells on a Friday night, ensuring he couldn't get an advocate until Monday morning.

As a Director of the Kenya Meat & Livestock Commission, and a man who refused to engage in corruption, Newton was convinced he would be the next target. After a period of avoiding being anywhere near Manera from Fridays to Mondays, he decided the family must leave Kenya for good. Robert, now at boarding school in England, was devastated. But his mother was relieved. Disillusioned by new Kenyan laws that only allowed her to remain in the country of her birth if she had a work permit or dependant's pass on her husband, she could finally find freedom and end an unsatisfactory marriage.

From England Newton watched sadly as all his hard work was 'ruined by others,' Robert told me. The subsequent downfall of both Soysambu and Manera, he said, broke his father's heart. From humble beginnings, on a six-month contract at Manera when money was so short, Newton had changed the tide for the Delamere businesses and was still hailed in 2018 by Philip Coulson and Wakaba as the best manager Delamere Estates had ever seen. Meanwhile, back in the 1980s, Kenya's rigid political landscape and the departure of Newton had been the start of inexorable decline. Soysambu's golden era was ending.

***

After A levels, Tom took a gap year before further studies, working on various farms in preparation for his destined career which was to be his eventual takeover of Delamere Estates. He gained a variety of experiences, working in many different terrains, including the wilder expanses of Laikipia, where he learned about camels from expert, Jasper Evans, and a farm on the slopes of Mt Kenya owned by Kenneth Matiba, an astute politician who repeatedly challenged Moi's repressive regime. Tom finally worked the summer of 1987 in Essex, where he joined two employees on 400 acres of cereals, his first experience of truly hands-on farming, as in Kenya there was cheap labour to do it for you.

That year Mary Delamere died in England, still insisting she had sole claim to the Delamere title, a claim Diana had always ignored. Meanwhile, still concerned that she owned too much land, Diana decided to sell Ndabibi. Hayes and Farrant are confusing on the issue; the former writes about some of Gilbert's former workers forming a co-operative to purchase the farm, which was sold instead to ADC (the Agricultural Development Corporation was a government parastatal established in 1965 to facilitate the land transfer programme from settlers to Africans), while Farrant claims President Moi himself bought Ndabibi, describing the Sunday Diana went to meet him at State House, dressed in her best. He kept her waiting, and Diana became so stressed that Desmond Bristow was obliged to deliver her to a friend's house and conduct the business himself. "The President had a bargain," wrote Farrant; "acres of wheat and maize, all kept in perfect condition and ready to sell, and including cattle." This was incorrect, Snoo told me; by the time of Diana's visit to Moi, Ndabibi had already been sold to ADC. Diana had been visiting him merely to ask permission for the money to be taken out of Kenya, which was granted.

Bristow remained on as manager until Ndabibi was subdivided, after which various scandals continued to emerge, with the President reputedly involved. By the late 1990s, the farm was supposedly the property of the nation, although the litany of political land-grabbing scandals and injustices dealt out to African smallholders remained a subject of discussion in the press. When I drove along the rough and dusty north lake road in 2017, Ndabibi's best land fronting freshwater Naivasha and its smaller cousin Oloidien was still farmed by those who'd been politically in favour during Moi's reign, with a handful of parcels of land later purchased by Europeans. I had lunch at Kiki Preston's former house, later purchased by Lord Andrew Cole, Galbraith's grandson, and now owned by a foreigner as part of the newer Mundui Conservancy. This grand home overlooked the idyllic riparian shores of Oloidien, which, like the main lake had become a battleground between landowners or tenants and an increasing number of illegal fishermen plundering the waters. Times were very different from those drug-fuelled parties in Happy Valley's heyday.

Typically, Gilbert had preferred to live in a very basic house further back on Ndabibi, amongst his cattle. We'd found it once in the early 2000s when looking for a shortcut from Ndabibi to Lake Elmenteita, and found it a depressing place, even if imagined in its former days without today's untidy patchwork of smallholdings, barely accessible down neglected tracks. Snoo told me that when she'd revisited Ndabibi, back in the early 1990s, she'd been heartbroken to see so many small plots so unproductive, struggling on land that was better suited to large-scale cattle ranching.

***

After savouring the sights of Madeira from Wickham-Boynton's yacht during the summer of 1987, Diana went to England stay with her sister Daphne, third wife of Inigo Freeman-Thomas, 2nd Marquis of Willingdon. On 3rd September, while planning her outfit for Royal Ascot, Diana had another stroke. She died soon afterwards. As it happened, *The Happy Valley*, a BBC drama, had shown the previous night, and the film - *White Mischief* - was in production at the Djinn Palace. The press hadn't forgotten her either. *Erroll case death* ran a sensational piece in the *Telegraph*, erroneously referring to Diana as "one of the central characters in Kenyan society of the 1930s." The following day it headlined another, *Femme fatale takes Kenya murder secret to her grave*, using an unflattering photograph that must have made Diana turn in her coffin.

Apart from her additions and changes to Main House, Diana hadn't left a significant imprint on Soysambu. She'd loved Tom and perhaps Soysambu, in her own way, but now, widely viewed as a hard-nosed woman who'd pursued and gained both wealth and social standing, Diana only left a legacy of notoriety. She'd been eleven years younger than Beryl, but both women had been part of a world that had also passed on. With glamour and promiscuity in common, they'd both led extraordinary – if very different – lives, but it was Beryl who would attract admiration after her death, continuing to be celebrated for her flashes of fame as pilot, trainer and writer.

It no longer mattered anyway, for Kenya had outgrown them both.

Snoo made the arrangements, so that Diana's body could return home. 'Any old box will do!' she told the undertakers, knowing there was a coffin awaiting her mother on Soysambu.

'But this is Lady Delamere,' they persisted. 'What about silk-lined mahogany?'

But Snoo refused all their attempts to charge her more, and Diana was thus flown home in a cheap coffin, duly transferred into another, and laid to rest a week after her death on Ndabibi, between two of her husbands. Her gravestone, less eruditely than Gilbert's, simply said, *SURROUNDED BY ALL THAT I LOVE.*

Charles Hayes describes a burial service conducted by Mike Harries, a farmer, pilot and part-time reverend from Thika. The pall bearers, he claims, included Hugh, David Partridge, Desmond Bristow, Tony Davis (auditor for Delamere Estates) and Charles Njonjo. Sherry was served in new glasses, according to Delamere tradition.

'Really?' Hugh said. Neither he nor Ann had any recollection of even being there.

'It was a quick burial,' Snoo told me, 'and they probably weren't.'

That December a memorial service was held at Nairobi Cathedral. Hugh recalled reading the passage from Ecclesiastes: 'There is a time for everything, and a season for activity under the heavens; a time to be born and a time to die...'

By now it had emerged that Diana had left her affairs in a muddle. 'Unfortunately nobody knew where she'd put her jewellery,' Snoo told me. 'It took them six months to find it - in a suitcase in a cupboard in her sister's house - and her will had never been sorted.' Leda Farrant writes of six unsigned wills, all relating to assets tied up in trusts to avoid tax, inadequately providing for Snoo and her staff, and leaving all her money to Tom, who was about to start at the Royal Agricultural College in Cirencester. It was Hugh who "informed Kleinwort Benson, the trustees, of Snoo's existence, thus enabling her to inherit the bulk of the estate," Farrant writes, further telling of Snoo's earlier visit to Diana in London, where she noted the disappearance of her mother's faithful lady's maid, Paterson. Snoo later found her in a penniless state in a charity home, but it was too late to assist; she died soon afterwards.

'Diana's Muthaiga house was sold to give David Partridge a pension,' Hugh told me, 'but he promptly killed himself in a car accident.' According to Farrant, Diana also left Partridge her fishing boat, *White Bear,* but, unable to afford her upkeep, he'd sold her on to the luxury beach resort named after Ernest Hemingway, where she was still taking out clients in 2017.

Tom put some of Diana's money to good use, raising the wall around the Ndabibi graveyard, and assisting Ann in enlarging a modest property she'd inherited from her parents in East Sussex. Snoo moved to Kilifi, where there was at least something she could do for Diana's old retainers. She paid off the more elderly ones. Then she embarked on her new life of fishing, returning to England for the racing season, keeping Villa Buzza open to visitors and family, and patronising the Delamere Cup, a fishing competition started by Diana in 1965.

***

More recently, when I visited Snoo in Kilifi, although she'd handed the Delamere Cup over to someone else, she still fished, chartering a friend's boat, sometimes taking Hugh's grandson Hughey. She hadn't changed Diana's decor, I noted when I retired to my room, surrounded by furniture and fittings that were fashionable in the 1950s. I turned off the rusting creaking fan so I could hear the sigh and swish of waves on sand. Lying beneath my mosquito net, I wondered about Diana and what secrets she'd kept? How much had she really known about Erroll's murder? As Hugh and Ann had disliked her, they weren't disposed to kind assessments, but I found it difficult to believe she'd pulled the trigger on a man she'd supposedly fallen for. Over time Diana has continued to be a hard nut to crack, and my instinct says it's highly possible that, along with her husband-of-convenience, Jock Broughton, and untrustworthy lover, Hugh Dickinson, she'd been caught up in a greater plot – very possibly one engineered by the British Government - that she'd failed to fully understand. Her silence would continue to spawn volumes on the subject, but I'd hazard a guess that she'd made a vow to keep the events of that night secret, for whatever reason.

Somewhere out there in the darkness - there were no security lights, which was most unusual in 2017 - lurked Jackson, an elderly Giriama night watchman, who'd been with Snoo almost 40 years, and Diana 13 years before that. Had he ever heard incriminating cries of horror, or confessions in her sleep? But he'd be unlikely to tell me either.

CHAPTER 24

Fresh Ideas and
New Beginnings

Hugh and Ann finally moved into Main House. Ann had added enough new shelves to accommodate their books, and an attic above the master bedroom in which to banish Diana's many clothes, and obliterated what she referred to as Diana's 'hideous yellow.' That involved completely redecorating the drawing room and repainting in turquoise all yellow pillars, doors and window frames. Hugh had a wall built around the pool to offset the cold wind, and added a roof to Diana's back patio.

'It was all rather expensive,' Hugh said. 'David Heath just did whatever I told him, which was a mistake. He should have said, "You can't afford it," because I couldn't.' As David Heath was a relatively new manager of Soysambu, this seems a lot to expect of him. Did I detect a whiff of regret here at the departure of Newton? Heath had moved rapidly up the ranks by virtue of his being a Kenya citizen. But not everyone liked him. Rowan left because he didn't get on with him, but also because as a British citizen, Rowan faced the increasing pressure from the government for places like Soysambu to employ Kenyans, with work permits for expatriates in the agricultural sector difficult to obtain without bribing.

'For a long time after we had no money at all. We still don't. We're used to it now - it's not cruel!' Hugh emitted a humourless chortle. 'It's like skinning eels alive - it's the only way to get the skin off. They've always been skinned alive, they're used to it.' The subject of money, constantly arising in conversations with Hugh, always seemed to hit a sensitive spot, this enigmatic metaphor hinting at a pain probably rooted in a childhood spent listening to an angry father raging about *his* father's perceived wasting of family money.

Coupled with Tom's thoughtless undermining of young Hugh's self-esteem, it's no surprise if he grew up feeling undeserving of wealth anyway. It's unlikely he'd ever received any useful guidance on the subject of budgeting, for Tom simply couldn't be bothered with his son. He'd been closer to Newton.

The previous night had seen another costly incident. Lions had walked along the track to my house, leaving multiple large paw prints in the powdery dust, before indulging in a serial-killing spree at a nearby *boma*. They'd circled the thick thorny barriers, terrifying the cattle into breaking out, at which point they'd pounced. It had been a noisy night of hyena whoops and jackal yelps, but the lions had been silent.

'Those cattle were worth 40,000 shillings each.' Hugh said furiously. Guy Combes, son of Simon, was busy raising money for new lion-proof cattle bomas, mobile ones that could be moved, but there weren't enough of them yet.

***

That August of 1989, Hugh and Ann threw a combined housewarming-silver-wedding-Tom's-21st-birthday party, commencing on Saturday with afternoon tea, after which we pitched tents in the paddock. There followed dinner and dancing on the patio, continuing into the small hours. Sunday morning saw brunch and Pimms beside the pool. It was a lavish affair, and in hindsight it seems that Hugh was simply putting two fingers up to his father by emulating his grandfather's extravagance.

After leaving Cirencester and briefly working with the Agricultural Mortgage Corporation in Andover, Tom returned home, initially to help out at Manera. He seemed more serious now, although he shared the often outrageous, sometimes sardonic family humour. Very tall and fair-skinned, like his father, he had a shock of strawberry blonde curls, already showing signs of receding, and although he wasn't classically handsome, he was eye-catching, dressing in stylish clothes that suited him. Like Hugh, Tom was kind and courteous, with the same gentle manner and interest in a broad range of subjects. He was intrigued when he unearthed some of D's old manuals for ox-drawn mowers and curious tools. Had his great-grandfather still been alive, indeed, he might well have found a kindred spirit in Tom, in whom his extraordinary memory, restless ideas and relentless energy had been reproduced with fiercer intensity than in either of the generations in between.

Tom then moved to Soysambu, where Pattie Fairweather's former residence became Tom's Cottage. His relationship with Hugh was already turbulent, as if some invisible line threading through four generations of male Cholmondeleys drew them into inevitable conflict. He'd left college armed with the enthusiasm and arrogance of newly-educated youth, but his staying power was lacking, a wild and restless spirit often leading him away from the job in hand in pursuit of adrenalin-filled adventures. When I visited Tom once, for afternoon tea on his veranda, we watched dust devils billow across arid horizons as he waxed lyrical about his 2,500 kilometre motorbike trip to Lake Turkana with his friend Paris Foot, where he'd fallen in love with the north of Kenya, as his great-grandfather once had - especially Marsabit.

By the early 1990s, with Kenya now politically turbulent and economically mismanaged and with a rising population, Tom was noting the increasing poverty around Soysambu and Manera. "I had seen that agriculture was no longer a safe way of life, but needed an innovative approach if it were to carry us into the future," he writes in his diaries, adding that working alongside his father wasn't easy. Hugh was prone to despondency, while Tom had a more optimistic vision of the future.

Like his father's and grandfather's, Hugh's heart wasn't strong. Feeling faint, he flew himself to see Dr Patel at Nairobi Hospital, putting his cigarettes and lighter on the doctor's desk. After the ECG he asked, 'Now can I have a cigarette?'

Telling this story, Hugh put on his best Indian accent to imitate the doctor's reply. 'No! And I must varn you if you carry on smoking you vill be dead in a fortnight.' He smiled wanly. 'Ann was there, so with great generosity I handed her my packet of cigarettes and my cigarette lighter, and I haven't smoked since. Everybody has to use will power if they want to change things. Ann used to smoke like a chimney, but I bullied her for a year until she stopped. I went to England almost immediately and had a triple by-pass. It was surgically fashionable.'

While his father was under the surgeon's knife, Tom was speeding round Kenya in the ageing Peugeot 504, a rally that proved to be its last. Fortunately Hugh's operation was more successful, and afterwards he embarked on a healthier lifestyle. Relieved to see his father regain his usual argumentative nature, Tom was ready to distance himself from the family fold, moving to Flamingo House, filling shelves with his collection of snake-skins, bones and skulls, enjoying his own space and planning new schemes. The grain grown on Ol Jolai had fetched good prices, although one in three crops had failed during drier years, but Anthony Rowan's efforts had left excellent fields for growing hay which could feed cattle during droughts. These fields also attracted large flocks of guinea fowl. Although the government had banned professional hunting in 1977, the shooting of certain game birds was permitted, so Tom proposed they set strips of bush aside for use by a bird-shooting syndicate as an income-generating project. Hugh was vehemently opposed, determined to remove every one of the blackthorn or *Senegalia mellifera* trees that made up the scrub, an acacia that spreads rapidly, choking the crops. Eventually Tom had his way and those blackthorn in the allocated shooting areas survived.

A decade of degradation on Kekopey had left Soysambu the sole refuge for wildlife, and it was now being overrun by increasingly large herds of zebra and other ungulates; a 1992 game count revealed approximately 5,000 wild animals. When the government introduced a game-cropping scheme, licensing the necessary firearms, Tom started a culling programme, naming the new business *Fair Game*. This soon paid for the building of a new slaughterhouse behind Flamingo House and the employment of fifteen staff. Tom noted the subsequent increase in wildlife numbers, which he put down to the added activity with vehicles in remoter parts of Soysambu, a deterrent to poaching. Various other illegal activities also came to light; he discovered brewing stills by the Mereroni and, on another occasion, walking with Hugh through lakeside forest, stumbled upon a marijuana plantation.

When they returned with the manager, it was to a handful of buffalo who'd eaten their fill and now lay in a contented daze. But Hugh wasn't enthusiastic about Tom's idea to create a 6,000-acre wildlife sanctuary around the lakeshore, although he agreed for two male Rothschild's giraffe to be brought in from Nakuru National Park. Being browsers, they wouldn't affect the grazing.

'We built a *boma* for them down by the lake and employed a young Maasai gentleman to keep an eye on them,' Ann told me. 'We told him that he could have the honour of naming them.' She imagined they might be nobly named, perhaps Batian and Nelion after former Maasai chiefs. 'Not a bit of it,' she laughed. 'He named them Rambo and Ninja. Rambo was the elderly one...Then we had a stink of a storm, buckets of rain and thunder and lightning and everything else - and he just fell over and died.'

As it happened, the day of Rambo's demise, the Nakuru vet, Hugh Cran, his wife and 23 of her pupils were hiking through Tom's newly-created sanctuary.

'I've never had the chance to P-M a giraffe before,' said Cran delightedly – and set to work. Two of the braver children stayed to watch as he diagnosed old age and pneumonia.

Ninja took up with a herd of buffalo 'as their sort of periscope, in case there was anything coming,' added Ann. Nakuru National Park donated eight young giraffe, ferried to the sanctuary in the back of a pick-up, coats wrapped around their heads to keep them calm. But these newcomers tried to flee. 'Tom spent the next month disentangling them from fences,' Ann said, 'until Ninja decided buffalo were rather boring and he herded them up around him.' The AFEW-funded Giraffe Centre in Nairobi then sent Barbara, a mature female, and they began to breed.

Hugh, who while Ann and I had been chatting had been busy telling another guest the history of gentleman's relish, broke in. 'We've got one-sixth of the world population here of Rothschild's.'

Driving home to lunch, I was delighted to find fourteen of their descendants, including three calves, taking shelter from the searing midday sun beneath the towering eucalyptus trees someone had planted many decades back.

***

Philip Coulson was now a qualified lawyer. He and Tom had parted educational ways after leaving Pembroke, but they'd remained good friends. Fun-loving, clever and multi-talented, Philip often accompanied Tom on safari, which was invariably arranged in what he described as 'true Cholmondeley disorganised fashion,' but always with exciting outcomes. Together they attended the coronation of the 36th Kabaka (or King) of the Kingdom of Buganda in Uganda and spent a night lost on one of Lake Victoria's midge- and reptile-infested Sesse Islands. But after Tom had invited Philip on a trip to Ethiopia, for which Philip had taken time off work only to discover Tom had forgotten and was in England, he vowed there'd be no more. Later he'd be relieved to have avoided some of Tom's misadventures, including being locked up at the Kenya-Ethiopian border.

At Manera in 1992, a new Manager, Nelson Rotich, helped establish a milk processing plant, and came up with the idea of drinking-yoghurt, which Delamere Dairies became the first in Kenya to produce commercially. With Tom, Rotich oversaw the reconstruction of Manera's modest milk shop, situated on prime land beside the Nakuru-Nairobi highway, into Delamere petrol station and farm shop. Like Hugh, Stephen Koigi remained sceptical; this sudden expansion, he maintained, had been the start of major financial problems.

Tom then mooted the idea of opening up Soysambu for tourism. This would entail building accommodation, to which Hugh reluctantly agreed, and Delamere Camp took shape at the north-eastern corner of the lake, beneath the same spreading yellow-barked acacias, *Vachellia xanthophloea*, under which Joseph Thomson had camped, Churchill had picnicked, and troops had trained during the 2nd World War. Long before white men came it had been home to the Sirikwa people, thought to have inhabited the central Rift Valley around 1000 AD from Lake Turkana in the northern part of the Great Lakes region to Lake Eyasi in the south. Soysambu protected many of the round depressions they had built on hillsides, up to 20 metres across and several metres deep, surrounded by stone walls or wooden fences in which they'd kept cattle. Excavations at Hyrax Hill near Nakuru had revealed more about this vanished tribe.

Creating the camp was a hands-on extended-family affair. Jay Hewett helped Ann make patchwork cushions, and Tom built a treehouse in the acacia forest west of the lake, where guests could enjoy a more exclusive night. East African Ornithological Safaris took up the lease.

Within a few years, Tom had become a Director of Delamere Estates, Chairman of Nakuru Wildlife Conservancy and an honorary game warden. He was keenly aware of an increasing need to protect Soysambu's wildlife; Kekopey was severely overgrazed and eroded, and by now failing to support well over a thousand families. Eleanor Cole's house had become a lodge, although views were changing from the rocky bluff with its stone obelisk commemorating Galbraith; vast flocks of itinerant Maasai sheep had eaten the landscape bare, but they wouldn't be able to stay here either - there were plans for a housing estate. Land that had been sold for 600 shillings an acre in 1979 was now worth over 40,000/-.

Believing dairy cattle had been a drain on resources, Tom saw no sense in pumping water to feed cows when cash crops could be more lucrative. Hugh didn't agree, but Tom invested the last of his inheritance from Diana in centre-pivot irrigation for newly-planted vegetables at Manera.

'Tom was mad about centre pivots,' Hugh told me in 2017. 'He said they wouldn't use much water - and he was right.' Hugh paused. The rains had been unreliable. A recent game count had revealed over 11,000 head of game, 5,000 of them zebra, competing with 7,000 cattle. The call of zebra wafted up from the plains below as large numbers trekked thirstily towards the cattle troughs. A sudden whirling gust blew dust at us as we sat on the veranda, blowing magazines and newspapers in all directions. Hugh blew his nose, before going on to expand on his latest schemes; growing rose geraniums to make oil, tapping into an enormous aquifer that lay somewhere beneath us to grow lucerne. He'd also heard that rose geraniums were a cobra deterrent and had asked his gardener to prepare me dozens of these shrubs, ready to plant around my property.

***

From his great-grandfather Tom had also inherited a reckless streak, although Tom's temerarious tendency surfaced more frequently than D's. There were stories of Tom mightily impressing his drunken audience at Gilgil Club by finishing off the dartboard with a pistol. Philip Coulson was there, enjoying the occasion in spite of his stepfather's being Chairman of the club. Other white Kenyans were quick to judge Tom as a spoiled, irresponsible playboy, displaying a fecklessness that ran through the family, although their sentiments were sometimes tinged with envy for this aristocrat who'd been born into fortune. Tom certainly wasn't too bothered if the old-Pembrokian types didn't accept him; having immersed himself in the broader, multi-racial scene of motorsport he had many friends of all colours and creeds, even though during an unsportsmanlike moment Tom had once shot his motorbike at the Rift Valley Motorsports Club in a fit of temper.

After being banned from Gilgil Club for a year, he turned his attention to higher pursuits - paragliding and women. There was no shortage of hopeful young ladies dancing attendance; Tom was charming and exceptionally courteous, with the added attractions of title and land. In Britain he'd developed a taste for 'little English roses,' as Snoo called them, noting that Tom hadn't been thrifty in his attentions.

Then one woman caught his attention because she was completely different. English-born Sally Brewerton, a doctor, had been volunteering in South Sudan when, in January 1997, she'd been held up at gunpoint, and subsequently sent to Kenya to recover. After climbing Mt Kenya, she met up in Naro Moru at the base of the mountain with a friend whose husband was a paragliding friend of Tom's, and Tom happened to be there too. Tired and footsore, Sally didn't feel very sociable, but Tom was very taken by her refreshing outlook, the fact she had no glamorous past, and above all her indifference. "She was without artifice or feminine wiles - no make-up, no outrageous clothes and a totally different outlook," he wrote. He kept in touch as Sally headed to Marsabit to take up a new job with *Medecins Sans Frontieres*.

The Rift Valley offered ideal paragliding conditions, and Tom had been pioneering new launching sites. He'd always had the ability to talk to anyone, and enjoyed chatting to local people in remote areas where his descent attracted much attention, surprising them with his command of Kiswahili and taking genuine interest in their problems. Amongst many other hills, he jumped off Ololokwe, sacred to the Samburu, and near the Maasai Mara he soared with two Tawny Eagles, ending with a perfect landing beside a tourist lodge, returning that June with another paragliding friend, Simon Dolan, and the trusty Waweru. They dropped Tom at the top, where he strode off through thick bush. He was aware of fresh spoor on the game trail but, watching the sky to ascertain air currents, he was ambushed by the young male buffalo charging out of the thickets. Aware they go for the abdomen to disembowel their victim, Tom turned his back, partially cushioned by his paragliding kit. He felt a strong push from behind, flinging him onto the rocks, and could hear the buffalo's breath as it failed to get a grip. Then came the pain as it dug its horn into his right leg, flipping him over its back. The world momentarily spun upside down; then Tom hit the ground.

First he noticed how badly his hands were bleeding. Then he became aware of his mangled leg. The buffalo bolted as he shouted for help. He managed to put his leg up on his paraglider to try and stop the bleeding, and made a tourniquet with his handkerchief. Luckily Dolan and Waweru hadn't yet driven away, and having heard his shouts came running, bandaging Tom's leg with a shirt as a group of Maasai *moran* suddenly materialised. Between them all they carried Tom back to the car.

Far below lay Keekorok airstrip. There was a plane there that had just dropped some tourists, but the pilot refused to take a profusely bleeding passenger. Simon Dolan parked the car in front of the nose wheel and argued with the pilot until he reluctantly took Tom to Wilson Airport, where an ambulance rushed him to Nairobi Hospital. There Tom found himself in the experienced hands of Imre Loefler, a highly recommended surgeon and conservationist, who'd already dealt with fourteen buffalo, seven lion and ten leopard attacks. There followed a series of operations and excruciatingly painful skin grafts.

Rumour and exaggeration had already created a more sensational story; Tom crashing his paraglider, gored by a buffalo as he crawled for help. And this had all supposedly happened in the north of Kenya, so when Tom eventually regained consciousness in some remote hospital the first person he saw was Doctor Sally, with whom he fell madly in love. The truth is more mundane. Sally returned to Marsabit after a trip to North Horr, heard of Tom's plight and visited him. Tom had no shortage of visitors (all of us most impressed to be shown his buffalo horn wounds), but Sally was the one for whom he'd been waiting, and when he was discharged, complete with cast and crutches, he persuaded her to accompany him home.

Sally was appalled at the lack of proper medical care in the area, noting that Soysambu clinic only had five litres of cough medicine, a tub of aspirin, and a bottle of chloroquine. She made some notes before returning to work. As Tom began to visit Marsabit regularly, Sally grew concerned about his leg, from which fragments of dirt from the buffalo's horn, as well as turf, earth and stone from the hillside in the Mara, would continue to work their way out for the next year. One of Sally's patients in Marsabit was a young Rendille girl whose severe burns had been treated the traditional way - fresh cow-dung and straw - after which infection had set in. Horrified, Tom drove her back to the Rift Valley and paid for her to be treated at Kijabe Mission Hospital, where she duly recovered. Perhaps it was partly Tom's great kindness to her patient that touched Sally's heart, and she finally agreed to move to Soysambu, where she immediately began to improve the clinic. That autumn she flew to England with Tom so that he could meet her parents, both medical consultants.

Some years later Tom would admit to his diary that he never fitted into Sally's English life; the lack of adventure and uncertainty bored him - the first indication of the gulf between their backgrounds. But still in the early flush of love, he was building them a new home; a straw-bale house he'd designed himself, set among the tumbled black rocks and leleshwa bush on the wilder side of Ol Jolai, the inaccessible south eastern end, overlooking the western edge of the crater that yawned out from behind Delamere's Nose. He named it Etutu House, using the hill's Maasai name - *Eutut,* the lover. Tom's Folly, as some called it, had high ceilings and windows, redolent of a genteel Georgian home, and required a great deal of cement.

'It is made of bamboo stakes and barley straw,' Hugh told me, 'which was very expensive - all the way from Mau Narok. It's a long way up and down that road. It broke the chassis of the lorry.'

Sally, roped in to ferry builders and materials to the site, was feeling unusually tired. A few evenings later, realising she was pregnant, she told Tom. She'd forgotten to take her pill on one occasion, and now she went through the options. While she was prepared to have a termination as she didn't want to trap him – she was 35; six years older than he – perhaps they should simply get married?

'Well, OK!' replied Tom.

'So I didn't have the bended-knee proposal, but I don't think Tom would ever have got round to doing that,' Sally laughed. 'I'm sure that some people think that I was desperately careless,' she added, 'being a doctor.'

Tom, whose pleasantly uncomplicated life was about to turn turtle, initially felt excited. They'd barely known each other for a year when they flew to England in April 1998, where he managed to steer clear of wedding plans, attending several stag parties with his friends. After the final fling, he arrived back in London late on 15th May, not particularly alert after trying out some magic mushrooms. His future mother-in-law took one look at him and frostily demanded to know *what on earth* he'd been doing? The marriage went ahead the following morning. Although it wasn't a typical up-country Kenya affair involving a two-day party, Tom enjoyed the novelty of the occasion and an excellent lunch. They honeymooned in Japan, where they tried out a traditional wooden bathtub, Tom memorising its dimensions and design meticulously; set among the lava beneath the stars it would be his piece de resistance for Etutu House.

But once they were back at Soysambu Sally was now concerned that her husband's dream house was too snake- and buffalo-infested for raising a child. In the meantime, she busied herself with her clinics. Having managed to secure support from a mission supplying cheap drugs, she trained up several assistants and began nutrition and vaccine surveys. Most local children, she discovered, had iron deficiency and needed de-worming. Then there was the high fluoride content in their drinking water. Often, she was outraged at the poor quality of care patients had received elsewhere.

Although he was delighted by Sally's medical work, noting that Soysambu now offered the only facilities in a valley of 100,000 people, one in Tom and Diana's old racing stables, the other at Mbaruk stores, not far from D's original huts, Tom's diaries reveal his early discontent. Evenings at Flamingo House were now spent talking about farm issues. His new wife had begun arguing with her in-laws over farm finances. She was astonished at the farm's lack of financial accountability, and critical of Hugh's habit of just shrugging off losses.

Rough roads had induced Ann's birth in Ceylon and now that Sally was overdue, Tom took her for a fast drive on rough roads to Ol Donyo Sabuk. Their son was born in Nairobi Hospital that night, on 9th November. Hugh Derrick, named after his two grandfathers, was nicknamed Hughey to avoid confusion. Although Tom was enamoured, indeed filled with hopes and dreams for his perfectly formed son, he quickly tired of domesticity, and reverted to his former restlessness, escaping regularly on long safaris. Sally was increasingly busy with her medical work, but Hughey received no shortage of affection and kindness from an extended family of staff, most notably Waweru, who also attended his baptism in the alkaline waters of Elmenteita. This was a wonderfully photogenic affair; a blond toddler and a small handful of other white faces that included a Catholic Father, flanked by a large congregation of Soysambu's African staff and their children. Transport was by ox-cart, and flamingos provided background sound effects. Looking at the photographs could lead anyone to believe that life was indeed perfect.

CHAPTER 25

Marriage and
Other Challenges

I arrived on Soysambu in September 1999. My daughter, Siana, almost seven, had just started boarding at Pembroke, very much against my wishes, but at least we now lived closer. My son Michael, aged eight, had survived two years of Pembroke already. On their first Exeat weekend, we drove down to the lake in my old Land Rover to admire the flamingos and pelicans. The latter were still breeding on the islands, and we watched them catch air thermals in the late morning, until they'd gained enough height to glide down to neighbouring Lake Nakuru. Here they would pack their pouched beaks with tiny fish and return to Elmenteita to feed their young.

That evening, Hugh took us on a scramble up the conical-shaped hill at the south-eastern end of Soysambu to admire the view. The flamingos were spread in streaks over a reflective green lake, rising up in sudden smoky-pink wafts. Hugh was busy amusing my kids with his stories about stones and trees.

'Excuse me, Lord Delamere,' Siana said, suddenly taking his hand. 'I love your farm.'

'Listen!' I said to my kids that night. We were sitting on the veranda, having blown out the candles to enjoy the light from an almost-full moon. They paused, mid-conversation, as we listened to the flamingos flying south to breed at Lake Natron in northern Tanzania. As they migrated, the moonlight gentle on their backs, they muttered gently to one another, a soothing rubbery sound, as if made by the shoes of passing angels. Knowing that as we slept, these special flamingo-vocals would be treading softly on our dreams, I felt enormously privileged to be here.

I hadn't been sure how my children would react to our small and very basic home, but they loved it, thrilled to be surrounded by so much space. Riding their bikes through the muddiest puddles when it rained, building imaginary farms and roads in the dust, and learning about a wealth of wild creatures that shared this expansive home with us would all prove far more exciting than television or play-stations. Although I missed them when they were at school, or with their father, I would never feel alone here in the middle of nowhere. I'd been lonelier living on the outskirts of Nairobi, even when surrounded by many friends. But now, immersed in so much beauty, I would find deep peace and fulfilment.

A few weeks later I was roped into Soysambu's bi-annual game count, assisted by Simon Combes, who'd returned to his childhood haunts, renting the house Diana had built for her secretary next to Main House; its small size more than compensated for by the vastness of the view. I knew nothing about counting wild animals but, as we drove onto the plains between a rising sun and a setting moon, Simon spotted hidden creatures with the canny perception of a leopard. At almost 60, his sandy-coloured curly hair whitening and receding, he remained youthful, fit, and strong, with an impish smile. Simon's childhood spent shooting and skinning animals had given him an intimate knowledge of animal anatomy, which made it easier to accurately recreate on canvas the inhabitants of the animal kingdom he revered and he was now an internationally acclaimed wildlife artist. He was kind, generous and astonishingly self-effacing, never too busy to inspire local farm workers and their children with talks and slideshows. These children walked to school barefooted and climbed a tree if they met a buffalo on the way, sharing pencil stubs and desks in the dark mud-floored classrooms where government teachers didn't always turn up and resources were almost non-existent, but at least they were getting better medical care, thanks to Sally. With his excellent command of Kiswahili, Simon would influence many of these young lives, nurturing an interest in conservation and proving to the more artistically inclined that they could use their talents. He was also a wise confidante for Hugh, having known him for much of his life.

Kat, Simon's fiancée, arrived from America soon afterwards. A tall and attractive, kind-hearted blonde divorcee, she'd met Simon through an art gallery in America, and now she would also fall in love with Soysambu. As my closest neighbours, five kilometres away, they would become good friends. When I had to power my laptop at Head Office, my kids wandered over to hear Simon's endless repertoire of entertaining stories; the time when he was a boy and took off all his clothes and sat on them during a rainstorm to keep them dry, the time he was charged by an elephant...not to mention his amusing limericks. On one occasion I found Michael helping Kat in the kitchen, while Siana was wielding a paintbrush in front of one of Simon's masterpieces, worth at least £35,000.

'I'm helping Simon,' she told me as she slapped some oil paint onto the forest-clad background behind a herd of buffalo.

She'd added even more to the background than Monet, Simon explained with a relaxed smile. Monet was a hand-raised Grey-backed Camaroptera, a small bird with green wings, usually perched on top of Simon's canvas, adding its own touches every time it emptied its bowels. I was looking forward to meeting Simon's son, Guy, who was arriving imminently. 'He's an artist too,' Simon told me, 'but he's much better than me!'

These happy days fell on the cusp of some troubling times for Delamere Estates. I'd heard Hugh worry about large-scale financial problems and had noticed Ann's stress, as well as a certain amount of strain between Tom and Sally. David Heath had left and there'd been an interlude with Renaldo Retief as General Manager. Now, in the new millennium, Retief was replaced by Kenyan Manager, Christopher Chirchir. The country was struggling through a desperate drought and Lake Elmenteita shrank to a sulphurous puddle. The ox-wagon passed my gate daily, piled up with dead cattle. Wild animals grew weaker until their emaciated corpses became food for circling vultures. It was Easter Sunday when a vast dust storm obscured all horizons, followed by a deluge of rain, battering the sun-bleached bones that hyena, jackals and vultures had scattered over the dry plains. We danced on what had been the lawn, dust transforming into slippery mud beneath our bare feet.

Sally was expecting their second child, returning to England for the birth. Tom followed with some reluctance. To lift his spirits - literally - Sally suggested he learned to fly at nearby Shoreham. They were thrilled when a son was born on 3rd July, although they'd been so certain of a girl (to be named Eleanor) that the baby was initially nameless, but a few days later they decided on Henry Gilbert.

On his return, Tom bought his first plane; a PZL-104 Wilga.

'It was a Polish plane - it had been used by Greenpeace or someone,' Hugh told me disparagingly in 2015. 'Tom likes extraordinary and complicated planes. It started on compressed air. The slightest leak and the bloody thing wouldn't start. But it could land on very rough stuff.'

Tom had crashed it. 'He is very stubborn, he wouldn't listen,' Hugh continued, 'he insisted on taking off in a crosswind. We had two runways on Manera - when we still owned that bit of Manera - so he didn't have to. I said, "This is a tail-dragger - it won't take off in a crosswind"...'

'Hugh was knocked out,' said Ann, 'and dragged out from under a leaking fuel tank by Sally.'

Tom's next plane would be a Cherokee 235, which he sold on as he fancied a Navian - the only one in Kenya. This would be eventually crashed by a friend of Tom's. The friend would walk away without serious injuries, but the uninsured plane was a write-off.

'It had belonged to a chap called Hall,' Hugh said. 'He'd painted a picture of a naked girl on its tail.' He looked up from his novel. 'Tom crashed my plane too. He landed on a road across the runway, instead of the runway, and hit a bump. Somewhere in Laikipia,' he added crossly - and returned to his book.

Ann glanced up from her tapestry. 'Do you remember those two eland with locked horns? You and Tom are like that.'

***

In 2001 a slump in tourism followed the 9/11 terrorist attacks in New York. Delamere camp faltered to a halt, even though Lake

Elmenteita was now internationally recognised for its great white pelicans, listed as an Important Bird Area.

The following year there was a feeling of great hope when Mwai Kibaki was voted in as president, finally ending the Moi-era. This wouldn't do service to Soysambu, though; by 2003, awaiting new government policy, Kenya Wildlife Service banned all game-cropping. *Fair Game* was obliged to close. A count revealed that Soysambu now had 13,000 head of wild animals, numbers it could no longer control. Old wildlife migration routes were now blocked by an expanding sprawl of human settlement, so these animals had nowhere else to go. If landowners were no longer permitted to cull those animals trapped on their land, their numbers would continue to grow.

To add to Delamere Estates' problems, the Kenya Revenue Authority were claiming large sums of money owed. Something to do with an accountant, Hugh told me, 'who didn't realise we should have been paying VAT...' Tom was obliged to use the remainder of Diana's money to pay off the farm's mounting overdraft.

Meanwhile, Maasai activists, their forebears having tried various routes since 1913 to appeal for the return of their Laikipia lands, were claiming that all 99-year land leases would expire on August 15th, 2004, in spite of the 1915 extension of leases to 999 years. Ranches were stormed, police were heavy-handed in their response and a compensation figure of ten billion shillings was mooted, but ultimately the Maasai and their Samburu cohorts didn't get anywhere. 'Elephants, zebras and all other herbivores are having a holiday in these so called settler ranches,' raged John Letai, President of the Organisation for Indigenous Peoples of Africa, noting that the drought was killing thousands of Maasai livestock, 'while the rightful owners whom history deprived of this gold mine are languishing in abject poverty.' Others complained of being squatters on their own land, even to the extent of supporting Robert Mugabe's policy of land seizures in Zimbabwe. But it wasn't an entirely black and white problem. In her book, *Unsettled; Denial and Belonging among White Kenyans*, Janet McIntosh refers to the 2004 Ndung'u report on the illegal and irregular allocation of land to the families of Kenya's former presidents, pointing out that

'Maasai may have felt it easier to attack "colonizers" - as a symbol antithetical to the nation - than Kenya's political power players.'

Late in the afternoon of 12th December 2004, a year after Simon and Kat had got married in a quiet ceremony on Soysambu, Simon laid down his paintbrushes in front of his half-finished canvas to take a walk with Kat and Mary Wykstra, an American cheetah researcher living at the northern end of Soysambu. They reached the highest point on Delamere's Nose and began descending towards the last rays of the setting sun when a large bull buffalo suddenly charged into their path. It went straight for Simon, and tossed him into the air repeatedly. Kat and Mary screamed, throwing water bottles and rocks at the buffalo until it melted into the darkening bush.

Simon had been badly gored in his chest and stomach. Kat held him on her lap, talking to him, trying to staunch the flow of blood. By now mobile phones had arrived in Kenya, with increasing coverage in remoter areas like Soysambu, but it was a public holiday and Mary failed to get hold of anyone. Eventually she managed to contact Simon's son, Guy, running a lodge on Lake Baringo, who called Flying Doctors. Mary then managed to get hold of Tom, who drove at top speed to the base of the Nose and then scrambled to the top, later returning with torches, blankets and water. Nobody knew where the buffalo was lurking as darkness dropped onto the rocky hillside.

It wasn't until late that night when the rescue helicopter arrived. Tom used his headlights to guide them, then showed the stretcher-bearers the way up the steep slopes by torchlight. As they moved Simon, he died.

I'd dreamed I'd heard a helicopter before I awoke to Guy's voice message on my phone. I stood at my kitchen window, looking out at the Nose beneath a crimson sunrise, throwing light on the sudden emptiness of a new day. As I drove to see Kat, the early sun caught the silvery spiders' webs strung between the thorn bushes, their suspended dewdrops shining like diamonds, as if Simon's generous spirit had spilled over the plains. The Nose was suddenly obscured by cloud, but Tom went back up that day, staying until he'd shot the buffalo.

A celebration of Simon's life was held on the spacious veranda of one of Mary Delamere's old cowsheds which Tom had converted into a research centre. Many mourners, including hundreds of farm workers and their families, listened to eulogies and appreciations from friends in English and Kiswahili. Aged seventeen, Simon had been called up for military training, the King's African Rifles sending him to Uganda where he taught future dictator Idi Amin. After independence he'd trained with Kenyan paratroopers in England, becoming their first commander in Kenya, painting portraits of people and wildlife as a hobby while sitting in the NFD waiting to be ambushed by Somali militia. Since becoming a professional artist in 1974, he'd been bitten by a tiger in Bengal and tracked snow leopards in Mongolia - and then a buffalo had taken him on home turf. A great man had been lost to his family and friends, as well as Soysambu. But Simon's death was also a sign of changing times. For five years we'd walked confidently through the bush and climbed volcanic hills without a second thought. But there were significantly more animals all over Soysambu now, especially buffalo, and this tragedy would make us all more cautious.

After the service, close friends and family slipped away up the hill to a glade overlooking the lake. Hugh, who'd turned seventy that year, read one of Simon's limericks. Guy read Kipling's 'If.' As the descending sun gilded the lake below and a military bugler played the Last Post, the pelicans did a final fly-past.

By now Lake Elmenteita was recognised as a Wetland of International Importance, listed as a Ramsar Site in 2005, which encompassed both the lake and a buffer zone of over a thousand square kilometres. But increasingly there were multiple ongoing environmental threats to its unprotected eastern and south eastern shores; degradation of the catchment area through deforestation and abstraction of water from springs, effluent from a timber-treatment plant, urban waste and raw sewage disposal into feeder streams, unregulated mining of salt and sand, pollution from the diatomite mines at Kariandusi and increased lakeshore and riparian development. NEMA, the National Environment Management Authority established in 2002, seemed powerless to stop anything, with conservation taking a back seat on government agendas. Nor were conservationists endearing themselves to the larger population; in January 2006 Joan Root, best known for the wildlife documentaries made with her ex-husband, Alan Root, would be shot on the shores of Lake Naivasha, where she had striven to protect the fragile riparian land from illegal fishermen. George Adamson, of *Born Free* fame, had met a similar fate in 1989, nine years after his wife, Joy, had also been murdered. Richard Leakey, the renowned paleoanthropologist and conservationist who'd revamped the wildlife service at Moi's request, creating the new Kenya Wildlife Service in 1990 and proving an outspoken chairman, had lost both legs in a plane crash in 1993, speculated to be sabotage.

On Soysambu the increasing numbers of wildlife taking advantage of the grass and water, not to mention the costly purchase of mineral supplements required for cattle to survive, meant Hugh had been forced to reduce cattle numbers. But Tom remained aware that overall wildlife numbers nationwide had dropped by 70% in only three decades. He realised it was vital to protect the wildlife, in spite of the odds, and so started the Greater Lake Elmenteita Conservation Area, signing a Memorandum of Understanding with KWS, and pursuing his idea of a wildlife migration corridor with the Italian owner of Marula, another large estate, situated between Soysambu and Manera, and protecting a large riparian area bordering Lake Naivasha.

"There is no room for aesthetic appreciation when on the breadline," Tom writes in his diary, "but the greater effect is that Kenya itself is using all that makes it unique to turn it into yet another rural poverty trap." Aware of the economic gulf between Soysambu and the surrounding small-scale farmers, who had little hope of success in this low-rainfall area, against a backdrop of Kenya's failure to develop at a rate to sustain her population growth, he witnessed daily incursions into Soysambu by tree-cutters, grazers and poachers. They stole cedar fence posts for firewood and used the wire to make snares, operating illegally but with a sense of entitlement on what they saw as a rich white man's land, stolen from their black ancestors. "Forty years ago we had seven neighbours," Tom would write in 2007. "We now have 350..."

Poaching on Soysambu reached horrific heights. On walks I found half-dead reedbuck, eyes glazing as their windpipes were constricted by tight wire nooses. As I drove to Pembroke, the sight of dead, dying and injured animals was becoming horribly common. I'd witnessed the massacre of over a hundred eland along a single fence line hung with snares, these vast majestic antelope lying in various stages of strangulation. It had reached the stage where Soysambu's policy when faced with poachers' dogs was to shoot on sight. One of my own dogs, a rescued stray and incurable wanderer, had been shot before they saw her collar.

Sally was involved in Voluntary Counselling and Testing clinics for HIV, extending these to Naivasha and training up counsellors. 'Lots of politics,' she later told me, 'although it was a good programme, testing almost 1,000 people a month.' Soysambu's two clinics now had VCT programmes, plus a post-test club; people who hadn't tested positive who could persuade others to take the test. She'd also started part-time work in a medical practice in the Nairobi suburb of Karen.

The marriage was less successful. Tom had been travelling extensively, visiting music festivals with a more hedonistic crowd, realising that he wasn't inclined to monogamy. He'd especially loved Mongolia, with its horse-riding, fishing and birthday celebrations of Genghis Khan. With his penchant for finding interesting people doing unusual things, he'd joined up with a gazelle researcher he'd met in a nightclub in Ulan Bator, and helped catch and radio collar a handful of the one million goitred gazelles that roamed eastern Mongolia.

Hughey had started nursery school near Nakuru, but after a car accident with Waweru driving, in which fortunately no-one was hurt, Sally moved with the children to Nairobi. Marriage counselling hadn't helped, and she'd resigned herself to an official separation. She wasn't to know that another twist of fate was about to plunge Tom, his family and Soysambu into further disaster, causing the old Happy Valley hype to rear its weary head all over again.

CHAPTER 26

A Fatal Shooting

The security situation in Kenya had worsened. Car-jackings and attacks had increased. In fifteen months there'd been four armed robberies on Soysambu and Manera. The workshop manager had been attacked twice, with the slaughterhouse manager also targeted.

On 19th April 2005, Tom had been up since dawn with a young Englishman, a friend of a friend, tracking down an old bull buffalo that had been chasing children as they walked to school. As honorary game warden, he was permitted to shoot it under the Problematic Animal Control Act. Having done the deed, and leaving his staff to load the heavy carcass into the back of his Land Rover to take to the slaughterhouse, he and his companion returned home. He was just dozing off after lunch when his phone rang. It was the General Manager, Christopher Chirchir, reporting that there was an armed robbery at the slaughterhouse, urging Tom to get there quickly, Flamingo House being less than half a kilometre away. His driver had been there, evading capture and managing to run to Lanet house.

Tom, suddenly pumped with adrenalin, hastily unlocked the gun safe. Handing his rifle to the young guest and asking him to cover for him, but to keep his distance, he took out his pistol, then strode the short distance to the slaughterhouse.

An unfamiliar white car with civilian number plates was parked outside, but otherwise there was no sign of anyone; just an ominous silence. Tom crept around one side of the building and crouched, his pistol ready, his heart pounding as he peered cautiously around the corner.

It all happened very fast. A man turned and fired a pistol, the ear-splitting noise resonating in Tom's brain as the bullet struck the corner wall four inches from his head. Flying splinters galvanised him into action; he fired back. The intruder ducked and ran towards the main farm road. There was a confusion of shots as Tom reloaded, his hands shaking uncontrollably. He crept backwards, halting abruptly as he spotted another armed man through a side door, aiming a large black pistol at the front door. As Tom shouted, 'Drop your gun!' a smartly-dressed lady with neatly braided hair emerged from the small office. Keeping his pistol pointed at both, Tom phoned Stephen to tell him to call the police.

The slaughterhouse manager and fifteen workers, all of whom had been made to lie on the wet floor amongst the cattle carcasses in various stages of dismemberment, now stumbled into the sunshine in a state of shock. '*Jambazi!*' they cried, all speaking simultaneously. Gangsters! One female worker was in tears; she'd been terrified by the thought of rape.

Tom kept his pistol pointed at the two intruders, who now claimed to be undercover officers from the Kenya Wildlife Service. Tom remained sceptical. Why weren't they in uniform? Where was their identification? The Elmenteita police arrived, congratulating Tom on capturing two thugs. But where was the third man? Then they found him, a short distance away, dead of a gunshot wound in his neck.

More policemen arrived, and some officers of the Kenya Wildlife Service, and things took a U-turn.

'This is murder!' shouted the Nakuru National Park warden.

Tom was horrified to discover that the dead man had indeed been one of three KWS rangers from Naivasha. Tom was placed under arrest, obliged to accompany the senior police officer to Gilgil Police Station, where he was relieved of one shoe and his belt - to prevent him running away or hanging himself - and locked in a cell. He slept fitfully, hip and shoulder pressing into the concrete floor, waking periodically throughout the night as various drunks were harvested from the streets, the smell of their urine permeating the cell.

The following morning Tom learned that the late Samson Ole Sisina, a Maasai, had been one of three rangers of junior rank from

Naivasha who, acting independently, had decided to mount an undercover anti-poaching operation. Tom wondered if it could have been something to do with the rogue buffalo - somebody with a grudge 'informing' on him?

Hugh and Ann were appalled to hear that a man had been shot while also very worried about what might happen to Tom. Sally was equally upset, ready to return and offer support. I heard the news from another tenant. At this stage there was a confusion of rumours and stories circulating, but I felt there was something about the whole incident that didn't add up.

Tom was moved to Naivasha, its Police Station perched high above the town, looking down towards the calmly reflective lake. There was little time to appreciate the view as he was hustled backstage to a dark corridor off which were four cells, and a stinking toilet at the far end where a cat-sized rat crept down a pipe. One cell was for women, kept firmly locked in, the others were free for all, run on a ranking system by their inmates; the farthest for the desperate, dirty, injured and insane. The middle, Tom wrote, housed "a rowdy bunch of toughs." The top ranking cell was kept for ten mature men. Tom was relieved to be locked into the farthest cell, alone. Waweru brought him a blanket from home, and he lay down on the foul-smelling damp floor, using it to muffle the stench. Any moonlight that might have filtered through the barred window was blocked by sheets of metal. He slept fitfully, awakening in his pitch-dark cell to the stench of home brew and a bloodstained criminal who demanded to share his blanket, pressing against Tom, who tried to move away. And so it went on until first light when the senior cellmates, intrigued at this relatively rare sight of a white man in the cells, invited Tom to join their dark dwelling.

Amidst the continual turnover of remand prisoners a daily routine took shape; one cup of tea and a plate of *ugali* (maize meal) a day, although families were permitted to bring food. Sally also brought flattened cardboard boxes on which to sleep. At morning, evening and midnight there was a roll call.

'Tom Choh...le..mod...leh,' the policeman would shout, stumbling over the name.

'*Tom Choh...le...mod...leh,*' echoed the noisy young toughs, creating much amusement. It was prudent to step quickly into the corridor and answer.

Nobody had any reading matter, so everyone talked loudly and at once, usually in Kikuyu or Kiswahili, unaware of Tom's excellent command of Kiswahili and understanding of some Kikuyu. He thus discovered that in the majority view, a white man who killed a black man must be killed, and his land given to landless small-scale farmers. There were plenty of fish poachers, picked up in the protected waters of Naivasha, coming and going with startling regularity, having been taken to court only to be released. They agreed unanimously about their entitlement to fish or hunt wherever they desired.

In spite of feeling keenly aware of a deep cultural gulf, Tom made some friends, including Stanley, a lanky Maasai, who came with a long story involving a treacherous woman and money, punching those he didn't like, keeping the top cell free of opportunists. He urged Tom to make reparations to the KWS officer Ole Sisina's family the traditional Maasai way, to avoid repercussions.

The tedium of Tom's days was alleviated by daily visits to the dusty CID office behind the police station to answer questions, or visitors. 'Tom Choh...le..mod...leh,' the policeman would summon, with the usual echoes - *Tom Choh...le...mod...leh*. He would then be escorted through the heavy metal door to the right of the front counter. Here he'd blink in the sudden brightness, humbled by a daily stream of well-wishers, from overseas friends to ex or current girlfriends, farm workers and even ex-employees. After a few days a policeman on duty commented on the fact that ninety percent of Tom's visitors were black.

Rather than overthink possible future scenarios, Tom concentrated on keeping sane, clean and healthy, as a fortnight passed, although he was aware of the public outcry; anonymous e-mails sent to those who did business with Delamere Estates, Maasai threatening to invade Soysambu, and the press branding him a racist.

When I visited with small treats - croissants or grapes and a re-supply of books - Tom, always composed and appreciative, told me he managed to read these under the corridor light. Afterwards, the clang of metal doors and drawing of bolts as they took him back to the cells jangled into my nightmares. Hugh and Ann took food, soap and loo paper, Ann writing in an e-mail to friends that Tom was "in good heart," that they were grateful to be permitted to visit, although she did admit that waiting for a hearing was somewhat stressful.

Upon the recommendation of Philip Coulson, Sally engaged Fred Ojiambo as defence lawyer. A British-educated barrister, Fred was a seasoned Advocate of the High Court of Kenya, his smooth British accent concealing a formidable presence; he'd chaired the Law Society of Kenya and was now a partner at Nairobi's leading law firm, Kaplan & Strattan.

On the day of his hearing, Tom was taken by police escort to the Nakuru courts, hustled away from the demonstrations outside and hastily led to the basement where there was standing space only in its row of barred cells, amidst strong smells of unwashed bodies and urine. Through the noise his escorting policemen reassured him and found him a seat; they'd taken to their quietly compliant, extremely polite prisoner.

In court all rose for Justice Muga Aponde, who'd seen almost two decades on the bench. He had a kind face, a way of listening that made it evident he was fully engaged.

'Not guilty,' Tom said, when it was his turn to plead. Through a roar of noise outside he just heard Justice Aponde say: '...to be remanded at Naivasha Prison until the next hearing in two weeks hence.' As they were driven back, Tom noticed with pangs of longing how fresh Soysambu looked after the rains; a golden sprinkling of impala leaping away through green-topped acacias. The policeman beside him cheerfully reassured him that all would be well as he imprinted the scenes on his memory to see him through the days ahead.

He could see Manera's dairy sheds from the prison gates. Handcuffed, head shaved to prevent transmission of lice, he waited as his details were taken before he was escorted beneath eighteen-foot-high walls to the remand block at the far end of a treeless courtyard. '*Karibu!*' shouted a host of men on the other side of the

247

last gate on the left, welcoming Tom as 92nd remand prisoner into their small concrete block.

Tom fell asleep amidst the general cacophony; people shouting across the hall and an evangelical group alternately singing and bawling in the end cell, waking to the first calls of birds, waiting to be unlocked over an hour later and served thin, grey-coloured *uji* (maize meal porridge) in tin cans. The morning was bright as prisoners squatted companionably in the sun, warming up slowly after a night on cold concrete. As they chewed the thick crust that formed when the porridge cooled, other inmates told Tom how much nicer it tasted now that *sugar* had been added. The Christian contingent began to sing and clap, joined by others, and the morning took on a festive air. That day he was moved to one of about 40 ten-by-seven foot cells, the small window's view blocked by a wall. Prisoners were issued with a blanket and even a mattress to sleep singly, or in groups of three or five. "This was to prevent buggery," Tom wrote, "although I was never allowed to mention this in my letters out." It was luxury compared to the police station.

Visitors involved complicated procedures; a message written in triplicate, signing of books, handcuffing, endless protracted greetings at gates during a slow 20-minute walk, accompanied by duty guards, to the visiting cubicles. Tom could then communicate for five minutes through a large reinforced glass window, one warder with him, two with the visitor. The handsets were broken, so he had to stand at the back of the cubicle and shout, his voice echoing off cement walls, along with those of other prisoners and their visitors.

Sally Cholmondeley remained calmly supportive, on one occasion bringing along a mutual friend, Sally Dudmesh, the latter reduced to tears at the sight of Tom's handcuffs. Sally Dudmesh was my age, slightly older than Tom, with blonde curls, green eyes and an attractive smile. She'd first visited Kenya in 1980, aged 18, returning several years later to complete her Social Anthropology dissertation on the Maasai, then staying on, designing and making jewellery. She'd first met Tom while they were both on separate safaris to northern Kenya. He'd noticed the pretty girl sitting atop a Land Cruiser and they were briefly introduced. As he'd stood beside the road between Wamba and Baragoi, hands in his khaki pockets of the short shorts that were fashionable in the 80s, talking to the driver of the Land Cruiser, Sally Dudmesh had no idea how closely their futures would become intertwined.

Tom would write in minute detail about his incarceration, partly with a sense of amazement, and he was genuinely fascinated by his fellow prisoners and their stories, but also because this was an entirely different experience for a significant landowner who'd been privileged to live in relative luxury with plenty of space around him. Main meals consisted of cold lumps of hard and gritty *ugali* (maize meal) with a scoop of soupy *sukuma wiki* (boiled kale) and two thimblefuls of rancid oil. Twice-weekly boiled beans and two chunks of rubbery boiled meat were served as extra treats, all of this eaten with the fingers. In spite of small amounts of salt and chilli powder secreted in by his visitors to spice up the bland food, Tom was losing weight. One prisoner contracted typhoid. There was one urinal and one toilet for 100 people; a stained bowl over which the user had to squat. The archaic flush system seldom coped with its load. In the same room a pipe stuck out of the wall under which a cold shower could be taken, an effortless way of washing the floor. Three sinks were used to empty the contents of the night chamber pots. Tom learned to brush his teeth while holding his breath so as not to gag. Others cleaned their teeth in their cells, spitting out into the hall, where bins of water were thrown out each morning at an attempt to clean them.

For daily exercise he walked brisk circuits around the concrete apron (55 by 20 paces), followed by a solo hour of self-styled yoga during the long nights. He was horrified by the old prisoner pens from the Moi-era, where three current cabinet ministers had been confined; cramped, kennel-like structures now covered in blankets and mattresses as they got a daily airing. Plenty of political prisoners had scrawled their lamentations on the walls, including those who'd been locked up for their supposed roles in the 1982 coup.

Among new arrivals was the bloodstained lyncher who'd tried

to share Tom's blanket in the police station. He plaited his beard and tried to endear himself to Tom, offering to clean his cell and - unnervingly - 'to do anything else' Tom might wish. Then there were two men who'd been involved in armed hold-ups, one of them while dressed in prison warder's uniform. The police beat them severely on arrival, leaving them handcuffed together for four days, making their nights and toilet visits most uncomfortable.

'Why are *white people* so frightened of knives?' one sneered at Tom, before telling him about the white girl he'd attacked, using a falsetto voice to imitate her: 'Don't hurt me, don't kill me...'

In his diaries Tom never mentioned the inter-prison football match he'd sponsored, which would become an annual event. I was told about it by Peter Ouko, a prisoner in the team sent from Kamiti Maximum Security Prison. It was the first ever held, involving three teams, the third from Nakuru Prison, and a two-day tournament. Visiting prisoners spent the night, and Tom arranged the slaughter of a Soysambu bull for the feast afterwards.

On 18th May it was time to return to court. Tom put on his suit, now hanging off him. Braced against the side in the rear of the windowless prison lorry as it hit every hole in the road, he arrived shaken and bruised. He was further shocked by the large crowd of young Maasai demonstrators, roused by a contingent of elders waiting outside the court building in the shade of some Jacaranda trees. White people in Kenya tend to be unfamiliar with how the rest of the population live, particularly those who are unfortunate enough to end up in prison, and Tom was only beginning to grasp how he'd underestimated public reaction, that this would ricochet into a sensational story, one with bigger ramifications than the Erroll murder. To the press this was headline news; a prominent white aristocrat in the dock whose victim was black! They didn't bother to fact check, most journalists referring to him as "Lord Delamere's grandson," interpreting his outward serenity as "expressionless" - by which they implied heartless. The implicit moral to most Kenyans was cast in the light of their perceived decadence of the white population in Kenya, a judgement based on the tainted Happy Valley story.

Relieved to escape the rowdy demonstrations, Tom was hastened into the cells below, where hours crawled by until it was time for his hearing. Fred had won his application for a team of ballistics experts to examine the two guns seized at the scene, and presented Tom's innocence with deft expertise. Philip Murgor, Director of Public Prosecution, then announced that the office of the Attorney General had recommended a *nolle prosequi* due to strong evidence against the murder charge. There was insufficient evidence to proceed, nor would a manslaughter charge hold water; it was clear that Tom had killed in self-defence. Justice Apondi sent Tom back to prison before his final hearing the following day. Back in Naivasha, Tom's fellow inmates were jubilant at the news and there was much hand-shaking and back-patting.

Packed into the back of the prison lorry the following morning, with three other prisoners and twenty warders, Tom felt alarmed by the driver's apparent haste. It was still a shock when the truck overturned with a loud bang, sliding along the tarmac for 100 yards. Lying on his back with three people on top, Tom waited his turn as they were helped out of the lorry, unnerved by the large gathering crowd. He realised he was drenched with blood, slowly working out it was another prisoner's; six people were badly injured. Various other means of transport materialised to take them all to hospital or court. Already in shock, Tom was now overwhelmed by the frenzy of shouting demonstrators waving fists, weapons and placards outside the court, and startled by the constant flash of cameras.

Finally the court formalities were over. After the Attorney General's recommendation of the dismissal of legal proceedings, and the Director of Public Prosecution's summing up, Tom was no longer accused. He returned to Naivasha Prison, where a friend collected him the following morning. He could barely swallow the beer he was handed; everything felt too much after the events of the previous day. By the time they left the tarmac to turn into Soysambu, he was shivering uncontrollably. At Main House, he escaped to wallow in a hot bath, longing to return to Flamingo House with Sally, who'd returned in a final bid to salvage their marriage.

***

Meanwhile there was a rumour that it hadn't been Tom who'd fired the fatal bullet, a story that persisted, although Tom was non-committal. In 2017, I heard the whole story again from the former slaughterhouse manager. He'd been on duty that Sunday, summoned to the slaughterhouse to speak to some tenacious visitors, who insisted they wanted to buy game meat. *Fair Game* had long ceased to operate and selling game meat was illegal, so the strangers eventually left empty-handed. On passing Tom's pick-up, dead buffalo in the back, they returned, produced guns and told the manager that he and his colleagues were under arrest. They shoved them roughly into the slaughterhouse, forcing them onto the wet floor. 'We are not afraid of *wazungu*,' sneered one man when the manager asked if he could make a call to Tom, adding that he had sixteen bullets, enough for them all. As Tom approached, the manager heard the armed man outside warning his fellow captors. From the floor where he sat, he saw Tom's head through the small high window, but didn't dare call out. He heard the first gunshots, saw Tom duck, then heard some return shots.

He'd been puzzled by shots coming from 'all around,' he told me, adding that in his view it hadn't been Tom who'd killed Samson Ole Sisina. 'He was shot from the wrong side,' he explained. He believed that Sisina had panicked and, thinking he'd shot Tom, run from the scene until he was shot down some distance from the slaughterhouse, out of Tom's pistol range. When they were assessing the crime scene, before the police had arrived, he'd noticed Tom's visitor, 'a young *mzungu*,' standing some distance off holding a .22 rifle. 'He wasn't a Kenyan white,' the manager concluded. 'I never saw him again.' He heard Tom tell the young man to return to Flamingo House, before turning to the manager and his colleagues, speaking to them in Swahili, "Say it was me."

Apart from withholding the truth, Tom had been on the wrong side of the law because his companion wasn't licensed to carry the firearm, this manager pointed out, but neither were the number plates on the white car the same as those on the insurance disc on the windscreen. Nobody had been acting within the law that day.

I noticed the tears in the manager's eyes as we sat quietly for a while in his office watching the late afternoon sun recede through the open door, listening to a flock of noisy brown babblers in a nearby tree, voicing their alarm.

Two years later I chanced to meet a KWS officer, who'd been based in Nakuru at the time. Tom, he insisted, had arrived with a rifle, walked up to the car and shot the driver as he was trying to run away. It was murder in cold blood, he told me firmly.

***

A few years after Tom's release from Naivasha Prison, a documentary called *Kenya Murder Mystery* was made by Michael Cunningham-Reid's daughter, Fiona. In it she refers to Tom as her cousin, telling how, as she watched events unfold, her initial poor opinion would change to sympathy. She interviews Fred Ojiambo. Before taking on the case, he explains, everything he knew about the Delameres was negative, but this changed completely when he met Hugh, and especially Tom. 'He is extremely sensitive to the needs of people around him,' Fred said, adding that he'd really grown to like him.

In another documentary, *Last White Man Standing*, in which Hugh describes the incident as 'a confused shootout' as Tom tried to defend his employees, Tom tells the interviewer, 'I'm going to go back home and be with family, and try to live as calm and uneventful life as possible.'

***

Tom's release instigated further demonstrations. The case had also tossed salt into the brew of something more political. Activists pointed out that the rich and poor were unequal in the eyes of the law. In Britain, *The Independent* related how teargas was fired at Nairobi protestors, who included 200 members of the Kenyan Human Rights Commission, adding that 500 Maasai armed with clubs and sticks were marching along the roads to the famed Maasai Mara. If Tom wasn't returned to jail, a Maasai councillor told a Kenyan journalist, they'd invade Soysambu, where they'd perform tribal rituals at the place their kinsman had been shot. A protestor shouted out, 'Proper justice would be for the Delamere family to go through the same pain as the Sisina family!'

While protestors and most journalists continued to frame the story as a black-white battle over 'stolen' land, a few acknowledged that it was more complicated. With a nomadic way of life no longer sustainable due to Kenya's dramatic population increase, a shortage of land was increasingly forcing Maasai into conflict with Kenyans all over the country. The traditional Maasai belief that their God had bequeathed them all land meant Soysambu was simply part of this deal, along with all God's water; during droughts Maasai frequently cut water pipes along the Nakuru road to water their stock, leaving precious water to gush wastefully.

But the Tom and Sisina story was a gift to popular opinion as well as lurid imagination. Journalistic accuracy was sacrificed for sensationalism, Soysambu - enlarged to 100,000 acres – was rebranded "Happy Valley." One journalist referred to Tom's "cockney" accent, claiming that his ancestor had sat in a well-known hotel quaffing whisky while he "mistreated black people for sport." Another claimed *Hugh* had married Diana (to his horror). *The Telegraph*, in Britain, who'd already titled earlier pieces 'Dark days put paid to Happy Valley's idyll,' and 'Happy Valley heir held for bushmeat murder,' got its generations muddled up too, as did the BBC.

'The state law office has decided not to please mass hysteria,' Fred Ojiambo calmly told the *Guardian*, 'but to act in accordance with the law.'

There was talk of Sisina's family taking out a civil action against the Delameres, and eventually, in a tacit acknowledgement of traditional Maasai custom, a settlement would be agreed with Sisina's widow and eldest son that included cows, land and education for all his eight children. It wasn't something Hugh and Ann would talk about, but a decade later, one journalist, Joyce Nyairo, would address the question of why the Delameres had done so. 'When push came to shove,' she wrote, 'Tom's father, Lord Hugh, resorted to his "Maasainess" rather than his English peerage.'

***

In this febrile climate of feeling Sally felt Tom shouldn't be on

Soysambu. She was angered by his continued correspondence with an English girlfriend, as well as busy juggling her work and life in Nairobi with the needs of their children, so she suggested Sally Dudmesh take him on safari to northern Kenya.

Tom and Sally Dudmesh thus followed a train of hired camels down the remote Seiya Lugga, accompanied by three Samburu men, who didn't care - or possibly even know - who Tom was. The monotonous wooden clang of camel bells and the singing of the men sank gently into Tom's troubled mind. And at night he could fall into the arms of Sally Dudmesh. It had been a traumatic month and excuses might be made about the effects of stress, or Tom and Sally Cholmondeley's incompatibility, but people were still shocked at Tom's latest infidelity, especially after his estranged wife had made the attempt to return after his release. When I talked to Sally Dudmesh in 2017, she was emphatic that she wasn't the type who broke up marriages, that the marriage had been over. As part of Tom's group of friends at a music festival, also travelling with them to Mongolia, she had frequently voiced her disapproval when he'd been unfaithful. 'Tom had *such* a bad reputation with women that I didn't want anything to do with him!' she told me as we watched the resident pair of Lilac-breasted Rollers noisily defending their nest from some unseen raptor. But that impression of Tom had been back in the 1980s, and now she'd fallen in love.

On their return to Nairobi, adamant she wouldn't be a *secret mistress,* Sally Dudmesh went to enlighten Sally Cholmondeley about their newfound love, a revelation that didn't go down well. Meanwhile Tom visited me in hospital, where I was laid up with a fractured femur. He wanted advice. Was it possible, he asked, to divorce without unhappiness and acrimony? My own experience hadn't been particularly positive, and I could only urge him to be kind. At a friend's insistence he was wearing a black wig over his baldness, but his height and high profile in the press made it impossible for him not to be noticed.

'*That* was Tom Cholmondeley!' gasped one of the nurses after he'd left. It was difficult to gauge whether she spoke in horror or merely astonishment. Most people imagined that he was British and had another country to run to.

A political row was raging. Various parties were gunning for the Attorney General, calling for his sacking. "Delamere's grandson, no doubt, has influential friends and help, locally and abroad," reported *The Standard*, "who could have pressured the AG to drop the case." The Director of Public Prosecutions, Philip Murgor, was fired. Years later, in 2013, asked by the *Daily Nation* about his *nolle prosequi* over the Cholmondeley case, he assured the reporter he'd do the same again. "The state counsel in Nakuru defied the Attorney General's directives and prosecuted in a rush," he was reported as saying, "From the evidence in the file, it was an unfortunate case of self-defence coupled with mistaken identity."

Tom and Sally Dudmesh had gone overseas, and by the time they returned to Soysambu in September the press had fastened onto other topics. Tom moved into the research centre, now renamed Jersey Hall, which Sally Dudmesh began decorating in between maintaining her Nairobi home and business. A little way up the nearby rocky ridge, Sally Cholmondeley brought her sons home to Flamingo House for weekends. To avoid confusion between the two, we dubbed them Sally 1 and Sally 2.

Nine months jogged by - the happiest of her life, Sally Dudmesh later told me. Tom busied himself in farm projects, although by now Delamere Estates' financial situation was critical. Bills, including tax, had been left unpaid, and board members resigned. Then, three years before the vast bank loan, payable over ten years, was due, the bank demanded payment in full, in spite of no default on the part of Delamere Estates.

'Farming doesn't work like that,' Hugh told me angrily – adding that he suspected foul play.

Tom asked his old friend Philip Coulson to meet him for lunch at a Chinese restaurant in Nairobi. 'I've known you all my life, Philip,' he said over the spring rolls and foo yong. 'My father and I don't agree on much, but we agree on one thing. We'd like you to help us.'

It would be an enormous task to get Soysambu and Manera back on their feet, but Philip replied without hesitation. 'Of course I will.'

CHAPTER 27

The Second Round

Early evening of the 10th April 2006, there was over an hour of daylight left as Tom and a friend parked beside the rough track and walked into the thick bush. Tom was looking about and listening; a large bull buffalo can creep up astonishingly quietly, although if the wind is right you can sometimes smell it first. Tom and Hugh still had firearms licences for security purposes, so Tom was carrying his Magnum .375 rifle. Tom loved planning future enterprises, and his friend was renting Flamingo House. As well as various ideas for cultivation on the higher, north western section of Soysambu, this friend hoped to build a house for himself in the leleshwa-clad hills towards the undeveloped northern end.

As they pushed through thickets, glancing back at the spreading view, watching all around for buffalo, the friend stopped to relieve himself. Walking on, Tom chanced upon a group of men armed with *pangas* (machetes), a spiked iron bar and *rungus* (clubs), carrying a Thomson's gazelle carcass. The poachers ran, but their dogs took the offensive, running towards Tom and barking. He opened fire on the dogs, killing two and injuring a third. In these moments of heated confusion and gunshots, Tom hadn't seen the one man who hadn't fled, hiding behind a bush.

'My buttocks, my buttocks!' the injured man screamed in Swahili.

Horrified, Tom rushed to give him first aid, staunching the blood flow, making him comfortable, reassuring him. Tom phoned for his other car to rush the man to hospital, then called KWS and the police. He carried the injured man to his car, and moved the carcasses of the dogs to a more open area before Tom's friend drove him and the injured man down the hill - it would be hard to describe their location, and if they were to save the man's life time was vital. As soon as they met up with the other car, the injured man was transferred to it and taken to hospital. Tom returned to the scene of crime to meet the police. As the night wore on, the temperature dropped dramatically. Tom and his friend were finally driven to Nakuru Police Station by the friend's father at around midnight. It was too late to record their statements, so they were locked in for the night.

The injured poacher, whose name was Robert Njoya, died three hours after arriving in hospital. After he failed to come home, his wife went to Elmenteita Police Station, where poachers caught on Soysambu were usually locked up. Here she learned of his fate.

Less than a year since his release from Naivasha, 37-year-old Tom Cholmondoley was back on remand. Sharing a cell, he and his friend inhaled the stench from drums of fermenting home brew Police had recovered from Nakuru's illegal drinking dens.

Philip Coulson heard the news at dawn, and drove straight to Nakuru.

'Will you still help us?' Tom asked, remarkably calm.

'Of course,' replied Philip. On his way back to Nairobi, he stopped in Gilgil to see his parents. 'I'm going to have to help the Delameres,' he said to them, expecting them to tell him to say, 'Stay well out of it'.

To his surprise they both replied, 'You are!' He would remain closely involved with the family, wearing different caps, as lawyer, trustee, trusted adviser and director, continuing his association, he later told me, 'out of deep love and friendship, but also a sense of duty.'

Tom's friend, who'd tearfully begged Philip to help him too, was released soon afterwards. His surname wasn't Cholmondeley, he'd never made headlines in the press, and he didn't own a significant amount of land. Realising that his own predicament could become serious, Tom felt concerned that he might be unable to see through the important work of protecting the wildlife on Soysambu. The next time Kat visited, he asked her to start the formal process of creating a conservancy. After Simon's death she'd stayed on Soysambu, in spite of her home overlooking the Nose, where he'd died, vowing to become a protector of the place that had been so close to his heart. And now she readily agreed to help Tom.

Hugh and Ann were in Sussex, staying in Ann's family home, as they did most summers, enjoying a very different lifestyle. Ann drove, did her own shopping, and Hugh cooked ('bacon butties' his speciality, he told me) in between spending time in his train room in the attic. Although they were desperately worried at the news, Ann had just had a cataract operation and was not permitted to drive, let alone travel. Thus they both remained stuck in England, extremely worried and distressed, relying on Philip's regular phone calls. Hugh wasn't well either; he'd seen a doctor about a tingling hand, although there'd been no diagnosis.

Sally Dudmesh rushed up country from Nairobi, feeling overwhelmed. ('I was completely on my own,' she later told me. 'I knew nobody in Nakuru, and I was just *left* with it. It was the toughest time of my life.')

Thirteen days after Tom's arrest it looked as if there was no case. There was no evidence for a murder charge, and Kenyan law stipulated that the police could only hold a suspect for 14 days before making a charge. On the evening of that 13th day the security manager later reported that the police appeared on Soysambu, bafflingly telling him that they needed to see the scene of the shooting 'after dark.' The result was another rapid turn of events. Some spent cartridges were supposedly discovered at the scene, and all guns on Soysambu would be confiscated by the police, including Hugh's double- bored .458 ('made to measure in Germany for £6,000,' he told me in 2018, when it remained in their keeping). At three o'clock in the morning on the 14th day Tom was moved to CID headquarters in Nairobi, and later that day taken to the high court in a police convoy. Responding 'Not guilty' to Justice Muga Aponde felt horribly familiar, except this time it was accompanied by an even larger media circus.

'I arrived in court and there were thousands of photographers,' Sally Dudmesh told me. 'I've never been so scared in my entire life. Hugh and Ann were still not back, and I was angry about that. I even paid the first lawyer's bill.' Afterwards she managed to inveigle her way downstairs to see Tom, trying to offer him reassurance.

It was dark when Tom arrived back in Nairobi's Industrial area remand prison, which he described as "a medieval Bedlam of small courtyards and narrow corridors with lots of small cells off them... Lots of heavy engineering and open drains." He shared a steel-doored, six-by-nine-foot cell with eight other men who showed him the illicit mobile phone charging socket behind the wallpaper of newspaper pictures. Sally Dudmesh managed to smuggle him in some food before he slept top-to-tail beside his fellow inmates.

Meanwhile Philip, true to his word, consulted some of his financial friends and, after seeking approval from Hugh and Ann, asked Andrew Gregory, a recently retired former partner in KPMG, to be 'company doctor.' By this time, Philip told me, 'the wolves were at the door and it was very serious, although the banks never foreclosed. This wasn't an official receivership as it was in the 30s.'

Once again the international media excelled themselves with fantastical flights of imagination. There seemed no end to their stories about the 5th Baron Delamere, his ancestors and his Kenyan Estates. The Hon. Tom Cholmondeley could hang, they wrote ghoulishly, reinventing him as an unscrupulous white landowner who'd killed an impoverished black stonemason, making much of the fact that he'd been educated at Eton, persisting in calling him "Lord Delamere's grandson," branding him a racist serial killer and dwelling on the thought of his "death sentence." The *Daily Mail* ran a piece on the 'Murderous world of the gun-toting Happy Valley set.' 'Cholmondeley, an Old Etonian, who favours cravats and Luger pistols,' raved the journalist, 'is the heir to the family who created the Happy Valley set, notorious for sexual debauchery, drugs — and murder, as immortalised in the film *White Mischief.*' It was hardly surprising when, in the face of a hostile vocal public baying for Tom's hanging, Sally Cholmondeley returned to England with their sons.

'Do you want a hot drink?' asked an unseen voice from behind the barred door.

Tom, who'd been locked up several hours earlier than anyone else, replied in the affirmative, and a plastic cup of vodka was carefully passed through the uncovered bars - and thus was Tom was welcomed into Kamiti Maximum Security Prison.

As he'd walked beneath a shaded avenue towards the fort-like prison compound, built by the British in 1955, Tom had thought it didn't look so bad. After the formalities at the entrance he'd been led across a bare earth courtyard where prisoners were shackled in pairs - those coming and going from court. Others who'd trodden this ground had included Mau Mau Field Marshal Dedan Kimathi before he had been sentenced and hanged by the British. A door in one corner, dwarfed beneath 24-foot stone walls, led into the more secluded remand block; a pleasant enough grassy yard, with some fruit and vegetables growing. Two hot showers and clean toilets lurked behind a curtain. Led into cell number ten, Tom had been pleasantly surprised to find a mattress on a bare but clean concrete floor, two blankets, a mosquito net and a small, wobbly school desk. As he sipped from his plastic cup, it didn't seem unbearable.

This wing of the prison, a world away from the overcrowded main section, had once housed the Kenyan businessman Kamlesh Pattni, whose company had been implicated in a political scandal when the government was found to have subsidised its exports of gold far beyond standard arrangements. The "Pattni wing" had housed some big names, including politicians in both Moi's and Kibaki's governments, and even some members of the judiciary.

Many criticisms might be levelled at Tom, but he couldn't be accused of arrogance. Always humble, he was now touched by the friendliness of other inmates. His excellent Kiswahili apparently came as a pleasant surprise, he soon made many friends and was quickly labelled 'an ordinary,' the term for both inmates and warders who knew how to handle others and to avoid drama. Kamiti's warders varied from kind and lenient, to zealously trying to catch prisoners out, involving detailed searches of cells and possessions. Money usually sorted any transgressions made; there was a system, and Tom had to learn to work it. Bells marked breaks, and in between Tom settled into a routine; writing his diary, reading, playing badminton and showering - if there was water. He began learning new tribal languages, regularly watching television for the first time in his life, giving up on trying to shave off slithers of over-boiled grey meat and gristle that tasted little better than wood shavings, preferring the vegetables and maize meal.

Visiting took up most of the day. Outside the tall iron gates of the main building a generously leafed fig tree provided shade from the sun or shelter from the rain, its tumbled roots offering seating as visitors waited, sometimes five minutes, other times several hours. Prisoners in faded uniforms would stop their labours to stare. Once summoned, if allowed to talk to Tom privately as visitors sometimes were, we could slip him reading material and carefully concealed food, which he always shared with his new friends. Patrick Waweru was a regular, and as soon as Hugh and Ann could fly back to Nairobi, Philip Coulson took them to Kamiti. Tobina Cole, who'd always been very fond of her godson, visited him weekly. She'd been a prison visitor with Margaret Kenyatta back in the 1960s, she told me, running a prison library for many years, when she'd been horrified to learn that one man had been stuck in Kamiti for 14 years awaiting trial.

But it was Sally Dudmesh's frequent visits that kept Tom going. "Nothing in her previous experience had prepared her to be such a pillar of strength," he wrote, "and so good at working through the legal minefield and keeping my spirits up. She was my anchor, the rock around which everything else orbited. She kept hopeful and bright even when everyone else was gloomy."

Perhaps none of us had fully grasped the attention this case had already attracted, and how it would now escalate. It was a shock to face the crowds outside the High Court at Tom's first appearance on the 25th September. We could only take one step at a time through the jostling, sweaty press, shouting questions.

'Please let us through!' I shouted pointlessly at the flashing cameras.

'Are you Lord Delamere?' they shouted. 'Are you Lord Delamere? Are you—'

Hugh had heard the question one too many times. 'No!' he snapped. 'I'm George V!'

A colourful mix of activists, friends and supporters of both parties crammed into the seats. Many stood, some were obliged to remain outside. There was a jury of three court assessors, although under Kenyan law the judge did not have to take heed of their findings. Fred Ojiambo was back as defence lawyer, with Teriako

Tobiko as Director of Public Prosecution, presided over by Justice Muga Aponde, resplendent in red robe and white wig, obliged to handwrite every word as there was no court stenographer.

The DPP stated his claim that the accused had attacked the deceased as retaliation or in revenge for trespassing or poaching in his land, also accusing Tom of tampering with the evidence to conceal his crime. Njoya's widow Sarah and his brothers gave evidence, the second the owner of a butchery. During his to-the-point cross-examination Fred implied the brother was doing a thriving trade in illegal bushmeat, and I wondered if his was the 'White Land Butchery' I'd seen at the mushrooming village of Kekopey (also known as *Nyama choma* - 'Burned meat', the Kenyans preferring theirs very well done).

That evening we sat silently in Hugh and Ann's room at Muthaiga Club downing a stiff whisky, watching Hugh's comment about George V as it was aired repeatedly on CNN. I found it impossible not to smile; back in colonial days, HM's prison - now Kamiti Prison - had been referred to by inmates as "*Kingi Georgie Hotel.*" Not that many of those reporters would know that.

On the second day one of Njoya's fellow poachers threw some light on the iron rod they'd carried; it was a 'killing stick,' used to finish off the animal the dogs had driven into the snare. He admitted they'd been trespassing - albeit 'in search of food.' Fred suggested they were there for commercial reasons, illegal game meat fetching good money, and got the witness to admit he was also a thief; he'd actually stolen the gazelle from someone else's snare.

But on the third day the trial took an unexpected and puzzling turn. It was time for the key witness, Tom's friend who'd been with him the afternoon of the shooting, to testify. He didn't seem the type to seek attention, let alone be embroiled in drama, standing awkwardly in the witness box, hands in pockets, at pains to emphasise that Tom had shot Njoya by mistake, and then striven to save Njoya's life. By the time of Fred's rigorous cross-examination, it was the afternoon and many journalists had left.

First arose the question of a third white dog at the scene of the shooting, which had been mentioned by other witnesses. Why hadn't this friend of Tom's told the police about it or mentioned it in his statement? Or was he a friend? He would now describe Tom as a mere 'acquaintance,' explaining that he was focused on the dying man, and later had been traumatised. It hadn't seemed relevant or important, he said.

Then, even though it was that time of day when it was easy to nod off in the stuffy courtroom, we sat up, startled, when Fred asked if he knew of a Beretta 9mm pistol, quoting its registration number?

The answer was affirmative.

Fred then suggested that the witness had been carrying this pistol - that indeed he'd finished off this white dog which Tom had wounded and left yelping in pain.

At Fred's ruthless questioning, his inference that he knew more than he'd revealed, the witness broke down in tears. Tom sat quietly, betraying no emotion. We drove back to Muthaiga Club, where Hugh poured us a stiff whisky. Fred's cross-examination had raised some totally unexpected questions. Had the white dog been killed by bullets from another gun, and if so, who had fired it? Hugh and Ann were clearly bewildered and upset, although it was hard to tell if this was because Tom hadn't been honest in withholding a potentially important part of the story. And indeed if this pistol story was true, then he'd also perverted the course of justice. They might equally have been worried about repercussions. The friend's parents were renting Suganoi House and Hugh and Ann considered them friends. Bizarrely, I was reading *The Curious Incident of the Dog in the Night Time*.

***

Sally Dudmesh later told me that it was she who'd told Fred about the white dog. She'd only heard of its existence after Tom had gone to Kamiti. A Soysambu manager had tripped over something in the dark behind a car, and identified it as the white dog by the light of his mobile phone. Earlier, when it had still been light, he'd noticed it lying separately from the corpses of two brown dogs. When he'd picked it up to add it to the rest of the evidence, Tom had told him to leave it where it was. Tom's reaction when Sally confronted him with the information in prison was to ask her not to tell Fred.

'I was furious.' She lit a cigarette and after a few puffs added, 'Tom made some very, *very* crap decisions.' It was clear that in Sally's view the story of the white dog should have been told from the start. She was astounded, unable to understand why he might have been hesitant to incriminate his friend. It was certainly puzzling to many of us that, for reasons only known to Tom, he'd possibly taken the course of withholding information from the police, his family and friends, and even his lawyer.

Stories were now multiplying among white-Kenyan cliques into which Tom had never been entirely accepted. 'He's made it impossible for people like us to live here!' said one to me. Others were furious with Tom for ruining their reputation for non-confrontation. He was called 'trigger-happy' and 'bonkers.' Tom's friends and employees, on the other hand, were unanimously on his side.

'Tom was very honest,' a black Kenyan manager told me a decade later, 'but his kindness and brotherhood always put him in trouble.'

'The bottom line is that Tom took the rap twice,' a close friend of his said in 2018. 'I am not sure that has happened too many times in the history of mankind.'

The key witness's father-in-law, meanwhile, was emphatic that Tom was a weak character, persuaded to change his initial, correct statement once he realised the gravity of the situation. When this gentleman had arrived at Nakuru Police Station the morning after the shooting, he told me in an email that he'd found Tom remorseful and apologetic. 'He repeatedly emphasized how sorry he was, as it was all his own doing!' Moreover, in his statement, he added, Tom had made it clear he accepted responsibility for the shooting, and that his friend wasn't to blame. After the unpleasant cross-examination in court Tom's friend had even received an SMS, in which Tom apologized again, 'saying he did not wish to implicate him, but just to cast doubt in the minds of the judges.'

In the documentary *Last White Man Standing* Fred also emphasised that they weren't incriminating a key witness - that wasn't their job - but wanted the court to know 'there was more to this than was initially said.'

The press were surprisingly silent on the issue.

CHAPTER 28

A Case to Answer

In between protracted hearings in Nairobi's High Court, life on Soysambu had to go on. It was a shock for Hugh when his workers went on strike, gathering angrily outside the gate of Main House, hoping to make their motives clear: They were fed up with the General Manager, Christopher Chirchir, whom they alleged to be dishonest.

'I had a big fight with Delamere about this!' Wakaba told me emphatically in 2018, the year after Chirchir had died. 'I said to him, "How many managers do you think I've seen here? Do you *want* people to steal your cows?"' But Hugh refused to listen, he said. A tenant also visited Hugh to tell him about the cattle thefts happening behind his back. Hugh shrugged it off and declined to talk to the angry workers. His attitude to theft seemed to harp back to his grandfather's. 'It's the Delamere burden!' he'd told me once. He and Ann had always defended their Kenyan managers, and whether they knew better, or simply weren't prepared to face any possible flaws in their integrity was a moot point.

The workers were perhaps unaware that Chirchir was working out his notice, having handed in his resignation soon after the second shooting. When he left, Nelson Rotich, whom Hugh and Ann also held in very high regard, moved from Manera to step into the position of General Manager. Meanwhile Hugh and Ann would remain good friends to Chirchir, who would continue in his role as Director of Delamere Estates, staying at Main House when he came to meetings.

They continued to make frequent trips to Nairobi for court hearings which, if they weren't postponed or somehow sabotaged, dragged by with excruciating slowness. I joined them whenever I could. As time trawled by, most journalists didn't bother to update their facts; it made a better story to claim Delamere owned 100,000 acres, add in a cocktail of irrelevant references to Happy Valley, and harp back to the so-called *White Mischief* trial. A *Telegraph* journalist lied his way into Soysambu and turned up at Main House. Hugh and Ann graciously offered him tea, during which he claimed he watched Hugh "sipping Earl Grey tea served by a white-jacketed servant..." They never drank Earl Grey, and neither did any of their staff wear white jackets. One journalist relocated Soysambu to Naivasha, "surrounded by foreign-owned flower farms drawing dirt-poor workers living in nearby slums," a glaring error repeated by Janet McIntosh in *Unsettled*. But there were indeed an increasing number of impoverished neighbours around Soysambu, as one offender from the poaching underworld would explain in court; after only being educated up to the penultimate year of primary school, then finding little else to do, he'd been introduced by Njoya to this easy money-making scheme.

By now we'd settled into a routine. I stayed with a friend near Muthaiga Club, driving through early-morning traffic to meet Hugh and Ann. At Hugh's request, I always had to remind him to put in his teeth and remember his cheque book. Ndung'u then drove us into the city centre in the 1970s Mercedes Diana had bought from Charles Njonjo, her silver bear remaining a figurehead on its bonnet. After a while, Ndung'u reluctantly agreed not to wear the old chauffeur's cap, which some of us felt might bear the stamp of colonialism - we certainly didn't want to feed the press any more Happy Valley ammunition. We dressed plainly - journalists seemed to delight in noting what everyone was wearing. There were no washrooms, the court ones remaining locked, so we had to cross several streets to find a friendly restaurant. Throughout the long day Hugh, Ann and Sarah Njoya maintained masks of dignity. Tom, handcuffed and attired in a suit, would acknowledge us with a raise of eyebrows or a nod from the side bench of the crowded courtroom, his height and upright stance singling him out, his gaze fixed above the scrum of press standing and kneeling a few feet away, somehow remaining the silent eye in a storm of palpable tension. Only once did I see him almost lose it, when he was so mobbed - in spite of the warders literally fighting off the media - that he tripped over a tangle of camera wires. His hands bound together, he couldn't save himself and, as his warders helped him up, Tom had to use all his self-control to regain his composure.

As another day in court crawled by, incompetence raised its weary head. A medical officer claimed that the hospital did everything possible to save Njoya's life, but Fred pointed out that Njoya could have been here to give evidence had doctors responded correctly; he'd been given cardiac massage before any attempt had been made to stop the bleeding. Tom, on the other hand, had done the right thing with his makeshift tourniquet. Fred's cross-examinations further established that some policemen had altered the scene, which they hadn't cordoned off. One witness even admitted to incorrectly marking cartridges. A lack of knowledge - or possibly integrity – on the part of certain police witnesses when it came to firearms was astounding. One constable claimed to recognise Tom's gun, but didn't seem to know the difference between a scope and a magazine. Another alleged 'expert' couldn't confirm if certain bullet fragments were actually from Tom's rifle. After gruesome photographs of Njoya's wounded buttock had been passed around, Fred argued that a high-calibre rifle would have smashed Njoya's pelvis to smithereens - and left an exit wound, and suggested that the police had deliberately misled the court, that they'd made up their minds what had happened from the outset.

'The Kenya Police continue to be the most corrupt institution in the country,' stated Philip Murgor, when interviewed by Fiona Cunningham-Reid for her documentary.

After only four days in court, 32 witnesses remained. The hearing was adjourned until 30 October, although the court would visit Soysambu the following day.

'I hope we see a buffalo!' quipped the DPP, Keriako Tobiko.

The following morning the judge, lawyers, witnesses, armed guards, journalists, television crew, and a motley bunch of hangers-on arrived at Soysambu. This bizarre convoy drove as far as it could, after which everyone stumbled and tripped up to the fated site, most of them in unsuitable shoes, even though the judge had asked people to dress 'smartly, but appropriately.' They found plenty of snares and did indeed see buffalo, fortunately at a distance. Tom felt a rush of joy at being home, albeit so briefly.

"The tragic beauty and fragility of the land itself, and the constant presence of animals within a landscape that seemed to belong to them but didn't, had a subduing effect," wrote Lawrence Osborne in *Men's Vogue: A Bloody Rift*. "The whole valley is a volatile tinderbox, with a handful of whites thrown by historical fate into a mix they have long ceased to control." 'The police in this country are very effective when they mean to be,' Philip Murgor told him, 'and hopeless when they mean to be.' If the entire Rift Valley became smallholdings, added Maina Kiai, a human rights activist, it would result in 'nothing but degradation and waste.' Kenya's best agricultural land was largely black-owned, Osborne pointed out, the biggest landowners being the Kenyatta family, "while much of the white land is like the Delameres' Soysambu: mostly semi-desert scrub better suited to big game than cash crops."

When court hearings resumed, witnesses continued to contradict themselves and each other. When the judge finally announced that the trial would adjourn until February, we drove home in sombre mood. Tom and his fellow prisoners returned to cells plagued with rats and bedbugs. Christmas came and went, Hugh and Ann dividing theirs between Muthaiga Club and Kamiti. By now Hugh had been diagnosed with Parkinson's Disease and become very depressed. He and Ann eagerly looked forward to conversations with Tom on the phone Sally Dudmesh had managed to smuggle in. Tom determinedly kept himself upbeat, laying traps and scrubbing his cell, raising the dust carried in by a second year of drought. The poorly insulated cells swung between extremes of hot and cold as another rainy season arrived. Water seeped down into the walls of his leaky cell and bubbled up beneath the whitewash, reminding him, he noted laconically, of "those miraculous statues that weep for the faithful."

It would take a long, slow year for all 38 prosecution witnesses to play their part. One particularly memorable witness was a Maasai herdsman from Soysambu, for whom a translator had to be provided. The elderly man looked baffled as he stood in the witness box, dressed in his traditional *shuka*.

'Do you know the accused?' the DPP asked. The old man threw him a look of disbelief before leaping across the courtroom to a handcuffed Tom, throwing his arms around him, talking animatedly in Maa. Tom broke into a delighted smile, replying in Maa amidst general laughter until the judge called for order and the witness was removed. The DPP, also Maasai, somehow suppressed a smile.

In his nine-by-six-foot cell, lit by a single energy-saving bulb, Tom relied on his stacks of books and learned meditation to keep himself sane. As the prosecution continued, Fred revealed that the investigating officer had decided Tom was a murderer before he'd visited the crime scene or even interviewed him. He'd also suggested that poaching wasn't a crime, producing a forged statement after Tom, somewhat naively, had signed some blank sheets of paper when requested.

In mid-March Gwladys's grave was dug up, her skull stolen. There'd been other lone bull buffalo seen guarding the graves since the death of the old bull who'd taken up sentry duty in 1931. A poacher had even been killed by a buffalo on Jolai Hill, but this hadn't acted as deterrent. Tom told me that D's remains had suffered the same back indignity in 2004, when he'd quickly and quietly reburied his great-grandfather, minus his missing skull, filling the graves with cement.

The *Daily Nation* reported this desecration with a note of sympathy for the Delameres, as it had reported the arson on Soysambu four months previously which had resulted in the death of two sisters and a child, plus the loss of 3,000 acres of hay worth 30 million shillings. A manager told the reporter that 30 cows worth over a million shillings had been caught in poachers' snares and pipes and fences were systematically being destroyed, all in spite of Delamere providing free water to local communities and donating land to schools. The writer quoted Christopher Chirchir's words the previous year: 'If they want Delamere to sell this farm so that it can be subdivided into small units and become a village where residents live on begging, well and good.'

Soysambu's problems were taking their toll. Manera was making a huge loss, Philip Coulson told me, 'so hard-nosed decisions were made.' Six hundred and forty acres of Manera were put up for sale to raise some desperately needed capital, and in December 2007 the land was bought by Vegpro, Kenya's largest grower and exporter of vegetables. After bad publicity the previous year had sabotaged marketing for Delamere Dairies, these had been leased out to Brookside, the dairy processing company owned by the Kenyatta family. It was now bought by them, its processing equipment transferred to their headquarters at Ruiru. Hugh found this particularly difficult to accept, insisting he'd been sold out by a former manager. When I later asked Nelson Rotich, he saw nothing sinister about the deal, although he admitted that perhaps there were those who took advantage of Delamere's misfortunes. All this had left Delamere Estates still owning about 1,200 acres of Manera, part of it leased by Vegpro, the rest used for growing lucerne, which as Hugh pointed out, could take the salinity of the water.

It was July 2007 when the judge ruled that the prosecution had established a *prima facie* case. Fred then confirmed that Tom would give an unsworn statement, and that seven defence witnesses would be called, including the chief inspector of the Central Firearms Bureau who'd already testified for the prosecution. Then unexpectedly Tobiko appealed for - and received - a dispensation for the defence to give all their evidence - including all ballistic, scientific and forensic reports - to the prosecution before things could proceed. Tom angrily recorded in his diaries that he felt that the DPP was "totally stripping" him of the right to a fair trial. "Fred rose to his feet in court and launched an interlocutory appeal against that," he wrote, "literally a case within a case. This created a lot of controversy, everyone asking me why I was casting myself into a certain lengthy delay."

'This is completely illegal,' raged Hugh, as we returned home. He and Ann had also heard that Sisina's widow was still trying to resurrect the old murder charge.

At the end of 2007 a controversial general election saw the incumbent Mwai Kibaki declared winner and hastily sworn in. His political rival, Raila Odinga, cried foul, and in the ensuing tribal violence over a hundred displaced and traumatised people took refuge at the basic staff accommodation close to my house. Soysambu provided them with relative protection, as well as milk, firewood and a water bowser, dragged by tractor from the far end of the farm as all our rainwater tanks had been sucked dry by a long rainless hot season. Everyone mucked in, sharing water, food and blankets. Outside Soysambu, roads were blocked, schools closed and travel warnings issued. Many Kenyans believed the violence was politically instigated, and as 2008 lurched on with the death toll rising, there seemed to be no solution in sight in spite of former UN Secretary-General Kofi Annan's best efforts to create some sort of deal.

"I didn't really grasp the extent of it until Sally came in to see me two days after it started," wrote Tom. "She was aghast as I merrily prattled on about my missing cup. She had been dodging angry mobs for two hours…This made me feel so utterly impotent."

What had begun with Kikuyu people arriving on and around Soysambu, seeking sanctuary with relatives, having lost everything to Kalenjin marauders further west, was followed with the arrival of Kikuyu mercenaries known as *Mungiki*, prompting non-Kikuyus to flee to their ancestral homes. There was a mix of tribes working on Soysambu at all levels, with the town of Elmenteita similarly diverse, but although its residents did their best to maintain peace, the machinations of a more powerful class had proved victorious.

'Please do everything you can,' Tom asked me over the phone. 'Get the displaced children a football and some books?' I could sense his frustration at not being there to help.

At Main House I found Ann reading an inflammatory document warning people to leave their homes before they were killed, brought by her Kikuyu friend, Leah, a retired teacher from Nakuru.

As people continued to leave their homes, Jolai *campi* soon had over 150 displaced people, with more arriving. Soysambu's managers agreed that for their own safety they must move to the newly set up Red Cross camp at Elmenteita Police Station. As we saw them off in a Soysambu lorry, several asked after Tom.

When I next visited Main House, Hugh, who'd heard the roads

from Nairobi were blocked by armed youths, was trying to phone Ann to tell her to go on the back roads. She was on her way home from seeing a doctor in Nairobi and I fervently hoped Ndung'u wasn't wearing the chauffeur's cap. She duly arrived in time for drinks, remarkably unflustered, relating how a group of youths had picked up large rocks threateningly. 'Ndung'u wound down the window and had a word with them in Kikuyu,' she said. 'I don't know what he said to them but they let us through. One even put down his rock and gave me a wave.'

Arsonists lit fires and we fought to extinguish the flames as they destroyed trees and pasture. Some creatures ran for their lives; others, including spring hares, aardvarks and pythons, retreated down holes where they suffocated. One night, after a long day of fetching water for beaters, driving between different fires on three corners of Soysambu, I exhaustedly watched the scarlet fiery tongue race up Jolai Hill in a self-generating wind. Behind us another fire had fanned itself back to life. The oily leleshwa shrub burns with a black, acrid smoke, although ironically its branches are good for beating. Suddenly the beaters started yelling, and our aching limbs were forgotten in our sprint from the enraged buffalo, followed by a beautiful serval cat bounding across the blackened waste. The fires burned 7,000 acres, spreading into Nakuru National Park, jumping fences and roads, destroying Kenya's largest forest of *euphorbia ingens*, more commonly known as candelabra. Fortunately Soysambu's pocket of similar forest survived.

Eventually Kibaki and Odinga agreed a power-sharing agreement and life began to settle back into some sort of routine, although families were fragmented, lives had been lost, property destroyed, and the tourism industry was on its knees.

When Tom was visited by Janet McIntosh, who interviewed him for her book about the white Kenyan community, *Unsettled*, she noted some of his reading material: *Histories of the Hanged*, detailing the execution of many Mau Mau leaders, and Ngugi wa Thiong'o's *Detained*. Tom described himself to her as 'the sacrificial anode for post-colonial Kenya,' a view also expressed by another interviewee, Richard Leakey, the renowned conservationist who'd formed

KWS and who saw in Tom's case a sense of 'beating colonialism,' with 'Tom as whipping boy,' Leakey also had a sympathetic understanding of what McIntosh calls "Kenya's ticking time bomb of inequality." 'There is no middle ground between those with lots of land and those with only a tiny bit,' Tom told her. Despite her preconceptions, McIntosh seems to have respected Tom, and she wrote about him perceptively.

In a double-page spread the *Daily Nation* highlighted the state of Kenya's prisons, giving space to Tom's many ideas for improvements. It quoted him as explaining that a borehole and seven pipes were needed to supply water to different parts of Kamiti and that Sally Dudmesh was assisting him in raising funds for these. Ann told me it was actually she who took all the water pipes and tools to Kamiti – twice, as the first project was abortive. Tom did all the plumbing work himself, delighted to be doing something so worthwhile for the prison. On her twice monthly visits, Ann also took Tom cleaning equipment so that he could keep his own surroundings clean, dustbins (which disappeared regularly and thus needed replacing) and once she took three electric fly-killing contraptions; one for Tom, the others for the prison kitchen and sick-room.

The *Nation* article continued to list Tom's suggestions: Conjugal visits (permitted for a century in America and since 1915 in the UK) would help to curb Kamiti's rife homosexuality and social problems. Communication for prisoners with the outside world should include computers and payphones. It was currently only legal to write letters, which were then subjected to slow and inefficient censorship, inevitably leading to illegal mobile phones being smuggled in. The report further unearthed some depressing facts and figures. In 1911, Kenya's 30 prisons had 310 staff members and 6,559 inmates. Now, according to the Ministry of Home Affairs, the 90 jails, with a capacity for 16,000 prisoners, had over 59,000, many not yet convicted. The internationally recommended staff prisoner ratio was 1:5; in Kamiti it was 1:16. The previous year 548 inmates had died of various illnesses, including cancer and HIV. Almost 200 prisoners were mentally ill. More than 300 warders had died in the past three years after contracting diseases from their working environment.

Lake Elmenteita was becoming increasingly important in protecting declining species. A 2007 avian census had yielded an average count exceeding 610,000 birds, belonging to more than 450 species, of which 80 were waterfowl, both resident and migrant. In 1999 Leon Bennun and Peter Njoroge's *Important Bird Areas in Kenya* had listed the Lesser Flamingo, Grey-crested Helmet-shrike and Jackson's Widowbird amongst Lake Elmenteita's globally-threatened species, with the Great Crested Grebe, Great Egret, White-headed Vulture, Ayer's Hawk Eagle, African Crowned Eagle, Martial Eagle, Yellow-billed Oxpecker and Long-tailed Widowbird regionally-threatened. In addition, it was increasingly clear that Soysambu's diverse landscapes, created by past volcanic upheavals, provided refuge for a unique blend of bird, animal, insect, reptile, and plant species, protecting rarer mammals including striped hyena, caracal, steinbok and aardvark. The threatened Rothschild's giraffes (which would be up-listed to Endangered by IUCN in 2010) were breeding well, and there'd even been a pair of wild dogs passing through. A recent game count had seen a total of 15,041 wild animals. Kat had kept her word to Tom, and on 1st May 2008, Soysambu Conservancy became operational as one of the largest remaining wild habitats in the Nakuru Basin.

But Lake Elmenteita's unprotected shores - those outside Soysambu's boundaries - were under unprecedented assault. That March I walked it with my son, Michael. We'd begun on Soysambu, on the northeastern side of the lake, where vast flocks of pelicans swam and bathed at the Mereroni river mouth or clustered noisily on the rocky islands, waiting for the sun to heat the air until the thermals could take them high enough to make their daily journeys back and forth to Lake Nakuru to feed. Heading south, we passed much to depress us: the rotting hulk of an abandoned and illegal jetty; the cutting of the shoreline woodland of giant and shady yellow-barked *Vachellia xanthophloea* and *Obetia radula* ('Stinging Nettle Trees') in spite of their coarse stinging hairs lining their leaves and stems; unplanned development and overgrazing and trashing of shoreline plants (including the ground orchid, *Eulophia speciose* with its large profusion of yellow flowers). The Kariandusi River was dry, and we'd seen no wild animals. Although we'd observed a variety of birdlife, it was disheartening to witness Elmenteita's natural beauty being elbowed out by man-made developments: an ugly housing development; various poorly built tourist lodges including one that was far too close to the water with – even worse - a rotting jetty jutting into the lake; and a deserted tourist camp spewing windblown litter along the soda flats. How had these obtained NEMA (National Environment Management Authority) approval to build on riparian land? NEMA had intervened to suspend the timber-treatment plant barely 100 metres from the lakeshore, but there'd been no follow-up, and now here it was, already operating! Was Kat right in connecting this with the many dead birds being washed up on the shore?

We walked towards where my Land Rover would pick us up, inside Soysambu's southern boundary, picking our way over more litter from a rush of new tourism ventures, buildings replacing Acacia woodlands, their former herds of golden Impala or occasional Bushbuck now gone. At the hot springs, where the surrounding wetlands, rushes and sedges had supported a wealth of waterfowl, we found only people washing.

It was now that Hugh and Ann agreed to *Mganga* David's proposal to perform his curious cleansing rites on Soysambu. I'd backed this as he'd been to cleanse my home two years previously, my initial scepticism dashed after various difficulties had seemed to miraculously disperse.

David was one of eight children, and when his parents had run out of money to complete his education, he'd devoted himself to what he called his 'power'. 'I heard voices when I was a child,' he'd told me, 'and I saw saints, even John, Moses and Jesus, surrounded by light and wearing white clothes.' This 'power' meant healing people of all religions, divulging problems, ridding compounds of bad spirits, protecting them, helping people to get work or have children, finding lost items and money. His work had taken him to Sudan, Somalia and even South Africa.

David already knew Tom; they'd got on well. But some of Soysambu's employees, even some managers, seemed terrified of what David might unearth. Waweru and I took him around the farm. He produced his bottle of potion, sprinkling it liberally as he paced about, stopping where he detected a need for stronger doses of magic, praying manically, sometimes in Kiswahili, at other times apparently speaking in tongues, throwing his head back, eyes rolling as he cast out bad spirits, the only discernible word being 'Jehovah' or sometimes '*Yesu*' (Jesus). I almost expected to see a puff of smoke whirling away as some spirit fled from David's admonishments. When we asked about this potion, he showed us some black rocks.

'These are God's stones from Mt Elgon,' he said. 'They are dissolved in water to get rid of the devil.'

David purged the spot where Sisina had died, before we headed to Melia, the northern part of Soysambu where Njoya had been shot.

'We are 15 kilometres from the farm boundary,' Waweru told us, navigating the car through the thick bush as far as possible before taking us in on foot. 'Njoya and the other poachers were also illegally burning charcoal. He was a thief and he used to beat his wife. Sarah is much healthier now!'

We drove on, past the boundary, a barren rocky area with missing fences, the Jerusalem thorn hedges planted by the previous generation now reduced to thickets with gaps making it easy for trespassers. David sprinkled his liquid protection around the Delamere graveyard, and further blessed the primary school where Tom had once targeted the Headmaster's chickens. Here, Waweru told us, Njoya's brother had incited the children to shout and demonstrate on television. Thankfully it was school holidays and all was calm. We drove under the bridge, beneath the main Nakuru highway, up to the north-eastern part called 'Triangle' with its springs and marvellous views, where the friend accompanying Tom that fateful day had been growing jatropha. We reached the top boundary, bordering the railway line. Waweru pointed to the land that Hugh's father had 'given' to his ex-employees, including his father. As we listened to the purr of a multitude of Ring-Necked doves, he smiled: 'I was born here!'

David was welcomed to meals at Main House in between his work. Conversation was conducted in Kiswahili as David spoke no English. Lunch always saw Hugh grinding the leftover croutons – 'fly-sinkers' as he called them - into the floor with an old broom for the host of birds. When an expectant glossy starling perched on the wooden griffin at the centre of the table, David admired the carving.

'It was given to Hugh by Tom when he had his heart operation,' Ann explained.

'Yes, it represents the griffin of the family crest,' Hugh added, his Kiswahili failing him over the griffin part. The conversation returned to easier subjects, cattle and sheep.

At the end of a second day of cleansing, we drove through the forest at the northern end of the lake, startling a pregnant bushbuck, admiring bewitchingly beautiful black and white colobus monkeys leaping between long-limbed golden acacias. Like the Rothschild's giraffes, they'd been translocated here – from former Happy Valley as it happened - where they were regionally threatened, killed for raiding the crops of subsistence farmers who had destroyed their natural forest habitat.

As we emerged onto open white-crusted soda flats beside a sky-blue lake, edged with flamingos, as if on cue, a Rothschild's giraffe paused to stare at us.

Suddenly David said, 'Tom, *atatoka*.' Tom will get out.

CHAPTER 29

Defence and Judgement

On 8th July 2008 Tom was bundled into the overcrowded prison bus, trying to maintain his core of inner calm as other prisoners debated their fates at top volume. He hadn't yet uttered a word in court, but today, two years and two months after his arrest, this delay partly due to Tobiko's unavailability, he would deliver his unsworn statement.

This was bound to be controversial, as Tom had changed his story. As his handcuffs were removed, I glanced at the clock. It was five past ten. He began to speak very quietly, as if the sound of his own voice in the courtroom might shake the fine line on which he teetered. Justice Aponde asked him to speak up, the pack of journalists leaning in, trying to gauge every nuance as Tom started again, answering the judge's questions, pausing regularly so the judge could write it all down. Beyond their two voices there was total silence in court.

The area where he and his friend had been heading to was thickly covered in leleshwa, a regular buffalo habitat, Tom explained, so he'd taken his rifle. He mixed gesticulations with words, bending down to pull up his trouser leg, showing the judge his own buffalo scar. When his friend had stopped, Tom had walked on, to be surprised by five men and a number of dogs. One of the poachers, he said, had called out, '*Hawezi kufanya kitu*' (He can't do anything). Their dogs - being used for chasing animals into snares, hence Soysambu's policy of shooting them - remained in the open, directly ahead, separated from the men. Tom then stated that he had dropped to one knee, aiming through his rifle's telescopic sight at the red-brown dogs, which he claimed to be the only thing in the telescope's field of sight. He shot two dogs in turn, and they fell instantly. He recalled the sound of the shots reverberating off the hills as he'd stood to re-load five rounds, during which time the men ran past, from Tom's right to his left, vanishing into the bushes. According to Tom, he then saw a white fluffy dog and fired two shots at it, although it didn't fall, but limped away. Once again it had been the only thing in the view of the telescope.

Tom then told the court there was something he'd left out of his statement to the police because that night in the Nakuru cells, his friend had been very upset as well as frightened he would get into trouble. Tom then proceeded to relate his version of events. He'd seen his friend approach from the left, holding a pistol in his hand, which he'd been unaware his friend was carrying due to his untucked shirt. Tom paused slightly before stating that he'd then observed his friend going over to a bush about 50 metres ahead before firing at the white dog that had been yelping. After this it didn't move again. It was then that Tom claimed he had heard the cries and was shocked to see a man lying on his front, as well as puzzled as to what had happened because the man was 20 metres away to the left. Tom then recounted how he'd picked the wounded man up under the arms, and the man had clasped his arms around his back. As he administered first aid he called out to his friend to get the car to take the man to hospital. After telling the court that he'd felt the weight of responsibility for anything that had happened, Tom's story drew to its end: 'I cannot see how I could have shot that person...' he concluded, before pausing. 'That is the absolute and utter truth.' He briefly closed his eyes before bowing to the judge and returning to his seat. It had taken time for him to say what he needed; it was now a quarter to midday. Afterwards he wrote of feeling a huge sense of relief at having unburdened himself.

Two days before Tom's court appearance *The Times* in UK had run an article with the extraordinary title: 'My love life's cursed, says girlfriend of Tom Cholmondeley: As the aristocrat prepares to give evidence at his trial in Kenya, his lover tells our correspondent of her own tortured past.' In this, Sally revealed how two past lovers had been shot, one of them being Tonio Trzebinski (son of Lord Erroll's biographer) who'd left Sally just before their planned wedding. Would readers of this strangely negative piece be left wondering what fate awaited Tom? I hoped he wouldn't read it.

Back now, in his restricted world, he sadly reflected how increasingly detached he was from the real world. He was particularly upset that he'd lost touch with his children. They'd visited Kenya with Sally Cholmondeley and been permitted to see him in a private room, but Tom acknowledged how difficult it had been for them, as well as for him, as he tried to fill in a two-year gap. After his little boys had left, wide-eyed at the whole set-up, he'd felt despondent.

A welcome distraction arrived in the form of the supposed leader of the *Mungiki,* a criminal organisation said to have originated in the 1980s, drawing inspiration from Mau Mau, and now banned for its violence, as well as its demands for protection money from households, businesses and public transport vehicles. A charming, smartly-dressed man, Maina Njenga was Tom's age. They'd met before in the court cells, and now Tom enjoyed his company and shared his sense of humour; he sent Ann an e-mail with a picture of his fly-zapper, a large heap of dead flies piled up like a heap of manure, entitled, 'Maina Njenga has accused me of genocide.'

But these lighter moments couldn't last. A prisoner in G block - the toughest block, where condemned prisoners were held - had been beaten to death for resisting a search. Somehow someone had recorded this on a mobile phone and managed to pass it on to human rights organisations, resulting in the prison governor's suspension. His replacement arrived from a hardcore prison in Kisumu and organised a massive search in which Tom lost everything that had made life bearable, including his phone, laptop and fly-zapping machine. "The complete callousness and indifference was probably the surest sign that things had changed badly for the worse," he wrote. "There was a lot of hate mail, and the prisons dept took great delight in showing my laptop on the television, claiming that it had been used for confidence tricks and drugs."

Prison conditions worsened. During the last few days of December a handful of Kamiti prisoners drank paint thinner, imagining it sufficiently alcoholic to offer pleasant reprieve. After being taken to hospital, some were pronounced permanently blind.

Tom's mood was further darkened when his fellow remand inmates, nine former prison warders who had become good friends, were sentenced to death after a seven-year trial. They were "ruined and angry," he wrote, while he felt deeply concerned for his own future after seeing the obvious "gaps in their case which were completely ignored by the judge."

By 3rd February 2009, when we were back in court, Tom told us with a wan smile he could pull his trousers down without undoing them. He sat motionless between his warders as Fred summed things up in a day. His main argument centred on the question of which gun fired the fatal shot, pointing out among many things that it was acceptable to remain silent, criticising the prosecution for providing contradictory information, the police 'by design or sheer incompetence' of messing up the evidence, and prosecution witnesses for lying and losing - or destroying - crucial evidence, and questioning the vanishing of the white dog and why the other dogs had been destroyed before bullet fragments were removed?

Outside the court Sarah Njoya and Ann shook hands.

'I'm so sorry about your husband,' Ann said softly.

'I'm sorry about your son,' Sarah replied even more quietly. 'I'm a mother too.'

Sarah, composed as always, was interviewed for *Last White Man Standing*, hanging out washing while her four children played in a dirt compound beside their mud-walled home. She was struggling to survive selling vegetables at the market, and finding it a challenge to get to court hearings, as it meant setting off before dawn and leaving her children behind. And yet surprisingly she told the interviewer, 'My heart is full of forgiveness.' She didn't want to see Tom punished severely, she said, or his family to suffer as she had.

Judgement day finally loomed on 7th May. I sat between Hugh and Ann. Sarah Njoya, in a new white headscarf, sat next to Hugh, returning his greeting with equal amiability, until a friend or relative seating himself firmly between them, ordered her to move. The general mood of optimism felt infectious as we rose for the Judge. The Lay Assessors had given their unanimous 'not guilty' verdict on 5th March. Now it was up to Justice Aponde.

In his 89-page judgement, Aponde pointed out that while Tom's companion on the day of the shooting had remained 'firm and steadfast,' Tom's change of tack had been 'an afterthought after realising the gravity of the case.' The judge further stated his conviction that there'd only been one firearm at the scene. 'I find as a fact that it is the accused who shot dead the deceased,' Aponde finally declared, before adding, 'The accused did not have malice aforethought...' Tom's charge was reduced to manslaughter. Final sentence would be handed out the following Tuesday, he said, and left quickly.

I detected a shine in Tom's eyes, as if holding back tears, before he was hurried out, Sally following, her face contorted with misery.

I had work in Tanzania the day of the sentencing, but I managed to find a television in the seedy bar of a village where some amused Tanzanians agreed to forego watching football in favour of viewing the sentencing of the Hon. Tom Cholmondeley, of whom only two of them had heard. On the small screen with its poor sound and indistinct picture, I could make out people thronging every available space, sitting on the floor, leaning against walls, squatting, kneeling and standing over Tom, the press with their lenses intrusively close. As I strained to hear, I thought I heard the judge say he was giving Tom a life sentence, but then he was talking about eight months. I'd misheard: a *light* sentence. Time, Justice Aponde continued, to allow the accused to reflect on his life and change direction appropriately. I glimpsed a composed Tom before he was engulfed by a blur of reporters. The camera focussed on shouting protesters wielding placards at the back of the court. 'Butcher of Naivasha,' I read on one, before the Tanzanians asked if they could switch channels.

Kat told me that before leaving court Hugh had put a hand on Sarah Njoya's arm. 'God bless, Sarah,' he'd said.

Tom had counted his days in custody: 1,097. 'I will have served 42 months of an eight-month sentence,' he joked with other prisoners and guards as the bus returned to Kamiti. But in spite of many Kenyans feeling he'd got off too lightly with a mere eight months, Tom felt despondent, then suddenly irrationally angry. He had simply not expected this.

'It was because of the political hit on the matter,' Tom's fellow prisoner Peter Ouko later told me. 'That's why the judge gave Tom a sentence.'

'It's been a difficult case,' Fred admitted in *Last White Man Standing*, 'dealing with someone not generally loved,' adding that he believed the frustrating amount of time the trial had taken to be intentional. 'A reasonable person would have foreseen the serious risk of shooting a person,' countered Tobiko, while Tobina Cole reflected that it was 'stupid but not evil' on Tom's part to open fire when he couldn't see clearly. The editor of the *Daily Nation* said the entire shenanigans had been a case of class; it was incidental that Tom happened to be white and of colonial descent - the point was his wealth. 'The rich have all the land in Kenya.' A television poll showed that 90% of Kenyans thought Tom had got off lightly. 'The message is clear,' concluded the documentary's narrator. 'If he survives in Kenya now it will be in spite of, not because he is a Delamere.'

Kenyan reporters were divided. Tom had made "a cowardly attack" Peter Kimani wrote in *The Standard* and should have been asked "to hand over his vast land or risk spending the rest of his life in jail." The *Nation*'s columnist, Gaitho, summed it up differently: "Once tempers had cooled the *White Mischief* headline was replaced by something much less judgemental. If Tom Cholmondeley were a wealthy black Kenyan accused of two killings within a short space of time, there would hardly be the same level of interest. Agitation on issues of landlessness and inequality in land ownership," he went on to note, "disproportionately tends to focus on the few remaining white farms and their vast holdings."

CHAPTER 30

Reforms and Repairs

Hugh, Ann and Sally were concerned that Tom would now be moved into the main prison, which indeed, after a few apprehensive days, he was. As he was marched away from the block that had become his safe place, he rang Sally, who immediately contacted the Head of Prisons, emphasising that as Tom had become so high-profile internationally, if things went wrong it would look extremely bad. Receiving a message on his phone, the warder escorting Tom suddenly stopped, then turned around. Such sudden adjustments highlighted not only the corruption in Kamiti, but also make it easy to understand why many Kenyans raged against the likes of Tom Cholmondeley with their ability to pull rank to gain privilege.

Relieved to be back in his familiar cell, Tom was thrilled to learn that he was to teach Business Studies to 12 very enthusiastic students ranging in age from 25 to 60, thrice weekly at the prison school. He prepared each lesson diligently, always looking forward to interacting with his pupils, enjoying this new exposure to the larger prison population. Other teachers (one of whom was Peter Ouko) were helpful and supportive. Realising there was a pressing need for computer classes, Tom approached the officer in charge and his confiscated laptop was finally returned. He'd already lost a laptop before that, on which he'd started writing his life story. He'd e-mailed this to me, but then my laptop had been stolen from my car. Tom had then handwritten a new version which Kat had been able to photocopy before it was confiscated too.

Since his incarceration, Tom had often talked to me about my writing his story. I'd suggested this was expanded into his family history in Kenya, for which I'd already begun my research in between working on *The Ghosts of Happy Valley*. While I wanted to include the whole story, it was still unclear to me why people outside Kenya might want to read about the Delamere family, let alone Tom who was so widely perceived in a negative light?

For now Tom was less concerned with his own story than arranging for four more laptops to be sent out from well-wishing friends in England with which he could teach his eager students. Although these computer classes continued to be viewed with some measure of suspicion by the authorities, the next months saw great progress as Tom's students learned to type their own legal documents and speed up their cases. In 2016 these computer classes would evolve into Zetech University, offering classes to all major prisons in Nairobi region, with more than 25 inmates taking law courses in three different prisons. This, Peter Ouko told me, 'was all from that small seed.'

In his spare time Tom created a flourishing vegetable garden, aiming to make the prison kitchens self-sufficient. 'It's still going,' Peter said. 'I was eating vegetables and fruits from there until I left...'

Tom was startled to spot another white man at the jail; Alexander McLean, the founder of *Africa Prisons Project*, was installing a library. Tom would become very interested in APP and its aim of assisting prisons to become places of positive transformation, promoting human rights and offering rehabilitation. Similarly inspired, Peter Ouko had formed an NGO called *Crime Si Poa* (roughly translated as 'Crime is not cool'), which Tom joined. This aimed to work in the slums to reduce crime and violence amongst vulnerable youths, (who made up 75% of inmates in Kenyan prisons), reaching out to them before they got into crime as well as rehabilitating released prisoners.

Tom left Kamiti very early in the morning of 24th October 2009, after five and a half months, under the normal remission for good behaviour. He didn't say goodbye - feeling it would be tempting fate. He left everything for his friends, apart from his old school blanket, its woollen fibres now infused with more frustration and emotion than he could ever have begun to imagine during those homesick nights at Pembroke. How would Soysambu look after three years of drought? How would it feel returning home, being with Sally

Dudmesh, seeing his boys?

Sally Dudmesh had made watertight arrangements. Even the media expected Tom's release on a different day. Maina Njenga was released on the same day, the *Daily Nation* reporting that charges had been withdrawn after Njenga had said he would publish the names of top officials involved in *Mungiki* activities. Now calling himself 'a follower of Jesus,' Njenga settled back home on his farm, giving out Bibles. His triumphant homecoming eclipsed any attention that might have been directed at Tom.

A friend brought Tom to Muthaiga Club where he had a hot bath, feeling self-conscious as he gulped down an English breakfast, unable to shed the feeling it might be his last. Sally wanted to fly straight to England, having organised Tom's visa, but Tom insisted on going home. He was flown by another friend to the airstrip behind Main House, where he was received by a huge crowd of farm employees. "I may have forgotten myself," he wrote later, "but no one else had forgotten me."

Soon afterwards they did fly to England; time for Tom to see his sons, to be rehabilitated back into the world beyond prison. But Tom hadn't forgotten his friends and obligations; within a week he set up the *Crime Si Poa* blog and paid for the domain address. Nelson Rotich told me that Tom had also made private arrangements to help Sarah Njoya to educate and feed her children, although it was not something he talked about.

After Tom's return from England, Ann asked me for lunch. 'We've got some guests...' she said rather vaguely. There I met Charles Quick, a tall man bearing a strong resemblance to Hugh. It turned out that Charles was Hugh's illegitimate son from the 'bus driver's daughter,' as Diana had called the young nurse from the Cottage Hospital. After her return to England she'd married the man who'd brought up Charles. In spite of a very different upbringing to one he might have had, Charles had inherited Hugh's love for model railways. Nor was it a surprise that he was a professor at Leeds University, immersed in the type of academic career Hugh might have excelled in had he been born into another life. Meanwhile Hugh was happy jamming on his guitar with his newfound grandson, Christopher, who played in a band in UK. I'd never heard Hugh play the guitar with such vigour, although he'd often enough given me a demonstration of his musical talents on the old pump-action organ in their library. It had been Bishop Hannington's, the unfortunate missionary who'd managed to get past the Maasai, but was murdered beside the Nile by the King of Buganda in 1885. Hugh told me he'd bought it off the Freemasons.

Connecting with Charles had been unexpected. Charles's friends had seen the photographs of Tom in the press coverage of his trial and noted an uncanny resemblance. He had thus contacted Tom in Kamiti, Tom had met up with him in England, and Charles had accepted Tom's invitation to visit Soysambu. The reunion was a happy one, though Charles was clearly uninterested in seeking a new life with these titled relatives.

In between spending time with his sons and travelling with Sally Dudmesh, whose jewellery business took her to interesting places, Tom returned to work. He was particularly pleased to find the conservancy up and running, an electric fence to separate his neighbours and wild animals being constructed along the problematic eastern boundary that flanked the main road from Mombasa to central Africa, and the two lodges he'd helped plan from Kamiti now taking shape.

In 2011 Soysambu enjoyed more than enough rain; my house was in a depression- 'a malarial swamp', Hugh called it - and my garden was under water for weeks, nirvana for the waterfowl that flocked in to swim and wade around my former lawn. Kenya Wildlife Service finally agreed to ease Soysambu's burgeoning zebra population by repopulating Amboseli National Park. A few hundred zebra were therefore herded into lorries, leaving Soysambu's green plains, hills and valleys sprinkled with wildflowers and driven the rough miles to the base of Mt Kilimanjaro to arrive at a lion-infested dustbowl. To Hugh's frustration the operation wasn't deemed a success, and there were no plans to repeat it. The Rothschild's giraffes had multiplied, too, and in 2011 some were moved to Ruko Conservancy beside Lake Baringo, travelling by lorry and boat, long necks sticking up from their crates, looking around with bewilderment at the vast body of freshwater surrounded by such arid scenery. It was 114 years since D had first seen Baringo and climbed the escarpment to Laikipia.

Soysambu now hosted paying guests at Sleeping Warrior Lodge - named after the more politically-correct alternative to Delamere's Nose - with its infinite views from the lava hills on south eastern Soysambu, or the Serena group's new luxury camp on the site of former Delamere Camp. An older lodge, Mbweha (Kiswahili for jackal), nestled beside Congreve's open plains alongside Nakuru National Park. Thanks to Kat's and Tom's combined efforts, Lake Elmenteita was in line for better protection as part of a proposed UNESCO World Heritage Site, together with Lakes Bogoria and Nakuru, due to their vast numbers of resident birds, as well as palearctic migrants.

But at the same time Kat was also battling to prevent a foreign-funded rubbish dump for the rapidly expanding Nakuru town on land adjoining Soysambu and Lake Nakuru National Park. Then in 2012, plans were announced to build an international airport between the lakes - in direct conflict with one of the world's highest concentrations of bird movements. Opponents were given just a month to respond. The Senior Warden of Lake Nakuru National Park and Simon Thomsett were equally horrified.

'This is one of the worst choices in the world for a large airport,' Simon exclaimed. The writer of the Environmental Impact Report for the Kenya Airports Authority had declared that bird migration happened only at night - ignoring the 5,000 pairs of Great White Pelicans breeding on Elmenteita, along with all the rest. A bird strike committee would be formed, continued the EIA, to deal with this 'bird menace.' A pelican, Simon pointed out, was one of the heaviest flying birds, and could easily take down a 747. Some years back, he told me, a similar committee at Jomo Kenyatta International Airport in Nairobi had opted to burn the grass to attract thousands of White Storks - which clean up pests, including army worm – in order to subject them to slow, unpleasant deaths by poisoning. This explained why the vast numbers of these storks when I had arrived on Soysambu, sometimes sleeping on my roof and in all the surrounding trees, had dropped to the occasional passing individual.

Eventually the proposed airport was dropped - for now. Kat then had to move on to other matters; the continuing threat of the timber-treatment plant, and leaking sewage from a new lodge across the lake.

Still unable to balance numbers of wildlife and thus profit from cattle, and with tourism not as lucrative as he'd hoped, Tom got busy planning a shopping mall, providing land on a former part of Manera in return for a 25% share. Some of Delamere's board had reservations, but in December 2012 Tom shook hands with Nakuru's Governor at the ground-breaking ceremony for Buffalo Mall, conveniently situated just out of Naivasha town, along the main highway to Uganda.

Other financial obligations loomed. Sally Cholmondeley, still living in Ann's oast house in Sussex, was asking for a divorce settlement, sufficient to educate her and Tom's sons in whatever careers they might pursue. One blisteringly hot Sunday I was cooling off in the turquoise waters of Hugh and Ann's pool. After drying off in Diana's arched gazebo with its inlaid Spanish tiles and worn out plastic pool loungers, I walked to the veranda, shadows of vultures overhead flickering across the sunburned lawn, to find Ann in tears. A gaping space on the dining-room wall revealed several dried-out gecko corpses. Hugh and Ann had already sold a Van Gogh painting to pay for the court case, and now their treasured Breughel had just been taken.

'We've had it since 1611,' Hugh said. 'I'm going to see if I can get Breughel to paint another one,' he added, his flippancy masking his sadness.

That October a *Telegraph* piece headlined 'Young bucks see better value in Old Masters' reported the sale of a winter scene by Pieter Breughel the Younger for £6 million. Hugh and Ann's Breughel was pictured. Thankfully there was no mention of the Delameres, or even any allusions to Happy Valley. Nor was there ever any sign of any improvements at Main House after Hugh and Ann had received their portion of the money and paid off Sally Cholmondeley. It seemed that the remaining millions had simply been sucked into Soysambu. Life would continue as usual, with Hugh constantly mentioning his ongoing cash flow problem. And yet he would – and often did – give those in need generous sums of money, including the unreliable son of one of Ann's longstanding Kikuyu friends, knowing he'd never see repayment. Such unconditional generosity on their part, sealed beneath a veneer of politeness, often made it hard to know when they'd had enough of visitors too. And there were plenty of those. On one occasion when I dropped by for afternoon tea I found Griff Rhys-Jones, filming a TV series about railways. The background interference of whinnying zebra, bellowing cattle and a Tropical Boubou belting out its monotonous note was frustrating the sound man, and five teapots, not to mention an array of biscuits and sponge cakes (Ann was determined to feed the entire crew) were patiently put onto a table, then back onto a trolley, for the third time.

'Why did you stay on in Kenya?' Rhys-Jones was asking Ann.

'Where else would we live?' she said.

'My family tends to settle for 400 years at a time in one place,' explained Hugh. 'Never be a pioneer - it cost my grandfather a fortune.'

I didn't see the television series, but heard that most of the tea-time footage had been cut.

Michael Cunningham-Reid died in February 2014, his obituaries pouncing on his lack of sympathy for Tom's shooting incidents. 'Once is forgivable,' he'd reportedly declared; 'twice is inexcusable.' In the minds of so many Kenyans and expatriates, Tom remained guilty.

For a while I'd observed what seemed to be an increasingly frantic edge to Tom's lifestyle, something I couldn't put my finger on. Was he happy? He'd always been a risk-taker, never afraid to try out new things, amusing us with stories of sampling cane rat, bamboo worm, scorpion and tarantula in Cambodia amongst other local delicacies, but now, in hindsight, perhaps his reckless living was an antidote to a deep feeling of foreboding. He wasn't in good shape physically either. 'Incident-prone,' Ann had once called him, and the second decade of the century had certainly seen a run of bad luck - or judgement. In the space of a few years Tom had injured himself falling off a horse and fallen off his motorbike competing in an extreme motorbike event in Scotland.

I'd thought about *Mganga* David often, knowing that he would have called me, sensing an imbalance in Soysambu, an urgent need for more cleansing. But he had died a couple of years back in his home in Kibera slums, in Nairobi. His daughter had phoned, asking for money for funeral expenses. I'd obliged. I asked her how he'd died?

'Malaria,' she'd replied dismissively.

Up until now Tom had not revisited Kamiti. I'd wondered if this was because his freedom still felt fragile, and he simply hadn't felt ready? Or was something else holding him back? Finally, in 2014, he returned, accompanied by Philip Coulson, to attend Peter Ouko's graduation, the first stage in his online studies for a law degree. Tom took him the graduation suit he'd bought for his friend in England.

'Tom and I went to Muthaiga Club afterwards,' Philip told me, 'and someone came up and said, "What are you two up to?" Without hesitation Tom replied, "I've just been to an old boys' reunion."'

I hadn't forgotten my promise to Tom to write the Delamere story. His attempts to find a publisher for his own part of it, for which he'd written a detailed proposal titled *Paradise Prejudiced*, hadn't been successful. But after the publication of my Happy Valley book in 2013, I'd immediately received a commission. Getting on with the Delamere story had remained on the back-burner. Finally, by early 2015 I was ready to focus on Tom's part of the story. But that March he vanished completely. Sally drove to Main House to ask Hugh and Ann where he was, but they didn't know either. It later turned out that Tom was in Thailand visiting another woman. Soon after arriving, he'd slipped and fallen from over half way up the steep path beside a ten-tier waterfall. Realising he was unable to move he was obliged to descend the treacherous slope on a stretcher.

In time, after hip surgery, Tom returned to Jersey Hall, where Sally struggled to bury her anger and hurt. But in between the relentless weekend parties, things no longer seemed the same.

By 2016, after various operations, including on his neck, Tom was hobbling around with a stick, now in need of a further hip operation. I'd noticed a change in him. He seemed calmer, quieter, more focussed. That June he visited Kamiti three times, the last time to hobble around for three hours taking water and soil samples, part of his plan to make the prison self-reliant by establishing a prison bakery and teaching its inmates farming skills so they could start generating their own incomes.

'Walking was difficult for him, but he just kept going,' Peter Ouko told me. 'In a short time he'd mapped it all out. He was so empowering.' Tom brought Peter fresh food as well as new ideas; he talked animatedly of getting a group of para-legals to work pro-bono or for minimal fee to provide legal help for prisoners, of donating 20 acres on the north-eastern corner of Soysambu for a halfway house for newly released prisoners (the necessity of re-adjusting something he truly understood), of a tree supermarket on the busy highway where ex-prisoners could plant and sell trees to replenish Kenya's depleted natural resources...

CHAPTER 31

...Nothing I Can Do

In July 2016, Sally Dudmesh persuaded a reluctant Tom to go to England to see an orthopaedic surgeon at the John Radcliffe hospital in Oxford. The consultant there was willing to operate on his hip the following week, but Tom declined; he was too busy to be confined for six weeks afterwards and his boys were coming home to Soysambu for their summer holidays. Sally Cholmondeley and Sally Dudmesh were in agreement that Tom should have the operation in England, but he was adamant about having it in Kenya, using the same experienced surgeon who'd replaced Ann's hip.

A few days before Tom's operation I joined him for sundowners by the lake. When I'd first arrived on Soysambu there'd been no lights across the lake, but now they stabbed the eastern horizon, their garish reflections crumpling in the water. I still hadn't got used to the change, but Tom would just smile and say, 'I pretend it's Monte Carlo!' There was a chilly wind. A large herd of buffalo was moving north along the western plain. As the sun set, softly gilding the lake, stars took turns to make their sparkling appearance in a deep indigo sky.

Tom was unusually quiet - as if he needed to absorb the beauty of the dusk. He told me of his plan to take Ann to India; she'd had a run of bad health and he felt it would be physically and emotionally healing. Their precious golden Labrador, Teddy, had died the previous year, and she'd taken it badly. I'd been trying to catch Tom for months, to get stories for the book, but he'd been impossibly busy. Now he said, 'I'll be stuck at home for weeks after the operation. Then you can come and interview me.' At last, perhaps, I could ask him more about the Njoya episode. What he would want me to write? From his demeanour, however, I could already guess the answer; he'd simply put it behind him. Tom didn't make judgements about people, cast his thoughts backwards, nor bear grudges. It was over and finished with.

I drove home along the track where sometimes I'd seen spring hares, or even aardvark or leopard, but tonight there was only a bull buffalo, statue-like in the middle of the road, glaring into my headlights.

On 16th August Sally told me that Tom walked into the hospital without his stick. 'At times like this I don't think I need that operation,' he told her. She lay on the bed beside him, sensing his nerves, holding him tightly until the anaesthetist arrived. As Tom was plugged into various machines, joking with the nurses, he remained adamant he didn't want an epidural.

'Are you sure it's OK to have a general anaesthetic?' Sally asked the doctor. 'He had one less than a year ago.' After she left, unbeknown to all of us, Amyra, Tom's girlfriend who'd been in Thailand with him at the time of the accident, slipped quietly into Tom's hospital room to spend the evening with him. They were planning a future together, she would later tell me, and Tom, she added, was happy and excited.

The operation was at nine the following morning. An hour and a half later Tom's blood pressure and temperature rose sharply.

Sally, who was doing errands in town, felt strangely uneasy. She'd just decided to head to the hospital when her phone rang. It was Philip Coulson, devastated, calling on the assumption that Sally had already been told. Now, to his horror, he realised he had to tell her.

Sally screamed the word back at him. '*DEAD*?'

"It has set me to reflect on the nature of death before its natural time," Tom had written in his prison diary, recalling the death of several friends (including his paragliding friend Simon Dolan) in a short space of time, "and how in Kenya we live fast and die before we should."

It was just after lunch when a friend rang me from Nakuru. 'I've just heard that Tom Cholmondeley is dead!' he cried - the news had already made it onto *The Star*'s website. 'It said he died during a hip operation.'

It was a warm afternoon, but suddenly I felt cold.

'It's true,' Kat said when I rang. 'I'm with Hugh and Ann.'

They were in the living room; Ann ghostly pale as she sat in her usual chair in a silent state of disbelief; Hugh, on the opposite side, in his. While Ann seemed paralysed by shock, Hugh's grief was immediate and heartbreaking.

'I shall miss him terribly,' he wept as farm staff came and went, their faces horrified, their condolences simple and heartfelt. 'We didn't always get on, but he had so many good ideas...and they would have worked.'

Snoo was in England, watching the racing, when she received a message from Kat to call urgently. 'My son is dead,' Hugh told her bleakly.

Over the next few days, stories began to unfurl. Kat told me that Ann had received a call from the distraught surgeon, telling her and Hugh to come to Nairobi as quickly as possible because something had gone wrong and Tom was in ICU. They'd called a neighbour to beg a lift in their plane, but then the phone had rung again. It was too late. Ann had called Philip. 'Oh, Philip,' she'd cried out in her pain, 'What have they done to my darling Tom?'

Sally Cholmondeley, Hughey and Henry happened to be staying at Villa Buzza. It was a relief to know they were together. There were calls from all over the world, including from Charles Quick. The house staff tiptoed around, their faces sombre. When I went to get more mugs from the musty pantry cupboards, I found Waweru in tears.

Later, sitting with Ann, Hugh, Philip, Sally Dudmesh, and a few friends, I heard the term *malignant hypothermia* as a possible cause of death.

'Shouldn't the hospital have been able to detect this?' someone asked.

Rumours rumbled around Tom's death; had somebody paid off one of the hospital staff and his resuscitation been sabotaged? Philip related how difficult the hospital had been, initially refusing to release Tom's body, determined they must do the post mortem. Frantic messages flying back and forth included one from 96-year old Charles Njonjo: 'Tell Coulson to *get him out*.' The law stipulated a government pathologist do the post mortem. This turned out to be the same person who'd testified during Tom's court case, and who now immediately suggested malignant hypothermia. With Philip's agreement he insisted he conduct the post mortem at a private funeral home, with Philip accompanying Tom's body.

The resulting report recommended toxic and genetic tests; specimens would need to be sent to Istanbul and London to determine whether the cause of this malignant hypothermia was molecular (in other words if Tom had a genetic predisposition) or toxicological. Philip warned Hugh and Ann of the cost of all this, but they felt it was important, to prevent possible disasters for future patients, although, as Hugh pointed out, it wouldn't bring Tom back. 'I keep thinking of something I want to say to him,' he sighed, 'and I can't because he's not there.'

Tom's picture was on the front pages of local newspapers, and the press only kept at bay by guards at Soysambu's Main Gate. It didn't prevent further regurgitation of the old Happy Valley stuff. *Tom Cholmondeley: Is he the last of the Happy Valley Ghosts?* asked Kenya's *Sunday Nation,* John Kamau retelling the story of Sally Dudmesh's doomed love life. He also quoted the wildlife activist Paula Kahumbu, a former board member of Soysambu Conservancy, who pointed out to those making negative comments on social media that Tom was not a racist, that he "spoke several African languages and had friends of all races and walks of life."

"Tom was quirky, formidably intelligent, impeccably courteous, calm and softly spoken," his friend Yoyo Vetch wrote in the Muthaiga Club magazine, paying tribute to his tireless work for his country. Other articles were less palatable; one reported the Sisina family's resolve to "block" Tom's burial until they'd been compensated. Eleven years on they were calling on the DPP to open fresh investigations. Another claimed that a Maasai council of elders had conducted a traditional ritual three weeks previously at Sisina's grave, cursing Sisina's killers and praying for justice. Now, they were saying, results had begun to manifest. The UK *Daily Mail* ran a piece about Tom's 'secret long-term affair,' picturing the forty-nine-year-old ex-girlfriend of Tom's holding the baby she claimed was his 'love child.' 'He was my life,' she sobbed, relating how they'd met at Cirencester, lived together at Flamingo House, that Tom had wanted to marry her, how they'd planned this baby when she'd visited him in Kamiti. He couldn't defend himself now, but he'd written in his diaries of how she'd moved into Flamingo House unbidden all those years ago, and had had to be persuaded to leave.

Indeed he'd been no saint. Fond as he was of Tom, Philip Coulson had often found him exasperating. He was 'a great mind, a visionary, but a reluctant follower of corporate governance if it did not suit him,' Philip told me in 2018. 'He could be a terrible flibbertigibbet too; he would agree to one thing and yet something else would emerge.' Snoo had often been exasperated by what she called 'Tom time,' recalling an occasion when he'd been 'six hours late for lunch!' Moreover, behind Tom trailed this legacy of mishandled affairs with women. Was this a refusal or possibly even an inability to emotionally connect? Sally Dudmesh once told me she believed Tom 'didn't understand hurt.'

But maybe he'd never found what he sought. To me it seems likely that Tom's veneer of old-fashioned courtesy, his innate kindness, made it difficult for him to tell a woman that she simply wasn't *the* one. Like his parents, perhaps he sometimes failed to get the right message across, even resorting to that Kenyan habit of avoiding a negative response. He certainly saw himself as Kenyan, never applying for the British citizenship to which he'd have been entitled when dual nationality became legal in 2010. "I have still got no urge to live anywhere else," he'd written after his release from Kamiti, "and I see my children still have a future and an important role to play."

A month after he died the *Daily Nation* ran a piece headlined, *Becoming Kenyan; The Delameres and the politics of being Maasai.* Tom had every right to carry a Kenyan ID, Joyce Nyairo wrote. She referred to Kenya's unacknowledged white tribe, who'd learned "to belong without shouting, to steer clear of political controversy," although Tom had "unwittingly succeeded in grabbing the headlines." And now, she continued, with dark-edged humour, "You can't get more Kenyan than a statement that the locally conducted post-mortem did not reveal a clear cause of death...To be a prominent Kenyan is to be a person whose cause of death leaves people engulfed in fretful whispers and torrid rumours."

Tom never doubted he belonged, noting in his diaries that he'd travelled the world extensively but never found anywhere that came close to Kenya. When questioned by other Kenyans about his origins, he wrote, he could "feel what black men in Britain feel when asked, 'Where are you from?'"

The funeral was planned for 26th August. Sally Dudmesh, overwhelmed by people and plans, opposed Hugh and Ann's wish to have Tom buried in the family graveyard, which she found 'a depressing place,' suggesting a funeral pyre by the lake. To ease the mounting tension, Kat, Yoyo Vetch, and myself went to look at the graveyard. Although the fence and gate were in a state of disrepair, we agreed it could be spruced up, with some of the bush cleared to restore its lake view. While we were there, two giraffes a little distance away watching intently. I looked at the old graves; D's flanked by Gwladys's (both with their headstones) and Florence's unmarked one. It's most likely these two gravestones were placed by the colonial government, probably some years before Tom moved his mother's remains. Either he never got around to adding a plaque for his mother, or maybe he thought it unnecessary. The other unmarked grave was a little distance away, presumably Eleanor's, Ann and Hugh's baby daughter.

'I've never seen her grave,' Ann told me after we'd returned.

'If you'd like to see it, I'll take you,' I offered.

'Not now,' she said.

The following morning, when I arrived at the end of breakfast to see where help was needed, Ann expressed her desire to go and find some giraffes, at which Snoo and Sally Cholmondeley both said they'd like to come. As soon as they went to their rooms, Ann said quickly: 'Let's go now. Just us.' The tragedy had tumbled her and Hugh back into wheelchairs. Henry, now a tall and handsome younger version of Tom, helped his grandmother out of hers into my car.

'Can we go to the graves?' Ann asked as soon as we were out of the gate.

I stopped the car beside the unmarked grave. Tom's freshly dug one was just below it. I walked away down the slope, leaving Ann to commune with the pile of rocks that covered her baby daughter, and the hole that would take the body of the son she'd known for 48 years. As we drove back, she was quietly composed, rewarded with a sighting of half a dozen giraffe, watching us as we watched them.

My children were devasted at Tom's death. They'd known him most of their lives. Michael was working in Iceland and couldn't get away, but Siana was able to come from London. On the way to Tom's funeral, we stopped at the graveyard to drop a Crowned Eagle feather in the waiting grave, given to me by Simon Thomsett. The lake below was sky blue, its ragged edges carpeted with flamingos. The narrow plateau behind the graves, studded with euphorbia, stretched south, its fresh greenness flecked with tail-flicking Thomson's gazelles, nonchalant zebra, a passing troop of baboon and clumps of shyer eland, in the foreground a bachelor herd of impala. There was a sudden poignancy in this beauty, causing my throat to constrict. Guy, son of Simon Combes, was unable to make the funeral, but he'd called me from California. 'Despite the fact that we've been through so many dramas during Dad's death and Tom's arrests,' he'd said tearfully, 'Soysambu kept us strong through all those years. If we lived anywhere else in the world we'd have fallen apart. It was our love for this place that kept us together.' We'd agreed it would again now.

The service was in a marquee, beneath the fever trees surrounding Jersey Hall. A vast number of people poured in, different colours and creeds, many forced to sit or stand beneath the trees. The Nakuru Governor and the 96-year-old Charles Njonjo were among the congregation, and Barbara Terry, holding a photograph of Tom at kindergarten. "Typically our burials are a study in performance theatre," Joyce Nyairo would write in the *Daily Nation*, where "local politicians trip over each other in the race for the microphone." But Tom's was quietly private "in that minimalist way that white Kenyans have learnt to belong."

'Time, like an ever-rolling stream, soon bears us all away,' we sang. The choice of hymns was a combined effort. Hugh had chosen 'Oh, God, our help in ages past,' Ann the Evening Vesper, and Sally Dudmesh 'Lord of the Dance.' There were prayers along with the tributes in English and Kiswahili, the latter provided by Fred Odhiambo. The timeless Desiderata was read:

'Speak your truth quietly and clearly;
and listen to others,
even the dull and the ignorant; they too have their story.'

Tom had always listened, always had time for everyone, whatever their background.

Peter Ouko, still in Kamiti, had written a eulogy which was read out. Even though everybody in Kamiti knew who Tom was, said Peter, "he wanted to be treated like every other inmate, had no airs and never threw his weight around...He was accessible to anyone who sought his counsel, a stance he continued with long after his release... What I found unique about Tom is that he never blamed anybody but himself. He did not pretend to be perfect, and readily said so." Ann, Peter said he'd been told, "would rather get the best lawyers and pay hefty legal fees than pay a single cent as a bribe to get him free. His family did not believe in shortcuts but in the rule of the law." He spoke of Tom's transformative work. "Tom appreciated that the secret of change was to focus all his energy, not on fighting the old, but on building the new." And above all, Tom, he pointed out: "did not see a country of blacks and whites, browns and yellows with shades of either in between. Tom saw and believed in a united Kenya...an equal country where no Kenyan has rights to claim to be more Kenyan than another Kenyan just because of their tribe or race, a country where hard and honest workers are rewarded and not pilloried, profiled and stigmatized because of their skin colour, status or creed."

Peter had been touched to read on Tom's Facebook page that under "Place of work," it read, '*Crime Si Poa.*' "Rest in Peace my brother, friend, mentor and Chair," he concluded.

Tom's long coffin ('incredibly heavy,' Philip later told me) was carried out by his sons, Nelson, and some of his closest friends, to David Bowie's 'Space Oddity.' The song's words, so pertinent in 1969 when history had been made on the moon, now took on new weighted meaning, especially as the singer himself was also dead. His lyrics stabbed us with emotion as Ground Control tried to call Major Tom. And while Bowie's guitar playing blended with his powerful voice and accompanying electronics, many of us broke down in tears. As the famed piece reminded us, Major Tom, even if he could hear, was now far above our small blue planet...

And there was nothing he could do.

Postscript

That year I accompanied Hugh to the Christmas carol service at Pembroke, the school Tom had attended all those years ago. As we sat in the candlelit chapel, enchanted by the singing of perfectly pitched childish voices, I noticed his tears. On the way back, having survived the insane Sunday traffic, motorists blinding us with their lights, we were grateful when the elderly driver, Ndung'u, turned off into the tranquil darkness of Soysambu. Hugh blew his nose again. Caught by our headlights two old bull buffalo moved slowly across the dusty road. A few miles further on Hugh asked Ndung'u to stop the car. There were three giraffe beside the road he wanted to talk to. 'In English,' he told me - once again the determined flippancy. 'Unlike buffalo, who respond better if talked to in Maasai.' The graceful giraffe stood looking down their long necks, beneath the light of an enormous moon. 'They like it when you talk to them,' Hugh said softly.

He hadn't been well enough to face a second memorial service for Tom, arranged by Peter Ouko at Kamiti. It had been held in the hall as the chapel was too small for the large congregation of prisoners. By now equipment for Tom's Bakery, as the prison enterprise had been named, had been provided by a well-wisher.

After Peter was released from prison after 18 years, I asked the reason for his imprisonment. His wife had been raped and murdered, he explained, and his in-laws, with whom he'd never got on, had had him charged, even changing his children's identities to ensure he couldn't trace them. But now, finally reunited with his adult kids, albeit still in court trying to clear his name, he'd found forgiveness. 'If you let go then you move on very fast,' he concluded, making light of the inner strength this must have required. 'When you become the bigger person it's the other person who's left on the back bench.'

On 6th June 2017 Patrick Waweru died. He'd driven Sally Dudmesh back from Nairobi, collapsed on arrival at Jersey Hall, and died soon afterwards. The post-mortem revealed a lung infection, although Sally remained convinced he'd had a heart attack. Kat, who'd accompanied Hugh and Ann to Tom's burial, told me that she'd walked away from the graveyard feeling this moment should be private for the family, to find Waweru standing in the flimsy shade of an acacia, also distancing himself, inconsolable. He'd cried like a child, wetting her shoulder. It was as if his heart had been torn apart at Tom's death, and now had finally broken. Another setback for Hugh and Ann. They'd gradually been regaining their strength, doing up Tom's old cottage for their grandsons - 'We've evicted Diana!' Ann told me triumphantly, referring to the portrait with the roving eyes - and focussing on the nitty gritty details of building a path across the lawn for Hugh's wheelchair. His Parkinson's disease was worse, no doubt exacerbated by stress. Aged 82 now, he'd begun using his wheelchair most of the time.

The paltry long rains were failing to sustain Soysambu. The climate felt hotter and drier, but the cold mornings were biting. Nevertheless, there was flooding in Nairobi. The drains were choked up by waste - mostly *Delamere* milk packets, Hugh pointed out to me with an ironic smile as we sat on their inward-facing veranda. My eyes had recently been drawn to advertisements on Nairobi billboards, advertising Brookside's products, still owned by the Kenyatta family, but using Delamere's name and logo alongside a pair of luscious lips, the colour of the relevant yoghurt flavour. *Delamere*, proclaimed the poster, *It's your time.* Earlier that year, when northern Kenya had been afflicted by drought, Samburu and Maasai herdsmen had driven vast herds of emaciated livestock onto the large ranches of Laikipia, many of which were still white-owned. There was talk of most of these herds belonging to wealthy politicians avoiding tax, and that it was they who'd armed these invaders. A white ranch owner had been shot, houses and a lodge burned, and eventually the government had intervened with a heavy-handed response.

Would the Maasai try to reclaim Soysambu too?

'The Maasai always said as long as the *Delameres* have this land it's OK,' said Hugh with an ironic smile. The loud coos of the Laughing Dove killed further conversation. An opportunistic White-browed Robin Chat, making such a low fly-past that it brushed the top of my head, reminded us it was lunchtime.

'Yes, please,' Hugh said, as I offered him a cup of tea. 'One railway-British-regulation-sized-cup. Rather a lot of sugar. Three please.' They normally drank mid-morning coffee, but I'd run out, so they graciously accepted the alternative this chilly July morning of 2018, its thick cloud and thin drizzle more common to Nairobi than the Rift Valley. Hugh was holding court on my veranda, seated on a bulky chair made out of his grandfather's old cedar fence posts, wrapped in two Maasai *shukas* to fend off the wind. I was always touched when they come to visit; Hugh didn't travel well, and he'd struggled to make his way on crutches to my veranda. Through the ordeals of Tom's two shootings, divorce, and premature death, they'd somehow retained their dignity. Hugh's white hair was thinner, his skin delicate-looking, blemished by the African sun, but he still had his imposing stature and lofty air of nobility. Ann had lost weight, but she'd somehow retained her youthful looks; her dark hair short and only slightly greying, her beautiful smooth complexion. She too had a gentle way about her, always managing to look neat and tidy when the rest of us were dusty and windblown. While facial expressions were usually kept to a minimum - a raised eyebrow perhaps or a witty comment while poker-faced - her keen sense of humour hadn't left her, and when she broke into laughter her entire face laughed too.

Hugh remained Chairman of the Board of Delamere Estates, greatly respected by Philip Coulson who still believed in the integrity of his decisions. There was a new CEO: John, son of Sam Weller who'd been a manager on Soysambu during its heyday in the fifties, had been tasked with preventing Soysambu's descent into bankruptcy.

'You know, when Grandfather came,' said Hugh, studying the arm of his fence-post chair, 'there were no trees here except along the river. He put up fences, 420 miles of them. But he only fenced what was necessary by law, which was the boundary of the farm, and then to divide the grazing he put one fence down the middle. Then the zebra smashed it all. I ought to send a monthly bill, 30 bob a head, to KWS. At least buffalo always use the same hole in a fence, but zebra don't - they just go on breaking fences all over the place.' The Kenya Wildlife Service's continued prohibition on culling of wildlife was making it difficult for Soysambu to be self-sustaining. Cattle had to generate enough income to pay for the aesthetically pleasing but currently economically useless wild animals. Earlier that year tourism had received a blow when Sleeping Warrior Lodge had burned down. With the old migratory corridors now so heavily populated, and Tom's proposed new corridor not yet a reality, the multiplying wildlife, which Soysambu was not allowed to manage, made it impossible to have anything close to the 11,000 head of cattle Hugh said were required to make a profit. In this daily conflict between farming and conservation, neither was it working for wildlife, with overcrowding of certain species at the expense of others.

Although Hugh had capitulated to Tom's insistence that Soysambu morph into a wildlife conservancy for the sake of its own survival, he was a farmer at heart, and it was with chagrin that he'd watched D's fence posts being systematically removed.

'Yes, well - people are making lovely furniture out them,' said Ann.

We watched a herd of goats tumble through the distance, frightening a giraffe which cantered gently out of sight. 'I need to increase the goat herds,' Hugh said. 'Goats don't compete with cattle. Like giraffe they eat bushes. Leaves have double the protein at 22%, compared to grass at 11%. They spent years teaching you that at Cambridge. I'm glad I can tell you something I've learned that I can remember!'

After having fallen out with the Delameres and being paid her dues as Tom's cohabiting partner, Sally Dudmesh left Soysambu later that year. Shortly before her departure she told me, her tea growing cold, that one drug in the concoction administered in the anaesthetic given to Tom had triggered malignant hypothermia and that this was in the toxicology report that was done in Europe 'The reports showed Tom had a chromosome which had a predisposition for malignant hypothermia,' she explained, blinking back tears: 'A doctor told me that it's a very Caucasian syndrome.'

After a lifestyle that invited many brushes with death, it still seemed extraordinary and impossible that Tom had died while undergoing a standard operation in hospital. It had then taken three years to obtain a death certificate; when the hospital had eventually released the necessary documentation, there'd been a further glitch when it was discovered that 'Cholmondeley' had been misspelt on Tom's ID card.

All over Soysambu, poaching and charcoal burning had escalated since Tom's death, and by 2019 there were further threats from Kenya's fast-growing infrastructure, the government forging ahead regardless of environmental impact. There was renewed planning of an international airport for Nakuru, this time at Lanet, lying just southeast of Lake Nakuru, another disaster-in-the-making for Soysambu, with a flight path that would be over Lake Elmenteita. But the most immediate concern were the gigantic new electricity pylons, their circuitous route making no economic sense, but said to be influenced by powerful politicians with their own agendas. These pylons, having already reached Soysambu's southwestern border, were set to bisect some of its loveliest plains, rocky ridges and woodlands, marching in front of The Nose, past my house towards Elmenteita town, before veering left towards Eburru. What effect would these towering structures, strung with high-voltage power lines, have on the pelicans as they flew low to catch the thermals? How would the flamingos see them at night?

Simon Thomsett was already busy enough, trying to rehabilitate an increasing number of raptors injured by other ill-thought-out power lines, or rushing to assist dying vultures in the Maasai Mara, poisoned by militant herdsmen targeting their efforts at those lions or hyena that had killed their livestock. Power lines were an emotive issue for him and Kat Combes; in the past decades half a dozen Rothschild's giraffe had been killed by low-hung lines that ran through the heart of Soysambu. More recently Soysambu's burgeoning lion population had also suffered from poisoning, their corpses found not far from the Delamere graves. It was a tragic day for conservation, and one that suggested the continued presence of a rotten core somewhere within Soysambu, as well as explaining the mysterious disappearance some time back of the original pair, Flir and Valentine. Now all that was left on Soysambu was one of their granddaughters, her three cubs, and another orphaned one.

Soysambu had seen dramatic change since 1906 when D had bought his first 10,000 acres alongside the pink lake, building this up laboriously into a sheep ranch where lion were considered vermin that must be shot. It had passed through two world wars, recovered from financial ruin and reinvented itself as a remarkable success in cattle breeding, booming and continuing to produce successful racehorses during Kenya's own war for independence. But by the 1980s an increasingly repressive political climate saw its decline again. Then came the time when it became apparent that its wildlife must be protected in the face of Kenya's increasing human population and associated destruction of surrounding ecosystems. While its water levels had always fluctuated, and the waterfowl had regularly come and gone, Lake Elmenteita, battling with heavy human influence on those parts of its shoreline outside Soysambu, was seeing a massive drop in bird numbers. Only a dozen years after 610,000 individual birds had been counted on the lake in 2007, there were 87,840. Out of the eleven sites where the counting took place in July 2019, throughout the Rift Valley and Central Kenya, Lake Elmenteita still had the second highest count. But would these pylons now see sufficient avian massacre for it to lose its World Heritage Status? And now, with Manera now too downsized to carry Soysambu Conservancy through those harder times, what lay ahead? Now, more than ever, I wished I could call *Mganga* David to urgently carry out his protection and cleansing rites on Soysambu.

After losing their father, Hughey and Henry had continued to return home to Soysambu during school holidays. They hadn't gone to Eton, Sally choosing two separate schools that suited their different temperaments. Like Tom, they sought adventure, enjoying off-road motorcycling, and they'd also inherited that Delamere ability to get on with all generations and types, a charm accentuated by good old-fashioned manners.

One morning in mid-2019, after he'd climbed The Nose,

Hughey dropped by for a cold drink. Now 20, tall and handsome, his hair darker than Henry's, he had completed a year of agriculture at Cirencester, where Henry planned to join him for a more business-related course. It was heartening to hear Hughey say that when he felt he'd acquired the necessary qualifications and experience, and in spite of all the politics and complications, he intended to return to Soysambu. They'd try to hold onto their remaining land, he told me, admitting that there were 'politics' and it might be 'tricky,' but going on to set out his intention for a more hands-on approach to its management, his conservation vision even greater than Tom's.

'Tom always had this bigger vision of things!' Kat had once told me. She remained on the Greater Lake Elmenteita Conservation Area committee, still working towards Tom's initial idea of a wildlife corridor in the face of increasing conservation challenges. And now Hughey was talking about opening up even more wildlife migration corridors than those his father had visualised. He left me with a sense of hope as he departed in Tom's old pick-up, his profile and parting gestures so like his father's.

I'd come to live on Soysambu two decades earlier, thanks to Tom's initial kindness, still remaining here on grace-and-favour terms, as an old family friend. This had been the most difficult story I'd ever tried to write, emotionally invested as I was in the place. I'd begun it, ended it, given up completely, tried again, tossed aside possible titles, going through all this repeatedly, often writing long sections that I knew would have to be left out. It had been through my own rejections and rewrites before I even tried to find a publisher. And now that I'd finally finished this extraordinary story, I was afraid that if I had to leave this harshly beautiful, crazily unpredictable place my heart might tear apart too.

I'd learned much about Soysambu and the Delameres' past - too much, perhaps – and seen where my own family history grated or resonated, understood the bigger picture. "Settler descendants would love to be judged on their own terms, based on their individual efforts and intentions," writes Janet McIntosh in the concluding chapter of *Unsettled*, "yet the colonial past and structurally entrenched white privilege that lingers on, keep rising up to interfere."

Would the Delameres, after Tom's two shooting incidents and unexpected death, be able to keep Soysambu? There was one positive indication that things had improved; Hugh and Ann had entertained members of the extended Ole Sisina family on their veranda. Many pots of tea and tins of biscuits were enjoyed, but more important, there was a ritualistic exchange of honey between the two families. This symbolic laying to rest of issues arising ever since the shooting of Samson Ole Sisina back in 2005, was beautifully summed up by his brother, John, in a text message: "Hallo Mrs Delamere," he wrote, "Am so grateful and happy indeed to here (sic) that you doing good. I must also acknowledge the previous successful meeting with us. It was a clear indication of forgiveness from both parties hence making our strong bond of unity…thanks." Although unrelated, I'd noticed the previous day that the road into Gilgil from the main highway had acquired a new name. *Delamere Road.* An unexpected nod to history.

Shortly afterwards, as I walked my dogs past one of Soysambu's old-style cattle bomas surrounded by rough walls of thorn, woodsmoke from the Maasai herdsman's fire sliding over the multi-coloured backs of the cows to disperse between brittle yellow acacias, I reflected that this scene could have been a hundred years earlier, in D's time. But a short distance away metal pegs had been punched into the ground, marking the place for a pylon to replace a swathe of woodland and destroy a hyena den, eradicating so many bird perches and nests I'd identified on daily walks.

As I walked on, a massive slice of rainbow suddenly appeared in the east, a curious clipped arc of warm colours blending gently into cooler ones, their iridescence floating in a bottomless baby-blue sky, like a hallucination above the sunburned plain. Its beauty resting in its impermanence, it felt symbolic. Change was inevitable. I'd never planned to end Soysambu's story this way, but a cruel twist of fate had proved what we all know; life is unpredictable. There was no knowing what the future held for any of us, or for Soysambu. But what I did know, right here and right now, was this overwhelming beauty.

As I walked on, the rainbow expanded against a brewing

backdrop of indigo storm clouds, arching over the ranch as if stretched by some unseen power. Kicking up dust, a herd of zebra moved through a copse of pale-yellow acacia *vachellia seyal*, a vulnerable beauty in every drought-exposed twig. The wind's breath brought that deliciously nourishing damp-earth smell of rain. Time to hurry home before the buffalo emerged. It began to rain softly; tiny drops, lighting up like jewels in the slanted rays of late sun, raising dust as they embraced the earth. The rainbow had shrunk again, now just a lingering arm above the Delamere graves.

Bibliography

Books:

Arensen, Shel, *And They're Off: More than 100 Years of Racing in Kenya*, Jockey Club of Kenya, Nairobi, 2017

Aschen, Ulf, *The Man Whom Women Loved: The Life of Bror Blixen*, St Martin's Press, New York, 1987

Barnett, Donald L, and Njama, Karari, *Mau Mau from Within* Modern Reader Paperbacks, New York, 1996

Barsby, Jane Clare, *Abraham's People: A Kenyan Dynasty*, privately published, 2014

Bennun, Leon, and Njoroge, Peter: *Important Bird Areas in Kenya*, Birdlife, 1999

Best, Nicholas, *Happy Valley: The Story of the British in Kenya*, Secker & Warburg, London, 1979

Bewes, Cannon T F C, *Kikuyu Conflict*, The Highway Press, London, 1953

Blixen, Karen, *Out of Africa*, Cape, London, 1964

Carberry, Juanita, *Child of Happy Valley*, Heinemann, London, 1999

Cole, Eleanor, *Random Recollections of a Pioneer Kenya Settler*, Baron, UK, 1975

Corbett, Jim, *Tree Tops*, Oxford University Press, New York and London, 1955

Cox, Richard, *Kenyatta's Country*, Hutchinson, London, 1965

Cran, Hugh, *Promises to Keep: A British Vet in Africa*, by Merlin Unwin, UK, 2015

Cranworth, Lord, *Kenya Chronicles*, Macmillan & Co. Ltd, UK, 1939

Delamere, Hugh, *Not in the History Books*, Old Africa Books, Kenya, 2016

Dinesen, Isak, *Letters from Africa 1914-1931*, Weidenfeld & Nicholas, London 1981

Douglas-Home, Charles, *Evelyn Baring: The Last Proconsul*, Collins, London, 1978

East African Women's League, *They Made it Their Home*, privately published, Nairobi, 1962

Elkins, Caroline, *Imperial Reckoning: The Untold Story of Britain's Gulag in Kenya*, Henry Holt and Company, New York, 2005

Farrant, Leda, *Diana, Lady Delamere and the Murder of Lord Erroll*, privately published, Nairobi, 1977

Fletcher, Lady Victoria, *Castle to Caravan: An Autobiography*, privately published, 1983

Fox, James, *White Mischief*, Penguin, London, 1984

Furneaux, Rupert, *A Crime Documentary: The Murder of Lord Erroll*, Stevens, London, 1961

Gavaghan, Terence, *Of Lions and Dung Beetles*, privately published, UK, 1999

Glyn-Jones, Richard, *Still Unsolved: Great True Murder Cases,* 'Who Shot the Earl of Errol?' (sic) Benjamin Bennett, Secaucus, NJ, 1990

Hamilton, Genesta: *A Stone's Throw, Travels from Africa in Six Decades*, Hutchinson, London 1986

Hayes, Charles, *Oserian: Place of Peace*, Rima Books, Kenya and Canada, 1997

Hewitt, Peter, *Kenya Cowboy*, Avon Books, London, 1999

Hopkirk, Mary, *Life at Vale Royal Great House 1907-1925: The memoirs of Mary Hopkirk (nee Dempster)*, sponsored by Cheshire County Council and Vale Royal Borough Council, Stuart Hogg, 1998

Hornsby, Charles, *Kenya: A History Since Independence*, I B Taurus and Co Ltd, London, 2012

Hughes, Lotte, *Moving the Maasai: A Colonial Misadventure*, Palgrave Macmillan, UK 2006

Hutchinson, Tim, 2006 *Kenya Up-country Directory*, Edition 2, privately published, Kenya, 2006

Huxley, Elspeth, *White Man's Country*, vols I and II, Chatto and Windus, London, 1935

Huxley, Elspeth, *East Africa,* William Collins of London, 1941

Huxley, Elspeth, *No Easy Way: A History of the Kenya Farmers' Association and Unga Ltd*, privately published, printed by East African Standard Limited, Nairobi, 1957

Huxley, Elspeth, *Nellie, Letters from Africa*, Weidenfeld & Nicholson, London 1980

Huxley, Elspeth, and Curtis, Arnold, *Pioneers' Scrapbook*, Evans Brothers, London, 1980

Keating, Molly, *The Kenya Connection: An account of the historical links between Northwich and Kenya*, Northwich and District Heritage Society

Kenya Information Office, *This is Kenya,* Nairobi, 1947

Leakey, Dr L S B, *Mau Mau and the Kikuyu*, Methuen & Co, London, 1952

Lovatt-Smith, David, *Kenya, The Kikuyu and Mau Mau*, Mawenzi Books, UK, 2005

Lovell, Mary S, *Straight on Till Morning, The Biography of Beryl Markham*, Hutchinson, London, 1987

Lovell, Mary S, (compiled and introduced by), *The Splendid Outcast: The African Stories of Beryl Markham*, Arrow Books, London, 1987

Markham, Beryl, *West with the Night,* Houghton Mifflin, 1942

Migel, Parmenia, *Titania, The Biography of Isak Dinesen*, Michael Joseph, London 1968

Mills, Stephen, *Muthaiga, Volume 1, 1913-1963*, Mills Publishing, Nairobi, 2006

North, Stephen J, *Europeans in British Administered East-Africa: A Biographical Listing 1888-1905*, privately published, UK, 1995

Osborne, Frances, *The Bolter*, Virago Press, London 2008

Paice, Edward, *Lost Lion of Empire: The Life of 'Cape-to-Cairo' Grogan*, Harper Collins, London, 2001

Parker, Ian, and Bleazard, Stan, *An Impossible Dream*: Librario, UK, 2001

Playne, Somerset, *East Africa (British): Its History, People, Commerce, Industries, and Resources*, 1908-9, Unwin Brothers, Limited, The Gresham Press, Woking and London

Roberts, Granville (Foreword), Public Relations Officer for Kenya, *The Mau Mau in Kenya*, Hutchinson and Co, UK, 1954

Roosevelt, Theodore, *African Game Trails: An Account of the*

African Wanderings of an American Hunter-Naturalist, Charles Scribner's Sons, New York,1910

Spicer, Paul, *The Temptress: The Scandalous Life of Alice, Countess De Janze*, Simon & Schuster, London, 2010

Topps, Tim, *The Umzindusi Letter*, by Matador, UK, 2017

Trzebinski, Errol, *Silence Will Speak – The Life of Denys Finch Hatton and His Relationship with Karen Blixen*, Heinemann, London, 1977

Trzebinski, Errol, *The Lives of Beryl Markham*, Heinemann, London 1993

Trzebinski, Errol, *The Life and Death of Lord Erroll, The Truth Behind the Happy Valley Murder*, Fourth Estate Limited, London, 2000

Vere-Hodge E R and Collister, P, *Pioneers of East Africa*, The Eagle Press, Nairobi, 1956

Watson, Rupert, *Culture Clash: The Death of a District Commissioner in the Loita Hills,* Old Africa Books, Kenya, 2014

Wheeler, Sara, *Too Close to the Sun: The Life and Times of Denys Finch Hatton*, Jonathan Cape, London, 2006

Wilson, Dr C J, *Before the White Man in Kenya,* McCorquodale and Company, UK,1952

Magazine and newspaper articles:
Historic:
Various issues of *Farmer's Weekly* and *Races Past* (Kenya)

'Kenya's Clouded Future: Can the European Survive?', Elspeth Huxley, *Daily Telegraph*, 1.3.63

The Kenya Church Review, The English Press, Nairobi, 1963

'Kenya on the Brink': Parts 1 and 2, *Sunday Times*, 10.8.75 and 17.8.75

'Femme fatale takes Kenyan murder secret to her grave', *Daily Telegraph,* 7.9.87

Kenyan:
'The Mysterious Death of Jim Elkington', Tom Lawrence, *Old Africa*, issue No. 24, Aug-Sept 2009

Julius M Huho and Edward M Mugalavai (*The Effects of Droughts on Food Security in Kenya*) online

Various articles *The Standard* and *Daily Nation*, including:

'Arrest puts the spotlight on a pioneer settler clan', Watoro Kamau, *Sunday Nation*, 24.4.2005

'Outrage as Delamere is free over killing', Nation team, *Daily Nation*, 19.5.2005

'Delamere: Now ministers step up pressure on Wako', 'Michuki takes police chiefs to State House', 'PSC summons Wako over Cholmondley (sic)', Nation team, 'Murgor rules out new murder charge', Nyakundi Nyamboga, and 'AG blames the police', Ngumbao Kithi, *Saturday Nation*, 21.5.2005

'AG, police in major row over Delamere', Douglas Okwatch, and 'LDP blames Kibaki for Delamere controversy', Eliud Miring'uh and Samuel Mburu, 'Anger mounts at rancher's release', Sunday Standard team, 'Security tightened as Maasai plan to invade Soysambu ranch', Allan Kisia and Kipchumba Kemei, *The Sunday Standard*, 22.5.2005

'LSK gives ultimatum to Wako', 'Police guard the Gilgil ranch' and 'Delamere farm loses Sh500,000 since death', Nation Reporter, *Daily Nation*, 24.5.2005

'Wako defends stand on cases', *Daily Nation*, 25.5.2005

'I've picked useful lessons in the school of life, says Cholmondeley', Peter Kimani, *Daily Nation* 27.5.2005

'Delamere son's new home and Kamiti friends', Dominic Wabala, *Sunday Nation*, 2.7.2006

'Rifle was moved from crime scene, court told', Evelyn Kwamboga, *The Standard*, 29.9.2006

'Who is haunting graves of the Delamere family?', Michael Njuguna, *Daily Nation*, 3.4.2007

'Revealed: Shocking details of the humanitarian crisis in Kenyan prisons', Kenneth Ogosia, and 'Humanitarian disaster behind the prison crisis, Opinion, and 'My life at Kamiti, by Cholmondeley',

Jillo Kadida, *Sunday Nation*, 11.5.2008

'Court ignored vital facts in case, says Cholmondeley defence team', Evelyn Kwamboka, and 'Cholmondeley: fingers crossed as Delamere grandson awaits fate', and 'Judge differs with assessors, gives guilty verdict', Wahome Thuku, *The Standard*, 8.5.2009

'Tense moments at final verdict', John Ngirachu, and 'Delamere son's verdict based on best friend's evidence', and 'Intrigues that made the case a legal masterpiece', Jillo Kadida, *Daily Nation*, 8.5.2009

'The black man's burden is carrying white man's guilt', Peter Kimani, *The Standard*, 15.5.2009

'It was a nervous, life-stopping moment but his prayers were finally answered', and 'A bit of 'white mischief'', Macharia Gaitho, *Daily Nation*, 15.5.2009

'Cholmondeley could be home for Christmas', Wahome Thuku, and 'Sisina's widow cry for justice, compensation', Judy Ogutu, and 'Rancher has faced Justice Apondi twice for murder', Nancy Akinyi, *The Standard*, 15.5.2009

'Delamere son being released on same day', Nation Team, and 'United in freedom', *Saturday Nation*, 24.10.2009

'Delamere heir's big plan for villagers', Simon Siele, and 'Mungiki leader turns to farming', Billy Muiruri, *Daily Nation*, 26.10.2009

'Philip Murgor: How Cocaine choked me out of Kibaki State job', Emeka-Mayaka Gekara and Julius Sigei, *Saturday Nation*, 10.8.2013

'Ground breaking: Sh700m mall for Naivasha town launched', *Daily Nation*, 13.12.2013

'Cholmondeley dies in hospital', John Kamau, *Daily Nation*, 18.8.2016

'Ranger's family 'to block burial'', *Daily Nation*, 19.8.2016

'Tom Cholmondeley: Is he the last of the Happy Valley Ghosts?', John Kamau, *Sunday Nation*, 21.8.16

'Ranger's family 'to block burial'', Nation Team, *Daily Nation*, 19.8.2016

'Becoming Kenyan: The Delameres and the politics of being Maasai', Joyce Nyairo, *Saturday Nation*, 10.9.2016

'Lion tales: Two lionesses who live in Soysambu are revealing a lot about themselves and their lifestyles', Rupi Mangat, *Saturday Nation*, 24.6.2017

'Lord Delamere: Trophy hunter who started modern large-scale farming', Odhiambo Ndege, *Saturday Nation*, 30.11.2019

International:
Various articles in newspapers and magazines including:

'Happy Valley heir held for bushmeat murder', Mike Planz and Caroline Davies, *The Daily Telegraph*, 21.4.2005

'Happy Valley heir denies warden's murder', Mike Pflanz, *The Daily Telegraph*, 29.4.2005

'A bullet in the heart of Happy Valley', Jonathan Clayton, *The Sunday Times*, 1.5.2005

'Aristocrat up for new slaying', *News 24*, 11.5.2006

'Expel the white settlers', *Reuters*, 18.5.2005

'Unhappy Valley', John Conyngham, *The Witness*, (SA), 25.6.2005

'Murderous world of the gun-toting Happy Valley set', *Daily Mail*, 22.9.2006

'White Kenyan tried for killing black man', Elizabeth A Kennedy, *Associated Press*, 25.9.2006

'Old Etonian goes on trial for murder of Kenyan poacher', *The Daily Telegraph*, 26.9.2006

'Trial begins for wealthy Kenyan accused of killing black man', Jeffrey Gettleman, *The New York Times*, 26.9.06

'British aristocrat on trial for killing poacher', Rob Crilly, *The Australian*, 26.9.2006

'Poacher 'needed food"', Rob Jillo, *News 24*, 26.9.2006

'Briton in Kenyan Court over Murder', *Daily Trust* (Abuja) 27.9.2006

'Cholmondeley 'tried to save poacher' he shot', Jack Kimball, *Telegraph* online, 28.9.2006

'Police admit errors at aristocrat's trial', Mike Pflanz, *Telegraph* online, 1.11.2006

'A bloody rift', Lawrence Osborne, *Men's Vogue*, Mar/Apr 2007

'Young bucks see better value in Old Masters', Hannah Furness, *The Daily Telegraph*, 21.10.2013

'How The Great War Razed East Africa', Edward Paice, *www.africaresearchinstitute.org*, 4.8.14

'Secret that the White Mischief Killer took to his grave: How the notorious Old Etonian had a love-child with his lifelong sweetheart just a few months before his death', Claudia Joseph, *The Mail on Sunday*, 21.8.16

Unpublished sources:
Cunningham-Reid, Michael, '*What Was, Was,*' typed memoir, courtesy of Errol Trzebinski

Cholmondeley, Tom, book proposals: 'Paradise Prejudice,' and '2 White Dogs,' and unpublished handwritten memoir

Long, Ernest Caswell 'Boy', Boy's Diaries, courtesy of the Weston Library, Oxford

Watson, Malcolm, typed memoirs, courtesy of Alfred Githaiga

Various letters, courtesy of The Lady Delamere

Letters to Gwladys Delamere, 3rd Baron, assorted letters and typed leaflets/press releases during Mau Mau, courtesy of the Weston Library, Oxford

Artist's impression of Vale Royal Abbey, built on a site consecrated by King Edward in 1277. (Courtesy of Lord and Lady Delamere)

Portrait of the Right Honourable Hugh Cholmondeley, 3rd Baron Delamere (who preferred to be called simply 'D.') (Author's collection)

A photo portrait of Lord Delamere in his later years. (Courtesy of Lord and Lady Delamere)

Lord Delamere at the races in Nairobi in about 1908. (Courtesy Steve Mills)

Photo portrait of Lady Florence Anne Cole by Sallie Charles, Mayfair. (Courtesy of Lord and Lady Delamere)

The Right Honourable Thomas Pitt Hamilton Cholmondeley, London, 1902. (Courtesy of Lord and Lady Delamere)

LORD DELAMERE'S EAST AFRICAN ESTATES.

FIRST CROSS EWES FROM NATIVE SHEEP WITH SECOND CROSS LAMBS,
SHORTHORN AND DEVON CATTLE, SECOND CROSS CATTLE, SHORTHORN AND NATIVE,
WHEAT HARVEST, MAIZE ADJOINING, PLOUGHING AT SAME TIME, NJORO.

A 1904 newspaper advertisement of livestock for sale. (Author's collection)

Lord Delamere's Equator Farm at Njoro in about 1908. (Author's collection)

Nakuru Hotel, built by Lord Delamere in 1908, and still in operation today as the Midland Hotel. (Author's collection)

*In 2015 cedar posts were all that was left
of Florence's wooden hut on Equator Farm, Njoro.* (Author's collection)

Vale Royal, formerly the Delamere family home, before its renovation in 1984.
(Author's collection)

*A young Thomas Cholmondeley
in England in about 1908.*
(Courtesy of Lord and Lady Delamere)

Early days on Soysambu, by Lake Elmenteita. (Author's collection)

Lord Delamere's huts beside the Mereroni River, looking towards Lake Elmenteita.
(Courtesy of Lord and Lady Delamere)

Thomas (right) with Lord and Lady Cranworth in England.
(Courtesy of Lord and Lady Delamere)

A photo taken in 2019 of one of the prefab houses imported from Norway in about 1911. (Author's collection)

The water pipeline on Sosyambu, the first of its kind in East Africa. (Courtesy of Lord and Lady Delamere)

Soysambu's first stone house, built by Edward Caswell (Boy) Long and completed in 1913. (Courtesy of Lord and Lady Delamere)

Soysambu's offices with a prefab house on the right, and Merino sheep. (Courtesy of Lord and Lady Delamere)

Dipping sheep on Soysambu.
(Liza Long collection)

One of the many Maasai herdsman on Soysambu, employed by Lord Delamere to look after the sheep.
(Liza Long collection)

Ruy Blas, one of Lord Delamere's stallions that he kept at stud on Soysambu.
(Liza Long collection)

The stables at Soysambu.
(Liza Long collection)

Motorcars arrive on Soysambu. Boy Long with a Maasai herdsman.
(Liza Long collection)

Lord Delamere's Rolls Royce, used for transporting sheep for which purpose he removed the back cover. The car was later sold and done up and photographed more recently in England.
(Courtesy of Lord and Lady Delamere)

A Kikuyu woman sewing beads.
(Liza Long collection)

The marriage of The Right Honourable Thomas Pitt Hamilton Cholmondeley, 4th Baron Delamere, to Phyllis Anne Montagu Douglas Scott, 14 June 1924.
(Courtesy of Lord and Lady Delamere)

*Lady Gwladys Markham
in a portrait painted in 1925
by Philip De Laszlo.*
(Courtesy of Sir David Markham)

One of D's cars stuck on his Laikipia farm, Ol Pejeta.
(Liza Long collection)

The Prince of Wales (subsequently Edward VIII) on a visit to Sosyambu in 1928. Left to right: Boy Long; HRH The Prince of Wales; Lord Delamere.
(Liza Long collection)

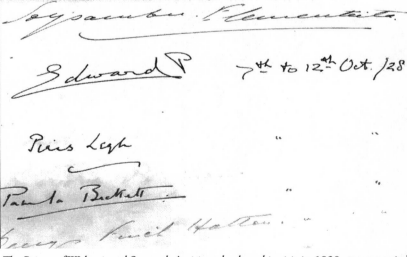

The Prince of Wales signed Soysambu's visitors book on his visit in 1928, accompanied by Denys Finch Hatton whose name is visible at the bottom of the photo.
(Author's Collection)

"Soysambu did not lay itself out to attract man, or seem to care whether he came, or to take much notice of him when he did. It had a vivid beauty of its own, a beauty which slowly saturated and possessed the spirit..." - Elspeth Huxley. (Courtesy of Simon Thomsett)

Phyllis, Lady Delamere at Vale Royal.
(Courtesy of Lord and Lady Delamere)

Phyllis, Lady Delamere, and her children in front of the Elizabethan Wing at Vale Royal in c. 1936. Left to Right: Anne Jeannetta Essex Cholmondeley, Elizabeth Florence Marion Cholmondeley, the Right Honourable Hugh George Cholmondeley.
(Courtesy of Lord and Lady Delamere)

Vale Royal in 2015, now part of a golf club. (Author's collection)

The three Cholmondeley children boating on the pond.
(Courtesy of Lord and Lady Delamere)

Left to right: Hugh, Anne, Phyllis and Elizabeth at Vale Royal.
(Courtesy of Lord and Lady Delamere)

The 4th Baron Delamere (Tom)
on Soysambu.
(Courtesy of Lord
and Lady Delamere)

Tom and Diana on Soysambu in about 1955. (Courtesy of Lord and Lady Delamere)

*Diana, Lady Delamere,
at Main House, Soysambu.*
(Courtesy of Lord and Lady
Delamere)

*The photograph of
Lord Erroll (known to
friends as Joss), that Diana
kept in a frame.*
(Courtesy of Lord and
Lady Delamere)

Gilbert Colvile, Diana's ex-husband,
sitting on the steps of the Djinn Palace
in Naivasha with the pug she gave him.
(Courtesy of Lord and Lady Delamere)

Diana receives the Uhuru Cup from Mzee Jomo Kenyatta,
Kenya's first Prime Minister and later President. Diana's horse Sea Port won that
inaugural Uhuru Cup in 1963 a week after Kenya's independence.
She and Tom had purchased the cup in England and donated it to the
Jockey Club of Kenya. (Courtesy of Lord and Lady Delamere)

The Right Honourable
Hugh George Cholmondeley.
(Courtesy of Lord and Lady Delamere)

Ann Willoughby Renison.
(Courtesy of Lord and Lady Delamere)

The marriage of Hon. Hugh Cholmondeley and Ann Willoughby Renison
on the patio of Main House, 11 April 1964. (Courtesy of Lord and Lady Delamere)

*The wedding party on the lawn overlooking the lake. Left to right: Peter Barclay;
Hugh; Ann; Diana; PC Mahihu; Tom.* (Courtesy of Lord and Lady Delamere)

*Hon. Hugh Cholmondeley and Hon. Mrs Hugh Cholmondeley
on the lawn at Main House.* (Courtesy of Lord and Lady Delamere)

*Tom, Diana and Diana's adopted
daughter, Deborah Colvile, at her
coming out in London, 1966.*
(Courtesy of Lord and Lady Delamere)

*Hugh and Ann outside Lady Eleanor
Cole's Church of Goodwill at the
christening of their son, The Honourable
Thomas Patrick Gilbert Cholmondeley.*
(Courtesy of Lord and Lady Delamere)

The view from the lawn in front of Main House.
(Courtesy of Lord and Lady Delamere)

The arrival of White Bear at Kilindini Harbour, Mombasa. (Courtesy of Lord and Lady Delamere)

Tom and Jomo Kenyatta, Kenya's first President. (Courtesy of Lord and Lady Delamere)

Pug on board.
(Courtesy of Lord and
Lady Delamere)

*The Hon. Thomas
Patrick Cholmondeley
(initially called Patrick,
although after his
grandfather's death he
became known to all as
Tom) in about 1970.*
(Courtesy of Lord and
Lady Delamere)

*Patrick with his friend
Rosa, daughter of
his nanny.* (Courtesy
of Lord and Lady
Delamere)

Patrick's Pembroke House School photo. (Courtesy of Lord and Lady Delamere)

Tom at his desk. (Courtesy of Lord and Lady Delamere)

Tom, Diana and Diana's crew.
(Courtesy of Lord and Lady Delamere)

David Partridge, Diana and George Webb with their catch of two black marlin and three striped marlin at Shimoni in 1978, a month before Tom's death.
(Courtesy of Lord and Lady Delamere)

Lions, two with radio-tracking collars, on Soysambu Wildlife Conservancy in 2016.
(Courtesy of Siana Bell)

Diana, the 5th Baron Delamere (Hugh), and Ann at the Ngong Race Course in Nairobi. (Courtesy of Lord and Lady Delamere)

*Tom and his dog named
Chaos.* (Courtesy of Lord and
Lady Delamere)

Tom on Soysambu.
(Courtesy of Lord and Lady Delamere)

*Setting Diana's table for lunch on
the Soysambu veranda. Muiruri is
on the right.* (Courtesy of Lord and
Lady Delamere)

*Diana and friends at
Villa Buzza in Kilifi.*
(Courtesy of Lord and
Lady Delamere)

Ann in the dining room at Main House.
(Courtesy of Lord and Lady Delamere)

*Hugh and Tom at the combined celebration of Hugh and Ann's 25th wedding
anniversary and Tom's 21st birthday in 1989.*
(Courtesy of Lord and Lady Delamere)

Tom paragliding.
(Courtesy of Lord and Lady Delamere)

*Tom's wife, Sally (nee Brewerton),
with their son, the Right Hon. Hugh Derrick
Cholmondeley (known to friends and family as
Hughey).* (Courtesy of Lord and Lady Delamere)

*A few of those who attended Hughey's christening on the Elmenteita lakeshore.
Nd'ungu is on the far right.* (Courtesy of Lord and Lady Delamere)

Sally with her and Tom's second son, the Hon. Henry Gilbert Cholmondeley.
(Courtesy of Lord and Lady Delamere)

Hughey (right) and Henry.
(Courtesy of Lord and Lady Delamere)

Hugh playing the organ that once belonged to Bishop Hannington.
(Courtesy of Lord and Lady Delamere)

*The author's house
after heavy rain.*
(Author's collection)

*Soysambu
devastated by fires.*
(Author's collection)

*Hugh looking over
Soysambu.*
(Courtesy of Lord
and Lady Delamere)

Tom teaching a class at Kamiti Prison.
(Courtesy of Lord and Lady Delamere)

Statue of 3rd Baron Delamere, which now stands in the garden beside Main House.
(Courtesy of Lord and Lady Delamere)

Hugh beside his grandfather's statue with children from Restart Children's Home in 2019. (Courtesy of Lord and Lady Delamere)

Crowned Eagle, rescued and rehabilitated by Simon Thomsett.
(Courtesy of Siana Bell)

Author looking over Soysambu. (Author's collection)

INDEX

A

Aardvark 49, 273, 275, 295
Abdullah (Bastard Baronet) 56-57
Abdullah Ashure (gun-bearer) 13, 16
Abercorn 70
Aberdare Mountains 22, 46, 78, 83, 111, 138-139, 141-143, 145
Abyssinia 15, 17, 41, 77, 129
Acokanthera fresiorum 198
Adamson, George and Joy 241
Aden 12-14, 18, 98
Africa Inland Mission 59
Africa Prisons Project 286
Aga Khan Hospital (Mombasa) 214
Agricultural Mortgage Corporation 223
Amies, Hardy 184
Amin, Idi 240
Anglo-Egyptian Sudan 77
Anglo-German Agreement 14
Annan, Kofi 272
Aponde, Justice Muga 247, 259, 263, 279, 282, 283
Arensen, Shel ix, 28, 178, 311
Armistice 70
Ashley, Ruth Mary Clarisse (later Gardner and Cunningham-Reid, before becoming Lady Delamere) vii, 123, 128, 131-134, 136, 140, 146-7, 157, 198, 216, 240
Athi River 19
Atkinson, Arthur Edward 13-18, 21, 24, 26, 30-32, 56-57 130
Atkinson, Eustace 24, 26
Austria, Vice Chancellor of 121

B

Bacon factory 41, 49
Baden Powell, Lord 120
Baillie, Arthur Alexander 54
Baker, Herbert 89, 92
Ballistics 250, 271
Baragoi (horse) 179
Baragoi (place) 248
Barbour, A. T. 123
Barclay, Peter 174
Baring, Evelyn 136-138, 141-

142, 153-154, 158, 162, 312
Bastard, Seagar 101
BBC 167, 170, 218, 254
Beard, Robin 212, 214
Behr, Dick (also son Peter) 183, 184, 213
Belfield, Henry 53-54, 67, 72
Berbera 14
Biplane 128
Bishop of Zanzibar 80
Blixen-Finecke, Baron Bror 61, 63, 102, 311
Blixen, Karen, Baroness (nee Karen Dinesen) 61-63, 66, 68-69, 84, 89, 94-95, 102, 311, 314
Block, Abraham 24, 105, 192
Block, Jack 192
Blood-brotherhood 34, 160
Blundell, Michael 141, 162, 169
Board of Agriculture 102
Bobbe, Alan 214
Boer War 76, 112
Bogoria 289
Boma Trading Company 41
Boran cattle 15, 68, 129, 168
Bowie, David 301
Boy Scouts 120
Breughel, Pieter (the Younger) 2, 290
Bristow, Desmond 204, 206, 212, 217, 219
British Carrier Corps 70
British Guyana 164
British Legion 118
British Museum 18, 20
British Treasury 169
British Union of Fascists 114, 120
Broadlands 131
Brookside (Dairies) 271, 303
Broughton, Evelyn 147
Brown, Leslie 158, 198
Brown, Monty x, 59, 134
Buffalo Mall 290
Buganda, (Kingdom of) 21, 227, 288
Buick 115, 118
Bull Box 54-55, 148
Bussilunhun 83
Byrne, Joseph 102, 109

C

Cambodia 291

Cambridge 43, 59, 123, 128, 131, 135, 143-145, 305
Cameron, Sir Donald 104
Campbell, Guy 142
Carnegie, Robert 42
Cathedral of the Highlands (also All Saints' Cathedral Nairobi) 118, 170, 207 219
Catholic Bishop of Nyeri 175
Cattle (also cow, bull, calf, calves, heifers) 2, 4-6, 10, 13, 15-16, 19, 21, 23, 25-27, 29, 33-34, 41-42, 46-48, 50-52, 54-55, 61, 65-69, 76-77, 84, 90-91, 95, 101, 113, 124, 126-129, 133, 141, 143-145, 157, 160, 163, 168, 181-183, 192, 195-196, 198, 204-205, 212-213, 215, 217-218, 223, 225, 226-228, 236, 241, 244, 250, 254, 266, 270, 278, 290-291, 305, 307, 309
Cedar 24, 39, 54, 73, 75, 146, 241, 304
Cells 140, 216, 244-250, 258, 260-261, 269-270, 280-281, 285
Central Firearms Bureau 271
Centre-pivot 228
Cessna 203
Ceylon 163-164, 233
Chamberlain, Robert 85, 104
Champagne 15-16, 89-90, 92, 191
Chanel No. 5 110, 118
Cherokee 235 237
Cheshire 8-9, 11-13, 89, 164
Chief Inspector 271
Chief Steward 178
Chirchir, Christopher 236, 243, 266, 270
Chiromo House 37
Cholmondeley, Ann (The Lady Delamere, nee Ann Willoughby Renison) vii, 2-3, 5, 10-11, 15, 30, 34, 52, 53, 55, 59, 75-76, 85, 87, 119, 127, 129-131, 135, 140, 145, 148-149, 156, 160, 163-167, 174-177, 180-181, 184, 186-196, 198-204, 207, 210, 212-215, 219-220, 222-224, 226, 228, 233, 236-237, 245, 247, 254, 259-260, 262-264, 266-267, 269, 271-272, 274,

Made in the USA
San Bernardino, CA
11 June 2020

73233709R00229